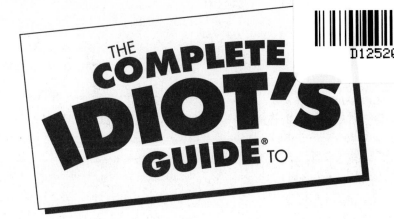

THE COMPLETE IDIOT'S GUIDE® TO

Intimacy

by Dr. Paul Coleman

ALPHA

A member of Penguin Group (USA) Inc.

For Jody

ALPHA BOOKS

Published by the Penguin Group

Penguin Group (USA) Inc., 375 Hudson Street, New York, New York 10014, USA

Penguin Group (Canada), 90 Eglinton Avenue East, Suite 700, Toronto, Ontario M4P 2Y3, Canada (a division of Pearson Penguin Canada Inc.)

Penguin Books Ltd., 80 Strand, London WC2R 0RL, England

Penguin Ireland, 25 St. Stephen's Green, Dublin 2, Ireland (a division of Penguin Books Ltd.)

Penguin Group (Australia), 250 Camberwell Road, Camberwell, Victoria 3124, Australia (a division of Pearson Australia Group Pty. Ltd.)

Penguin Books India Pvt. Ltd., 11 Community Centre, Panchsheel Park, New Delhi—110 017, India

Penguin Group (NZ), 67 Apollo Drive, Rosedale, North Shore, Auckland 1311, New Zealand (a division of Pearson New Zealand Ltd.)

Penguin Books (South Africa) (Pty.) Ltd., 24 Sturdee Avenue, Rosebank, Johannesburg 2196, South Africa

Penguin Books Ltd., Registered Offices: 80 Strand, London WC2R 0RL, England

Copyright © 2005 by Dr. Paul Coleman

International Standard Book Number: 978-1-59257-387-5
Library of Congress Catalog Card Number: 2005926960

12   11   10   8   7   6

Interpretation of the printing code: The rightmost number of the first series of numbers is the year of the book's printing; the rightmost number of the second series of numbers is the number of the book's printing. For example, a printing code of 05-1 shows that the first printing occurred in 2005.

Printed in the United States of America

Note: This publication contains the opinions and ideas of its author. It is intended to provide helpful and informative material on the subject matter covered. It is sold with the understanding that the author and publisher are not engaged in rendering professional services in the book. If the reader requires personal assistance or advice, a competent professional should be consulted.

The author and publisher specifically disclaim any responsibility for any liability, loss, or risk, personal or otherwise, which is incurred as a consequence, directly or indirectly, of the use and application of any of the contents of this book.

Most Alpha books are available at special quantity discounts for bulk purchases for sales promotions, premiums, fundraising, or educational use. Special books, or book excerpts, can also be created to fit specific needs.

For details, write: Special Markets, Alpha Books, 375 Hudson Street, New York, NY 10014.

Publisher: *Marie Butler-Knight*
Product Manager: *Phil Kitchel*
Senior Managing Editor: *Jennifer Bowles*
Senior Acquisitions Editor: *Renee Wilmeth*
Development Editor: *Jennifer Moore*
Senior Production Editor: *Billy Fields*

Copy Editor: *Tricia Liebig*
Cartoonist: *Shannon Wheeler*
Cover/Book Designer: *Trina Wurst*
Indexer: *Julie Bess*
Layout: *Angela Calvert*
Proofreading: *Mary Hunt*

Contents at a Glance

Contents

Foreword

I have read a *lot* of relationship books during the past three decades—most everything published on the topics of love/relationships/sex/romance … and *this* is one of the very best. Congratulations on picking it up. You're about to enter into an adventure of a lifetime: the adventure of intimacy.

I consider this one of the best books of its kind because of three things: the *quality* of information it contains, the *quantity* of information it contains, and the *manner* in which it is presented.

Regarding the *quality* of information that Dr. Paul Coleman has compiled: first-rate and up-to-date. This is great stuff, people! Paul Coleman is a practicing psychotherapist, a real Ph.D. His insights come from a combination of real-life experiences and serious study. This book isn't just a compilation of concepts that he thinks are cool.

Regarding the *quantity* of information in this book: good lord, just take a look! Over 300 pages of solid stuff.

Regarding the *manner* in which this information is presented: honest, straightforward, easy to read, no razzle-dazzle, no psycho-babble, no obnoxious attitude. (Don't you just hate that attitude of "Let's treat the opposite sex like they're idiots/children/fools"? I do. Here's an insight into the world of publishing and promotion: that obnoxious/ condescending approach is great for PR. But in terms of actually helping real people? It falls flat.) Oh! Another thing: Dr. Coleman has a talent for presenting information in a *simple* but not *simplistic* manner. His insights are true insights (not pseudo-insights like "Men and women are different")—insights that will really improve your love life.

As I read the manuscript for *The Complete Idiot's Guide to Intimacy* I was struck again and again by the many great insights and topics addressed. Here are some powerful statements from the book: "The truth is that rich, meaningful intimacy doesn't just happen, it must be cultivated." And "Intimacy also protects you from stress. Think of the levels of intimacy as layers of clothing that shield you from the elements." And *here's* a great concept: "I.Q., or Intimacy Quotient." —Cool, huh?

I don't know about *you*, but *I* certainly want to know: "What *men* want *women* to know about intimacy" and "What *women* want *men* to know about intimacy." Women: Do you want to know "A man's key underlying conflict?" Of *course* you do! Men: Do *you* want to know "When to make your relationship sexual"? Well, duh! And what about "How intimacy can go from warm to hot in mere seconds." Sounds good to me! And who wouldn't want to know "How to make sensual connections when time is at a premium"?!

The Complete Idiot's Guide to Intimacy explains and explores the magic of intimacy—and untangles this most important concept from its brother and sister concepts, love and romance. You will learn that intimacy is intimately related to—but separate and distinct from—love, sex, and romance. Dr. Paul Coleman explains how they all work together, and why intimacy is the key to relationship success.

—Gregory J.P. Godek, author *1001 Ways To Be Romantic*

Introduction

Love may be the heart of your most important relationships but intimacy is the soul. Intimacy is the energy center of how you relate to others and how they relate to you. Without intimacy, there is no meaningful togetherness.

Have you had a string of lovers that just didn't work out? Intimacy is the underlying factor that needs your attention. Are you single, unattached, and afraid of a serious relationship? Intimacy issues are lurking. Are you in an established relationship that has everything going for it but still something isn't right? You guessed it: You have a slight problem with intimacy.

I'll say it here: Everybody, and I mean everybody, has something to learn about achieving intimacy. Intimacy is all about knowing someone—really knowing them—and really being known. It's closeness with a capital "C" but in a manner that allows you to be a separate person, too. Just about everyone would like to feel closer to the ones they love. And yet just about everyone shrinks from intimate encounters at various times. People have a love-hate relationship with intimacy. But this book will help you understand intimacy from the inside out, as it shows you dozens of ways to improve the quality of intimacy in your life.

Intimacy is nothing to be afraid of. It's really all about being you.

So many books teach you to communicate better or improve your love life. But the driving force behind any effort to make yourself and your relationships more satisfying is the quality of intimacy. I've counseled thousands of couples. No matter what their problems or concerns, I've discovered that if they improve the quality of their intimate encounters their "problems" start to diminish. "I want to have a more exciting sex life!" some people tell me. "We need to handle money better!" some couples say to me. "I'm in a relationship rut!" I hear others cry.

What they all want is genuine, wholehearted, delicious intimacy to be part of their lives. They just don't fully realize it.

Intimacy has many facets, as this book will reveal. The good news is that if you improve intimacy in one area you will probably make gains in other areas of intimacy, too. But the reverse is also true. If you let one area of intimacy slide, other areas will weaken.

If you focus on improving the quality of intimacy in your relationships, I can guarantee that you will be happier and more fulfilled and that any problems you encounter in life won't carry as much weight. Everything will feel lighter.

How This Book Is Organized

The chapters in this book are divided into six sections that show you step by step how to build and sustain intimacy in your life.

Part 1, "The Magic and Madness of Intimacy," reveals the four major pathways to intimacy. Men and women often handle intimacy differently, and these chapters explain those differences and give suggestions for bridging the gap. The most common (and often hidden) obstacles to achieving intimacy are also uncovered in these pages. If you've ever wondered why you seem to choose the wrong person, this section discusses the four key reasons why that can happen. Finally, you'll read state of the art advice on how to sustain your intimacy gains over the long haul.

Part 2, "Intimacy Through Thought," takes a fascinating look at how your thoughts and your overall thinking style work either for you or against you when it comes to creating intimacy. Take some short quizzes and you'll be amazed to learn that with just a few attitude shifts you can be on your way to greater intimacy. "Linking by thinking" is not just a catchy phrase—it's powerful medicine with hurricane-force potential. How you think about yourself, your friends, and your partner creates a condition that will lead to goodwill or ill-will. Intimacy thrives when goodwill is present.

Part 3, "Intimacy Through Talk," is not your run of the mill chatter about how to communicate effectively. Even if you're not a talker by nature you'll learn a bunch of easy-to-use "power phrases" that will boost intimacy with the snap of a finger. You'll learn how to have foolproof conversations that even the most shy and reserved person can handle with ease. You'll discover how nonverbal body language can add to intimacy in ways that verbal language can't. And finally, if any conversation goes sour, you'll find how to make easy repairs that will U-turn you back to intimacy.

Part 4, "Intimacy Through Touch," helps you get physical in ways Mom and Dad never talked about. First you can take a quiz to help you learn things about the opposite sex you perhaps never knew, especially as it pertains to sexual arousal and attitudes about sex. Then hold onto your hat! "Hot Intimacy" is all about having sizzling connections that go from 0 to 60 in a matter of seconds. Hot intimacy isn't just about sex, but it is about fantastic intimacy that takes off like a rocket. This section wouldn't be complete without talking about obstacles to sexual intimacy and how to overcome them. You'll learn about seven sexual myths that you should stop believing right this minute. And you'll discover the tremendous power that affection has in creating and sustaining intimacy.

Part 5, "Intimacy Through Togetherness," helps you figure out how to spend more time with those you want to be intimate with. Take a quiz and find out your "Togetherness Quotient." It will reveal whether you're weak or strong when it comes to having quality time with those you love. Learn about dynamic togetherness and how it can transform what might be ordinary "spending time together" into something more heartfelt and cozy. Is friendship an important part of any love relationship? You might be surprised at the answer.

Part 6, "Intimacy During Trying Times," is a must read for whenever life turns upside down or you're going through some ordeal. Intimacy needs fluctuate wildly when you're under stress. Unless you handle it correctly, intimacy will suffer and you'll experience even more stress. This section covers important topics such as how to keep intimacy thriving when you or a partner have a chronic or debilitating illness. Going through new transitions in life such as parenthood or middle age? Your intimacy needs will vary, and these sections tell you what to do to keep yourself and your partner happy. Lastly, if you've ever been betrayed and you're having trouble rebuilding intimacy, you'll learn some key intimacy steps to take that will make your life a whole lot easier.

Extras

If you're like me you'll love these handy-dandy information boxes that will pop up all over this book. They contain wonderful tips and advice in a quick and easy format.

 Intimacy Boosters

Here you'll find snappy suggestions on how to enhance intimacy.

 Just Ask!

Other people just like yourself have questions I'm sure you'll relate to. You'll find the questions and answers here.

Exercise!

In addition to the many exercises mentioned throughout the book, I've highlighted some all-important and easy-to-do exercises here. They will absolutely help you in the intimacy department.

 **Close Calls**

Caution! Watch out! This box alerts you to problems and pitfalls you might not otherwise know about when trying to improve intimacy.

Acknowledgments

First and foremost I thank my wife Jody for her continuous love and support in all my endeavors. Writing a book takes a lot of time that might otherwise be spent with family and friends. Thanks to my children, Luke, Anna, and Julia, for tolerating my hogging the computer and for asking me what page I'm on.

Any writer would be lucky to have a fantastic literary agent. I have two: Mike and Pat Snell. We have a 16-year history together and I'm well aware that no matter how good a writer I try to be, so many of my books would not have seen the light of day if not for Mike and Pat. I never fail to appreciate their insights, their enthusiasm, and their friendship.

Speaking of friends, let me thank MSG Shawn Morgan, a soldier who is currently protecting America's interests in Iraq. Even before he had to leave his young family behind for a one- to two-year stint in Iraq, Shawn would still take the time to ask me how the book was coming along. I'm reminded that it was the soldier, not the writer, who gave us freedom of speech.

I'd also like to thank the gang at County Players Theater in Wappingers Falls, New York. County Players is a diamond in the rough, a wonderful community theater company that produces powerhouse entertainment. I've had the pleasure of being cast in several plays there and the greater pleasure of making so many new and lasting friends.

At Alpha Books I'd like to thank Renee Wilmeth, senior acquisitions editor; Jennifer Moore, development editor; Billy Fields, senior production editor; and Tricia Liebig, copy editor, for their hard work, insights, and enthusiasm for this project. I did my best writing this book and they made it even better. Maybe we'll do it again some-time?

Trademarks

All terms mentioned in this book that are known to be or are suspected of being trademarks or service marks have been appropriately capitalized. Alpha Books and Penguin Group (USA) Inc. cannot attest to the accuracy of this information. Use of a term in this book should not be regarded as affecting the validity of any trademark or service mark.

Part 1

The Magic and Madness of Intimacy

Ever try to create more intimacy in your relationships only to see the "sizzle" you're aiming for simply "fizzle"? Or maybe you're convinced that the person you've been dating is absolutely your soul mate—only to question your judgment later on? Have you noticed that your last two or three relationships ended for similar reasons?

Achieving intimacy is essential for a fulfilling relationship. Although some days it seems like an easy thing to accomplish, lasting intimacy is elusive for so many people. You can love another person but be aching for greater intimacy. You can have the world by the tail in practically every area of your life yet seem unable to sustain closeness with the person of your dreams.

The first part of this book is designed to help you understand what genuine intimacy is really about and how to begin walking the path toward greater closeness in your most important relationships. You'll learn about the common (and hidden) roadblocks to intimacy and how to step around them. You'll discover why bright people often choose the wrong person for an intimate relationship, and how to keep intimacy alive over the long haul.

Understanding Intimacy from the Inside Out

In This Chapter

+ Defining true intimacy
+ Achieving above-average intimacy
+ Discovering the four pathways to lasting intimacy
+ Finding your IQ (Intimacy Quotient)

Intimacy is pure magic. When you experience it quietly with a friend, it fosters caring. When you experience it with a romantic partner, it generates something even more profound: growing love, passion, and devotion. Many people, however, single and married, trip up when trying to find the right formula for achieving meaningful intimacy. And long-time couples too often let the intimacy in their relationship lose its sparkle. It usually doesn't require strenuous effort to get intimacy to grow and blossom, but it does require tending, much like a garden.

When a relationship is fresh and exciting, many people view intimacy as a given, as something that automatically happens: you talk, you feel romantic, and you do things together. Easy, right? Well, not quite. Sure, intimacy sometimes starts easily, such as putting on a cozy, snug slipper. But how many people seeking a brand-new relationship discover that lasting intimacy eludes them? And how many people in a long-term relationship still feel lonely at times? Or misunderstood? How often do they settle for periods of isolation and disconnection when what they really want is to feel more connected?

The truth is that rich, meaningful intimacy doesn't just happen, it must be cultivated. This chapter helps you clear away the confusion and discover what intimacy really is (I guarantee it's more than you think it is!) and how to make it the centerpiece of your important relationships.

Make Intimacy Your Main Goal

Karla and Ryan had been dating for eight months and were contemplating living together. They told me all about their "communication" problems and their tendency to get into power struggles over little things, but I knew they'd missed the boat in defining their real problem: Their intimacy levels were well below average. Mostly they had it backward. They thought that if they improved their communication skills, for instance, they would automatically upgrade their intimacy and stop arguing. Possibly. What they didn't realize was that their communication efforts were sub-par in large part *because* intimacy was low. They needed a positive shift in intimacy, especially their attitude about intimacy. Until then, lasting change probably wouldn't happen.

Just Ask!

My fiancée and I sometimes argue about small things such as who should do which chores and how much money to spend. If we can find a way to agree more and argue less, will that automatically improve our intimacy?

Not necessarily. About 70 percent of all couples' arguments are not really about the topic being discussed. The topics are a stand-in for the real underlying issue: "We aren't as close as we should be; are we really a 'we?'" If you and your fiancée agree on chores, it might not automatically fix the deeper intimacy problem. It's better for you to find ways to improve intimacy more broadly. You might discover that arguments over chores are no longer a chore.

Karla and Ryan were putting the cart before the horse. Good communication skills do not necessarily lead to better intimacy. But when intimacy grows stronger and deeper, communication automatically improves. Why? Because when intimacy is deeply felt, it is much easier to be an effective listener. I told them we had to come up with a plan to cultivate a greater desire for intimacy and closeness—not for developing better negotiating skills—and things might fall into place more easily.

Your primary goal should be to achieve greater intimacy in your most important personal relationships. Let's imagine two couples whose intimacy levels have gone flat. Couple number one wants to strengthen their sense of closeness and intimacy and decides to go on a vacation where they can spend meaningful time together. Intimacy is their goal; where they go to bring that about is secondary. Couple number two has a slightly different focus. They haven't been getting along well and their careers have been causing stress, so they decide to fly to a beach resort and relax. Which couple is more likely to succeed at building more intimacy? The first couple. Why? Because they made intimacy their destination, not a hoped-for by-product of reaching their destination. It is a small but significant distinction, similar to a ballplayer missing a homerun by inches. If achieving greater intimacy is at the centerpiece of your relationship vision, you are more likely to steer in that direction and not veer off into areas that appear promising (such as good communication skills) but may miss the mark.

What Is Intimacy?

Intimacy does not exist without a connection to someone. The connection can be brief, such as chatting with someone you never met before at a party (although simply chatting is not by itself an intimate act). Intimacy is not merely a feeling inside you. It is not about one person at all. It is about interaction and the magic that happens when two people give something of themselves to one another.

Intimacy can't be defined in a single sentence. It has many facets. Typically, when people think of intimacy they think about having sex or perhaps a very personal discussion. These are two ways that intimacy might occur but they are not the only ways. Haven't you ever had a close, intimate moment where no words were spoken? Where there was no sexual contact?

Whatever the intimate encounter might be, it must possess three qualities that render it truly intimate: connecting, caring, and sharing. Let's look at those three factors more closely.

+ **Connecting.** This can be either a physical interaction or a soulful-emotional connection, such as feeling connected to someone who is far away.

Intimacy Boosters

Of the three factors required for intimacy—connecting, caring, and sharing—which is strongest for you? Which is weakest? If you connect with your mate but not always in a caring or sharing way, intimacy suffers. Identify your weak spot, aim to improve it, and intimacy will grow.

- **Caring.** Some form of love, compassion, or very positive feeling—often passionate—must be involved. If a person matters to you solely for the purpose of using them for a gain, that is not genuine caring.

- **Sharing.** The connection is mutual. It is not one-sided or selfish. Even if you are alone and just thinking about the person you love, there is a sharing in that the other person probably thinks tenderly about you, too.

Unless all three factors are present, there is no intimacy. Think about it for a moment. You might connect with someone at the supermarket, but without caring and sharing you wouldn't call it an intimate encounter. Or you might care about a celebrity you see on TV, but without a connection and a sharing, there is no intimacy. Being examined, unclothed, by your physician may appear to be an intimate encounter, but there is no sharing, and the degree of genuine caring is probably limited.

Determining If Intimacy Is Real or a Cheap Imitation

Your goal of finding and deepening intimacy will get sidetracked if you misunderstand what intimacy really is. Watch out for these common mistaken views of intimacy:

- Believing that liking is the same as caring.

- Believing that an intimate moment must be intensely felt.

- Believing that genuine intimacy also requires commitment.

- Believing that intimacy can be one-sided.

Let's look more closely at each of these intimacy mistakes.

Intimacy Imitation #1: Liking = Caring

"We were intimate last night," Hank said to me in a therapy session. He was describing his first date with Michelle. They ended their date by having sex. Was that true intimacy? Well, they were definitely connecting. And yes, they were sharing. The real question was this: did they genuinely care about one another? "Well, we enjoyed each other's company," Hank said.

Is that true caring? Probably not. It lacks the depth of genuine caring. If Hank is with someone for purposes of pleasure only, he might like her and enjoy her, but it is stretching the truth to say he really cares. It is really a "pseudo-intimacy." When liking is mistaken for real caring, relationships often end with at least one partner wondering, "What happened? We seemed so close."

Intimacy Imitation #2: Intimacy = Intensity

Another mistake is the belief that the intimate encounter must be powerful or passionate. Not so. A couple alone on a porch, embracing each other wordlessly as they think about their many years together are sharing an intimate moment. No words, no bells and whistles, but packed with intimacy. A simple kiss could be intensely intimate—or not at all intimate—depending on the level of true caring. However, adding passion to intimacy creates a level of romance that can be exhilarating.

CAUTION

Close Calls

If your need for intimacy is routinely at least 25 percent higher than your partner's, you will feel frustrated, tired, and worried. Demanding more intimacy won't help (you would have succeeded by now) and has probably become part of the problem. Pull back to a level nearer to your mate's and see what happens in the next few months.

Intimacy Imitation #3: Intimacy = Commitment

Can intimacy be powerful and genuine even if there is no commitment? Of course. Commitment is one component of true love. Combine it with intimacy and passion and you have a high-voltage relationship. But intimacy does not require commitment. However, when commitment is present, intimacy can go deeper because the depth of love is probably greater.

Intimacy Imitation #4: Intimacy = One Person's Experience

Lastly, intimacy is a shared experience, not one-sided. Someone caught up in the need to be in love or to find a close friend may reveal too much of themselves too soon or misinterpret politeness by the other person as a sign of wanting a deeper connection. If you tell the details of your life story to someone who listens but doesn't care, or to someone who won't reveal any aspects of his or her life, genuine intimacy is stunted, if not absent altogether.

When trying to figure out if intimacy is real or just a cheap imitation, remember that having contact doesn't mean you're connecting; talking isn't necessarily sharing; and liking someone doesn't mean that you really care.

Your Level of Intimacy

Intimacy doesn't come in a one-size-fits-all package. What works for one person doesn't always work for another. But after a relationship is established, a couple's way of being intimate becomes predictable. A pattern develops. Every relationship has a level of closeness and a level of separateness that must be balanced. Couples who argue about intimacy are really arguing over where to draw the line. The more stable the relationship, the more predictable and acceptable the level of intimacy becomes.

Intimacy also protects you from stress. Think of the levels of intimacy as layers of clothing that shield you from the elements. Below-average intimacy levels are like wearing shorts and a tee shirt. Fine if the weather is warm but that's all.

Couples with lower intimacy levels have infrequent, meaningful connections. Hurts and resentments are on the forefront of their minds. These couples also have a harder time coping with life's hardships. Weak intimacy acts like a weak immune system and fails to adequately protect them from outside "viruses" such as job strain, money worries, health problems, and so on.

Moderate levels of relationship intimacy are similar to wearing a coat over your clothes. You are better protected but still vulnerable to severe conditions. Couples with average intimacy levels find time for each other somewhat regularly, but outside influences such as work or child-rearing often interfere. Resentments may pop up now and then but are unlikely to last long or get in the way.

Couples with above-average intimacy are well protected from the elements. Their immune systems are strong. Time together is frequent and satisfying. Devotion always overrides resentments or misunderstandings.

Couples with above-average levels of intimacy have the equivalent of a huge savings account. If any hardships arise, they can be dealt with and paid for without much effort.

Exercise!

If your relationship is below average when it comes to intimacy, one of you has to get things rolling with a sustained effort. Decide to make thoughtful gestures every day for at least a month with no expectation of return. After that, have a talk with your partner about making mutual efforts to improve the quality of your relationship.

Don't Rest on Your Laurels

The moral is simple: Aim to be above average when it comes to intimacy! The good news is that it doesn't take a tremendous amount of effort to go from fair to good and from good to great. A Hall of Fame ballplayer achieves greatness often by just getting one more hit in every 10 at bats than the average player. You can do it. It may only take a 10 or 20 percent shift to make all the difference in the world.

The Four Pathways to Genuine Intimacy

Intimacy may take many forms but it follows only one of four paths. For intimacy to be strong in your current or future relationship, you should use all four paths a great deal. If you examine any special relationship you've had in recent years you will probably discover that you used only one or two paths most of the time. That won't make your relationship great, merely good.

The paths are listed here and explored in greater detail throughout this book. The purpose now is to acquaint you with them so you can begin to identify where your intimacy strengths and weaknesses lie.

The four pathways might be called The Four Ts: Intimacy through Thought, Talk, Touch, and Togetherness.

Intimacy Through Thought

Every act toward or away from intimacy begins with a thought. Your attitudes about intimacy and about that special person will determine what you think and how often. But thinking a certain way not only leads to greater intimacy, it can create an intimate feeling inside you even when you are alone. Imagine you haven't seen your best friend or romantic partner in quite a while. You anticipate a happy reunion later in the day and you can't wait to see each other. As the hours pass all you think about is that person. Doesn't your sense of closeness and intimacy grow?

Does it pass the connect-care-share test? Well, you are certainly connecting on some kind of mind level when you think so positively toward someone. And you feel a depth of caring and love. But is there a sharing? Yes. Even though you aren't together, you each have thoughts of being together again. Can you deny that such an experience has a positive affect on intimacy? As another example, imagine you have a co-worker whom you like but not in a romantic way. Imagine that the co-worker is totally infatuated with you and has a great many intimate thoughts about you. Is that genuine intimacy? Well, you are connected, and you may even care about that person. But unless you have passionate thoughts, too, the intimacy is not shared. Your co-worker is involved in fantasy, not intimacy.

Intimacy Through Talk

If the stranger sitting next to you on the plane tells you her life story, is that intimate? Not unless you care about that person and you share your life story, too. For the typical couple, intimacy through talk can be the most profound and fulfilling type of intimacy. Sadly, it is almost always the weakest part of the relationship.

> ### Intimacy Boosters
>
> "Pillow talk" is a delightful form of intimacy. It may last just a few minutes but it is something special for the two of you that isn't shared with anyone else. Spend a few minutes each night making small talk just before you and your partner fall asleep. Do the same in the morning, if you can.

> ### Close Calls
>
> If conversations fall apart, one partner is usually attacking more while the other withdraws. Then each one blames the other for the inability to communicate. Take responsibility for your side of the discussion. Stop attacking or being harsh and don't automatically retreat when the going gets rough.

Men have a tendency to shut down conversations quickly when the discussions get heated. Women usually desire more intimate conversation and can tolerate any emotional discomfort that might arise. However, women are much more likely than men to discuss problem areas more harshly, especially at the beginning of the dialogue.

Intimacy blossoms when conversations allow each person to truly say what's on their mind and to feel accepted—not rejected—in the process.

Intimacy Through Touch

Affection and sex are important ways to build and sustain intimacy. A physical connection alone, without at least one other form of intimacy working in the relationship, is probably not true intimacy because you don't know the other person well enough to genuinely care about them. Again, liking someone is not the same as having a depth of caring.

That is why it is rare for couples who are unhappy together to still have a great sex life. Typically, at least one partner will not feel very desirous of having sex if she does not also feel cared about in the relationship. Ironically, men often need to have sex to feel cared about.

Intimacy Through Togetherness

Many couples act like passing ships in the night. Their lives are so hectic; perhaps they even work different shifts, and they rarely have time to connect. They may care deeply about one another but without the opportunity to connect on a regular basis, intimacy will be stifled.

After a pattern of "We're too busy to spend time together" has taken hold, attempts to change it can be as difficult as losing that last 10 pounds. Many couples in this situation try to maintain a hectic schedule and somehow squeeze each other into their lives. It's like wolfing down fries and a burger and calling it a fancy dinner. This kind of "drive-through" relationship pattern will not sustain a couple over time. If your schedule is too hectic, something has to give.

Close Calls

The four types of intimacy are inter-connected. If you are weaker in one area, it can cause a reduction in intimacy in one or more of the other areas. Don't let that domino effect happen. Build intimacy across the board.

Quiz: What's Your IQ? (Intimacy Quotient)

Respond to the statements below using the following scale. If you are not currently in a relationship, respond as you would have if you were mid-way through your previous relationship.

4 Occurs most of the time

3 Occurs often

2 Occurs sometimes

1 Occurs rarely or never

1. I think lovingly and positively about my partner many times during the day when we are apart.

2. I remember when my partner has a medical appointment or special meeting and always ask about it later.

3. If my partner does something that annoys me I'm more likely to cut him or her some slack than think badly.

4. I really enjoy small talk with my mate.

5. If we disagree we can usually talk it out to our mutual satisfaction.

6. I can speak as openly with my partner as I can with my best friend.

7. We show affection at least eight times a day to each other.

8. Our sexual relationship is mutually satisfying.

9. We each initiate affection and sex at about the same rate.

10. We have at least 20 minutes a day where we feel warmth and connection as a couple.

11. We look forward to time alone together.

12. I don't feel threatened by my partner's outside interests.

Scoring key:

45–48 You have a high degree of intimacy. Congratulations!

37–44 Intimacy is good but could be better.

28–36 Intimacy is sluggish. Get moving!

19–27 Yellow alert! Improvement is absolutely essential!

12–18 Sorry, there is no intimacy.

Your score is a guideline, not a precise measure. Even if you scored a perfect 48, there are probably some weak spots in your Intimacy Quotient that went undetected in this test. You may also have strengths that were overlooked, even if your score was very low. Still, your score probably comes as no surprise. You know if you need some improving.

Your Personal Roadmap to Healthy Intimacy

When you try to add more intimacy to your life, be systematic in your efforts. A disorganized approach is one where you flip through the pages of this book and read something that pertains to you. Then you say to yourself, "That's a good idea. I should do something about that." You may or may not apply your new knowledge.

The better idea is to be at least somewhat organized. Identify the key areas you need to improve and write down the specific steps you can take to improve them. Monitor your progress weekly and make adjustments when necessary.

Identify Strengths and Weaknesses

The Intimacy Quotient test you just took is a great place to begin identifying your strong and weak points. There are 12 statements broken down into the four pathways. Statements 1 to 3 assess Intimacy through Thought; 4 to 6 assess Intimacy through Talk; 7 to 9 assess Intimacy through Touch; and 10 to 12 assess Intimacy through Togetherness.

Which of those four areas did you score highest in? Lowest? What steps are you willing to take to achieve a perfect score of 48?

Make an Intimacy Pact

You can make this pact a personal one or you can make it an agreement between you and your partner. You might want to include the following agreements:

- I will improve efforts at intimacy every day.

- I will not allow routine hassles or events to interfere with intimacy.

- I will focus on what I need to do to improve, not what my partner needs to do.

- If I lose my focus I will get back on track quickly.

- I will make progress checks with my partner.

You can add more statements that fit with your specific needs. Write the pact on a paper or index card and place it in your car, on your bathroom mirror, or anywhere it will serve as a reminder.

The Least You Need to Know

- Genuine intimacy involves three factors: connecting, caring, and sharing.

- Don't confuse liking with true caring.

- Improve your ability to have intimacy through talk and you will dramatically improve your overall intimacy.

- Identify which of the four pathways to intimacy are strengths and weaknesses: Intimacy through Thought, Talk, Touch, or Togetherness.

What Intimacy Really Means to Women and Men

In This Chapter

◆ Learning what men want women to know about intimacy

◆ Learning what women want men to know about intimacy

◆ Examining the fundamental conflict men and women each have about intimacy

◆ Finding the right balance of togetherness and separateness

Intimacy is required if you eventually want to have a relationship that matters and a relationship that lasts. Close encounters with your mate, your best friend, or the new person in your life must occur if your relationship is to survive. And they must occur somewhat regularly if your relationship is to thrive. People say that love is the glue that keeps people together. True. But the glue is useless unless it is applied. In other words, love needs to be shown, not merely felt. Intimacy is the way we show love and caring. It is the application of the glue.

And that is where all the madness comes in. Just about everybody wants intimacy. But how much? And how often? And in what ways? And what can be done when your desires for intimacy don't match your partner's? This chapter reveals what men and women really think about intimacy and what it means to them. And you guessed it; there are major differences between the genders. This chapter also reveals the core conflicts a typical man and woman have when it comes to achieving intimacy and how to begin eliminating those conflicts.

Do Men and Women Really Want the Same Thing?

Linda was determined to make her evening with Jim a memorable one. The cozy inn she found tucked away near a lake had the perfect combination of romance and privacy. Their dinner was succulent. The stroll by the water's edge made her feel like they were the only two people on Earth. True, Jim wasn't much of a talker, but he did hold her hand as they walked. When they found a bench swing overlooking the property, she cuddled next to him.

"This night is perfect," she said. The next thought that crossed her mind seemed a bit silly but she spoke her mind anyway. "I couldn't live without you in my life," she said. She looked into Jim's eyes and waited for his reply. And waited … And waited … "Well," she said. "Aren't you going to tell me how you can't live without me, either?"

"No," Jim said. "I mean, I don't *want* to live without you but I know that I could if I had to." He watched her face turn from soft and loving to hard and angry. He suddenly realized he had given the wrong answer so now he had to think fast and worm his way out of the situation. "I'm just being logical, Linda. That's all. Don't take it personally."

The rest of the night didn't go very well.

Linda and Jim are like many couples. Jim works hard and enjoys an active life. But when it comes to stoking the fires of intimacy, Linda is the prime mover. Jim would be content with their life as it is. Linda's efforts to increase affection and time together seem unnecessary to him. Aren't they happy enough? His attitude frustrates Linda. Sure he's a good guy but he has about as much sentimentality as a calculator. Doesn't he understand what a true, intimate, loving relationship entails? Doesn't he get it?

Intimacy Boosters

Intimacy gone flat? A night out or a romantic getaway is a fine idea but don't be surprised if some moments are awkward or disappointing. Keep expectations optimistic but modest. If the time together was mostly good, overlook any down times and emphasize the positive.

Men's Expectations of Intimacy

Men are raised to compete and achieve, not to nurture relationships. Men certainly can be nurturing and want relationships to be warm and close, but their instinct is to provide and protect, not communicate and cuddle. Think of it as a default drive. Any man can learn to become more open, communicative, thoughtful, and tender. But under stress or tension, his default drive kicks in and he is likely to think more than talk and to withdraw more than connect.

Often a man who emotionally disconnects from a woman during an argument or stressful time is not indifferent or uncaring. In fact, he is flooded with emotions. However, he tries to manage those emotions by distancing himself. What looks like aloofness or callous withdrawal is really his attempt to regulate intense feelings. When he detaches in that way, he starts judging his feelings. He wonders "Are my feelings appropriate? Are they manly? Am I feeling what I am supposed to feel?" Although a woman might want her man to talk about his emotions, the man may feel inadequate when it comes to expressing himself. In fact, he may feel ashamed about his inability to convey his thoughts and feelings fluently, so he shuts down even more.

To avoid feeling inadequate for being "intimacy challenged," a typical man will blame the woman for being too demanding, needy, or unappreciative. This is where couples get into a kind of emotional gridlock. She pursues more closeness, he pulls back. Each views the other as the source of the problem so each one is unwilling to see the role they are playing in the perpetuation of this tug of war.

As I said in Chapter 1, there are four primary pathways to intimacy. The Four Ts are Intimacy through Thought, Talk, Touch, and Togetherness. On average, men prefer intimacy through touch (especially sex) and togetherness more than through talking. And although a man may think about the woman he loves during the course of a day, he is more apt to get preoccupied with work or hobbies and forget all about her. This description of the average man is not ideal or flattering, but it is reality.

Intimacy Boosters

Do you offer a lot of advice during conversations with people you want to get closer to? By doubling the amount of listening and cutting away 90 percent of your advice, you might discover that conversations are easier and that people will feel more comfortable with you.

What a Man Wants a Woman to Understand

Before anyone can change their ways and make improvements, it is helpful to feel understood and not judged. Therefore, the typical guy would dearly love it if the woman he is wild about understands the following about his views of intimacy:

- He wants intimacy just as much as she does, but he often looks for it in ways that are different from her ways.

- He is willing to improve intimacy if he is not made to feel inadequate in the process.

- He tends to downplay (or hide from) his softer sides. But it is precisely that side of him that must emerge during many intimate moments. Therefore, he often escapes from intimacy sooner than a woman might.

- He truly regards any hard work he performs (his job, home repairs, and so on) as a way to show love. He is also doing it for her and not only for himself.

- Sex is not merely lust. It is a way to express nonverbally what he may have a hard time expressing verbally. Men who crave more sex with their lovers are often craving intimacy.

Interestingly, these insights about men are often just as revealing to some men as they are to women. Men are less apt than women to examine their motives and deeper feelings about these issues.

Exercise!

If you are feeling confined by your partner's push for greater intimacy, make a short list of the things you feel you are losing by being more intimate. Time alone? Money? Freedom of choice? Now ask yourself, "Is that really, really true?" You may discover that what you fear is really exaggerated.

A Man's Key Underlying Conflict

Each person in a relationship must find an acceptable balance between togetherness and separateness; between maintaining an independent sense of self and a sense of union. The problem for many men (or any person who is more competitive or achievement-oriented) is that they tend to focus on ways to maintain their personal identities more than they focus on ways to build their relationship identity. They lean more in the direction of separateness and rely more on their partner to lean in the direction of togetherness.

The conflict a lot of men face when trying to sustain intimacy is how to achieve it without losing their sense of self; without feeling controlled. What they don't often understand is that when a man pulls away from intimacy, a woman is likely to push for more intimacy, causing him to think she is trying to control him. In fact, he is trying to control her just as much. After a man realizes that he in no way loses any of himself by becoming more intimate, more open, or more tender, he can relax and enjoy intimate moments more than he already does.

Women's Expectations of Intimacy

Despite these socially enlightened times, women are still raised to be more relationship-focused than men. Achievement may be important to a woman, but after she is involved in a significant relationship she is a bit more likely than a man to alter her career path or relocate if it means keeping the relationship alive.

If children enter the picture, a career woman's inner conflicts rise. In a classic study, married professional women were asked to rate their own and their husband's performance with child rearing. These women rated their husbands highly but were displeased with their own performance as mothers. But in fact, they were still doing more for their children than the men were! Clearly, the pressure to fit the caretaking role remains strong in many women.

Just Ask!

Haven't sex-role stereotypes changed dramatically over the years? Aren't men and women freed from the stereotypes of two generations ago?

Not exactly. Although you are more likely to see a woman performing a role that was once only for men, you are not as likely to see men in roles once primarily held by women. Women are still raised to be caretakers more than men are. And men are supposed to reveal their "softer side" while still feeling a strong pressure to be tough and independent. Popular women's magazines primarily focus on relationships, child-rearing, or on how to balance a successful career as well as a successful relationship. Men's magazines emphasize sex (the lustful kind, not the loving kind), sports, competition, financial investments, and body building.

When times are stressful, the average woman—unlike her man—will try to connect with him. She will usually want to talk. Think of it as her default drive. Her instincts are to move closer and to strive for togetherness, especially during anxious times.

Often, that is in direct opposition to the man, who wants to withdraw and mull things over by himself when he is tense and under duress.

Statistically, women are clearly ahead of men in all the Four T's of Intimacy. They especially use talking and touch (affection). With a wider range of intimacy tools at their disposal, women often view the typical guy as deficient in intimacy. Women therefore pursue men for more magical moments together and get frustrated more easily when those moments don't happen.

When a woman craves more intimacy, her man might perceive her as needy or over-emotional. What he doesn't understand is that her efforts to connect to him are her way of managing her emotions and bringing them under control. When a man feels flooded with emotion, he pulls away in order to manage his emotions. He doesn't understand that she is regulating her emotions, too, but in a manner totally opposite from him.

It would be funny if it weren't always so stressful, but many couples debate with one another as if one person's way for achieving intimacy and managing emotions is obviously best and the other person's way is obviously flawed. It reminds me of an incident when I was a small boy. I had just been given some goldfish but they soon died. Why? Because I fed them every time I was hungry. I assumed that what was best for me was best for them.

Just Ask!

I've been with Doug for three years. I've tried and tried get him to spend more quality time with me and to talk more. Nothing works! He just gets more aggravated. He tells me I'm supposed to just accept his ways. Should I?

Acceptance is a two-way street. If your man tends to be more aloof or less affectionate and he wants you to accept him, then he must accept you, too. Fair is fair. But accepting you means a willingness to meet your needs. Put it another way: he can meet his needs to be alone or disconnected all by himself. He just has to pull away. But you cannot meet your needs for togetherness and connectedness alone. It requires his cooperation.

What a Woman Wants a Man to Understand

When couples come into my office I am more likely to hear the woman complain that she has told the man something important many times but that he hasn't fully heard her. Feeling misunderstood and ignored or unheard, these women are aggravated and even lonely. Down deep a woman may be passionate about her man, but she would be so grateful if he would comprehend the following about what intimacy means to her:

◆ Wanting more closeness, more intimacy, more togetherness, and more affection is not a sign of dependency or overactive neediness. It is her way of showing love and feeling loved.

◆ She fears that if she cut back on efforts to keep intimacy alive and kicking, he wouldn't find common ground and try to meet her intimacy needs.

◆ If she was given more of what she wanted in terms of closeness, she would easily tolerate those times he wants distance because she would trust he would provide closeness later on.

◆ She enjoys playful, sexual affection but not exclusively. When a man offers sexual affection, she may feel attractive but not necessarily beloved. Tender, nonsexual affection by her man tells her she is beloved and cherished.

◆ Her desire for sexual intimacy is a natural consequence of feeling loved and cherished.

The average woman has a lot of insight into her intimacy needs but does not convey those insights in a clear way. She is more likely to be indirect, hoping her man "gets it." Often as not, she is disappointed.

A Woman's Key Underlying Conflict

When it comes to establishing, building, and maintaining intimacy in important relationships, women are the prime movers. Whereas a man may err on the side of reduced intimacy to maintain a sense of self, a woman will err on the side of losing some of her identity to keep a relationship alive. Of course this isn't always true. Still, in the push and pull of relationships, a woman will look for ways to build a relationship identity and be willing to sacrifice some of her personal identity in the process.

A woman may not even realize she is doing this because so often her own identity is already tied to the concept of building a relationship. The less a woman has a clear sense of her own personal (nonrelationship) needs, wants, dreams, and goals, the more she will need to be in an intimate relationship to feel more alive.

Whose Rulebook Do You Follow?

Close Calls

Statistically, men are less adept at detecting relationship weaknesses than women. When a woman feels the relationship is off-track and a man says everything is fine, it's a mistake to accept his assessment fully. He's probably wrong.

That's a trick question. It implies that one way is better than the other way. One way is not necessarily better or worse. But some ways are fulfilling and some ways are not fulfilling. If your goal is to not bicker over having more or less intimacy but to understand one another's wants and needs and to do your best to meet them as often as possible, you may believe that your expectations of intimacy are proper and normal. But if you push to get your expectations met without trying to understand your partner's opposing needs, you both will be unfulfilled and you both will lose.

Bridging the Intimacy Gap

In the recipe for achieving an intimate relationship, whether it is friendships or serious dating or marriage, you have two "selves" combining to make one relationship. In the extremes, if someone is too self-focused and puts up barriers to intimacy, there can be no relationship and no intimacy. Similarly, if someone completely loses him- or herself in the union, then you have a relationship—but still no intimacy.

You can't have intimacy if you possess no self for the other person to be intimate with.

If any person in a relationship (often, but not always the man) fears that greater intimacy will cause a loss of self, then that person will resist efforts to improve the quality of the relationship. The trick is for him to discover that the most spectacular form of intimacy allows a deep connection and union without loss of one's personal identity.

If any person in a relationship (often, but not always the woman) fears that having a more defined self will cause a loss of intimacy, then efforts to improve self-esteem via personal achievement will be resisted. The trick is for her to discover that the more warmly she regards and respects herself the more the relationship truly becomes a union of two distinct people, not a merging of one person completely into the other.

Tips for Women

These tips are not exclusively for women but for those who are more apt to sacrifice their "selves" too much for the sake of a relationship. You know you fit this category if most of the following apply to you:

❏ You are best described as a people pleaser.

❏ You more often say "Yes" when you'd like to say "No."

❏ You easily slip into a caretaking role.

❏ You feel drained, unappreciated, and complain about it but still end up doing most of the work in the relationship.

Take time to develop a new hobby or interest that you think you'd have a passion for. Carve out time for it even if it means cutting back on time with loved ones. Also, get acquainted with people who are struggling with the same issues you are. Encourage and support each other.

Make a list of important qualities about yourself and your skills. My guess is that you will describe yourself mostly in ways that connect you with others. You will point out how generous or loving you are, for example. But you will have far fewer descriptors that do not imply a relationship. Your job is to add to the list of descriptors that do not involve having a meaningful relationship.

Tips for Men

These tips are not exclusively for men but for those who are more apt to settle for less intimacy for fear of losing their "selves." You know you fit this category if most of the following apply to you:

❏ You often meet your needs ahead of meeting others.

❏ You feel more comfortable saying no to requests that inconvenience you.

❏ You are more apt to let others take care of themselves than to be a caretaker for them.

❏ You may feel drained or not fully appreciated for all the work you do outside of a relationship.

To make changes that will improve intimacy, start cutting back somewhat on hobbies or activities that take you away from your primary relationships. Or, if the special person in your life wants to spend time on a personal hobby or interest, assist her with her other responsibilities so she can free up her time.

Make a list of your better qualities and skills. You may discover that qualities that involve relationships (patience, thoughtfulness, compassion, tenderness, and so on) could use some expansion. Your job is to try to enhance those qualities.

The Least You Need to Know

◆ True intimacy does not cause you to lose some or all of your personal identity.

◆ Having a strong and clear personal identity will not interfere with achieving intimacy.

◆ The highest quality intimacy happens when two people with a strong sense of who they are find the right balance of togetherness and separateness.

◆ You can't achieve lasting intimacy if you think mostly of yourself or mostly of the relationship.

Common Roadblocks to Achieving Intimacy

In This Chapter

- ◆ Understanding the affect of fatigue on intimacy
- ◆ Discovering the myth of quality time
- ◆ Defining the three intimacy killers
- ◆ Looking like intimacy when it isn't
- ◆ Shedding light on hidden intimacy concerns

Having trouble forming a new relationship or figuring out why your last relationship didn't work? Does your current relationship need an intimacy tune-up? You need to clear the pathway of obstacles before you can walk down Lover's Lane. The impediments to intimacy are more than you imagined. Some are small and easily avoided; some are bigger and must be pushed aside.

This chapter identifies the common roadblocks that halt intimacy from the get-go. You have to start somewhere before you can build more intimacy. But if the roadblocks aren't cleared away, you won't get far.

Barricades to Bonding

When a couple is dating, happy, and falling in love, intimacy—in all its forms—seems as natural as breathing. You think about each other constantly, eagerly waiting for the next moment you will be together. Talking is a breeze. Even if one of you is quieter by nature, somehow the spell is broken and you find yourselves staying awake to all hours in a nonstop, intoxicating conversation. Togetherness? Not a problem. Sex and affection? You probably can't keep your hands off of each other.

 Just Ask!

My relationship ended four months ago and I still feel devastated. When will I know that I'm emotionally ready to move on?

Jumping into a new relationship now isn't wise. Take time to sort through the reasons why the relationship ended and what you learned. When you feel eager for a new relationship but not desperate or frightened, that's a good sign. Your ex may have hurt you deeply but when your attitude is a (somewhat) sincere "I wish him (or her) well," you have gotten past much of your anger and are probably ready to look to your future.

So what happens to make intimacy falter? Why does cozy togetherness seem impossible to achieve?

Small Obstacles

Sooner or later, most people experience three very common obstacles to intimacy. I consider them small obstacles (even though they can have large negative effects) because they are more easily overcome.

- ◆ Fatigue
- ◆ Not enough time together
- ◆ Believing "We'll make improvements … tomorrow"

Too tired? Fatigue is perhaps the number one reason for lack of intimacy. It means you are too busy and not taking better care of yourself. It probably means you are saying "Yes" to low-priority events and obligations when you could be saying "No." When fatigue interferes with your relationship on a regular basis, it means you have put your relationship on the bottom of your list of important things. It means you are taking your relationship for granted.

If fatigue has persisted for more than a month, do the following:

◆ Get a check-up from your physician. You could have an iron deficiency, a blood sugar problem, or a host of other ailments.

◆ Buy any book on nutrition that you believe makes sense and follow that diet plan for a month. Chances are your eating habits are abysmal and are contributing to your fatigue.

◆ Exercise more, even if it is just 10 minutes a day.

◆ Get to bed at the same time every night and wake up at the same time.

◆ If you drink alcohol, stop, especially before bedtime. Alcohol may make it easier for you to get to sleep but it will increase your chances of having early awakenings.

Part 5 of this book gives you many ideas on how to make time for one another. For now, understand that although many couples are too busy to have quality time together, making that time is a *must*. Actually, quality time is a myth and won't cut it. Quantity time is also key. A nice, quality night out once a month, however romantic, won't fill you up with warm fuzzies about one another. One solid clue that you haven't been spending enough time together is if you are cranky. If you are, you can bet that is the reason. Cranky couples complain about small things. They whine. They flinch when their partner tries to show affection. They sigh a lot. What's really going on is that the lack of togetherness creates a feeling of entitlement. You feel owed. So you complain about anything and everything when what you really want is to spend relaxed time with each other.

Exercise!

If your boss said that you would have to make phone calls from home for about a half-hour every night for the next month, you would moan and groan but you would also find the time. So do the same for your relationship. Sit down for 10 minutes with your partner. During that time, come up with as many ideas as you can to carve out 20 minutes a day of relaxing time together and at least three nights out in the next month. No excuses. What can you do for 20 minutes? Rub each other's back, hold each other in bed, go for a walk, listen to a new CD, have a glass of wine or a cup of coffee. It doesn't matter. Just do something. Find a babysitter who will agree to three babysitting jobs in the next month.

The final small obstacle to intimacy is procrastination; assuming you'll start making improvements soon but not right away. Busy couples with hectic lives always find time for their bosses, their children, and even themselves—but postpone finding time for each other. Put the relationship on the top of the list. Now. Otherwise, more time will pass and your relationship will pay the price.

Bigger Obstacles

If you see any of these obstacles, watch out:

◆ Retaliation

◆ Contempt

◆ Unreliability

Karla and Tim had another one of their arguments about spending. Tim purchased a truck—Karla knew they needed one—but he paid about $5,000 more than she expected by upgrading to a classier vehicle. Karla was furious because two months earlier she had a chance to purchase two tickets for a cruise to Bermuda at dirt-cheap prices. Tim was adamant they could not afford it, so they did not go. But now he managed to justify spending thousands more for a fancy truck. How did Karla handle her feelings? She gave him the cold shoulder. She stopped all affection; spoke only in crisp, short sentences; and slept as far away from him in bed as she could. For his part, Tim stayed later at work without informing her he'd be late and somehow his clothes ended up on the floor each night instead of in the clothes basket where he usually put them. What was going on? It is a common ailment—retaliation.

> **Exercise!**
>
> Get rid of contempt using two key strategies. First, agree *never* to speak to each other in a mocking or ridiculing tone. Second, every day for a month you should end the day with something praiseworthy to say aloud to your mate. Contempt can kill a relationship. Praise and admiration will strengthen intimacy.

When a partner retaliates it is as if he or she is saying: "Now you will know how unhappy I am and this will make you feel badly for what you've done." But retaliation rarely, if ever, prompts a mate to respond with compassion and understanding. Retaliation only leads to resentment or annoyance. Retaliation is an understandable response but it is not a useful one. Part 3 of this book teaches you more effective ways to manage differences without retaliating. A better response is simply to state "I'm angry at what you did and we need to discuss it now or very soon." If you're not in the mood for a talk, say "I'm angry at what you did and I want some space to think things over for now."

When retaliation occurs frequently, couples often start feeling contempt for one another. Contempt is a form of anger but it also includes a feeling of disrespect. Sometimes it shows up as mocking, as when you roll your eyes in disgust or when you repeat your partner's words in an insulting tone. Contempt is very poisonous to a relationship and must not be allowed to continue.

The final big block to intimacy is unreliability. If your partner doesn't keep his promises or fails to follow through on important decisions, intimacy will suffer. Sometimes an unreliable partner means well but is disorganized or has taken on too many responsibilities. Common indications you may not be reliable are as follows:

❑ Forgetfulness, especially when it is important to your mate that you remember

❑ Household repairs that have been incomplete for months

❑ Irresponsibility with money

❑ Inability to maintain a job

❑ Last-minute excuses

❑ Thoughtlessness, such as failing to call when you are running late

❑ Making time for others but not for your mate

❑ Recreational overuse of alcohol or drugs

Someone who is unreliable in any of the above ways may still think of himself as trustworthy because he is faithful and monogamous. But trustworthiness goes beyond sexual fidelity. Unless you are reliable, it is hard for intimacy to blossom because your partner can't rely on you to be there for her in ways that are important.

> **CAUTION**
>
> **Close Calls**
>
> If your mate has ever bitterly complained that you "act like one of the kids!" then he or she views you as irresponsible and not very reliable in at least some matters. After your partner starts to feel like your parent, passion and intimacy can fizzle.

Intimacy Killers

Forget about building intimacy if any one of these three intimacy killers is present:

◆ Alcoholism or other addictions

◆ Physical, emotional, or verbal abuse

◆ An ongoing affair

CAUTION

Close Calls

If you are being abused in your relationship, do not go into counseling together. The abusive partner will use punishment or intimidation to keep you from being completely open and honest in therapy. No progress will occur. Sessions together may be warranted when the abusive partner has been nonabusive for several months.

When one of these factors is present, one or both partners often believe what I call "The Big Lie"—that by improving intimacy, the addiction, the abuse, or the affair will stop. WRONG! In fact, it is the other way around. Until the addiction, the abuse, or the affair stops completely, intimacy will be thwarted.

If one of you has an addiction, a rehabilitation program may be necessary. A 12-step program such as Alcoholics Anonymous can be extremely helpful. Beware of the addict who refuses to get help. Sobriety is difficult and requires humility—a willingness to admit weakness. Refusing to seek help is a sign of arrogance and a denial of the severity of the problem.

Abusiveness of any kind can be highly traumatic. If you are a victim of abuse (or if you are an abuser who was abused as a child), seek therapy with a professional who specializes in Post Traumatic Stress Disorder.

Affairs are not an automatic death sentence for a relationship. A couple who is motivated to overcome the immense pain of betrayal often makes large strides in therapy. However, if the affair is ongoing—even if there is brief, nonsexual contact by the participants (via phone calls or e-mails)—progress will grind to a halt. Chapter 28 gives you many more guidelines on how to rebuild intimacy after an affair.

Love's Illusions: False Intimacy and False Detachment

Intimacy can fool you. So can detachment. Imagine coming home late at night and your spouse, who is watching TV, ignores you. What does that mean? The answer depends on your overall view of the relationship. If you are happy, you'll give your spouse the benefit of the doubt and assume she is engrossed in a movie. If you are unhappy, you'll see it as her way of not caring.

Before you learn more about improving intimacy, I'd like you to consider the ways you can be fooled. If you think that some behaviors qualify as intimate—but they really aren't—you will falsely believe the relationship to be stronger than it is. If you don't recognize intimacy when it is really there, you will suffer many missed opportunities for closeness.

It Looks Like Intimacy But It Isn't

Don't be fooled by these common intimacy decoys:

- Frequent need for reassurance
- Receiving clichés instead of real understanding
- Sex (to avoid intimacy)
- Politeness without passion
- Possessiveness

If your mate clings to you and frequently needs reassurance that you really love him or her, insecurity is smothering intimacy. An insecure person will be afraid to be honest and open if such openness might lead to rejection. True intimacy is not based on fear.

If your mate makes flat, uninspired statements such as "Life is hard" or "It will all work out" when you're feeling stressed, that's not intimacy. Intimacy involves understanding and acceptance, not pat phrases designed to make you move on to another topic.

How can having sex be a way to avoid intimacy? Easy. Anybody can go through the motions but it doesn't mean they feel a depth of caring for the person they are with. One woman who was headed for divorce put it this way: "I had sex with my husband last night. But I wouldn't kiss him. Kissing is too intimate." If you really want to meet someone and develop an intimate, loving relationship, delaying having sex is correlated with long-term stability in the relationship. In other words, the sooner you have sex, the less likely the relationship will last. Why might that be? True intimacy comes from a depth of caring that can only happen when you get to know someone over time.

Some couples act like polite strangers at a cocktail party. They talk, they smile, they snack on cheese and crackers, but they lack a depth of caring. They do not cherish one another. Because they rarely argue, these couples pretend they have intimacy when they don't. A polite relationship is not really intimate if it lacks a genuine caring or the occasional spark of passion.

Intimacy Boosters

Just because you're feeling in the mood for attention or affection doesn't mean it is the most opportune time for your partner. If your mate looks busy, agitated, or preoccupied, keep your intimacy attempts short and sweet. If your mate wants more, you'll know.

Finally, a possessive partner claims he loves you but his insecurity and need for control make it impossible for genuine intimacy to thrive. A possessive partner might demand to know where you've been when you're late and inquires about your daily activities with the detail of a police investigator. Possessiveness does not pass the connection—caring—sharing test. He might be connected to you, but possessiveness is a form of control, not real caring. And it isn't mutual. A possessive partner would not tolerate you being demanding and possessive.

It Doesn't Look Like Intimacy But It Is

Couples whose relationship is a bit strained often overlook these efforts by their partners at caring and intimacy. What often happens is that one person's attempt at closeness just doesn't show up on the other one's radar—or worse, the well-meaning attempt is downright annoying. If your partner does any of the following, view them as subtle but genuine efforts at achieving intimacy:

- Giving you space when you are in a bad mood

- Complaining

- Pressuring you to try new things

- Doting or fussing over you

- Wanting sex soon after an argument

The typical guy is an expert at giving a woman time to herself when she is in a bad mood. That's because when men are in a bad mood they want to be left alone, so they think women deserve the same courtesy. However, it comes across to many women as indifference or withdrawal. In these moments, if you want his company, you must ask for it.

How can complaining be remotely connected to intimacy? First, a complaint is not an attack. It is a statement of dissatisfaction made to improve the situation. Women complain more frequently than men, on average. That is because women have a better handle on the state of the relationship and are more alert to potential problems.

It may be annoying when your mate tries to talk you into activities you really don't enjoy. ("Hey hon, I know you're not fond of heights but wouldn't it be fun to try out the new rollercoaster at the amusement park?") He or she just wants a little adventure or change of pace. Don't always be a party pooper. Besides, you might enjoy it more than you think.

If your mate reminds you to wear a coat because it's cold outside, is she being a nag and acting like your mother or is she simply demonstrating that she cares? Often, behaving "motherly" or "fatherly" is not a put down or an attempt to control. It's a way to express concern and love.

Finally, men more than women will seek sex as a way to repair a rift in the relationship. Women think, "How can you think of such a thing?" and men think "When did I ever stop thinking of such a thing?" The bottom line is if you're not interested in sex after an argument, fine. But if your beloved other is interested it is probably because he is trying to mend fences through physical intimacy, not simply to fulfill an urge.

Shedding Light on Hidden Intimacy Needs

Sometimes you may be unaware of what you really want in a relationship. Or maybe you try to convince yourself that your current relationship is fine but a nagging doubt persists. Perhaps your partner says he or she is happy with you, but you can't help but wonder if that's completely true. Fortunately, hidden signs are sometimes available to clue you in to unanswered questions you may have about your own or your partner's intimacy needs.

Over several days, pay attention to any complaints you have that have nothing to do with your relationship. (Or monitor your partner's complaints.) The list might look something like this:

"I'm tired ... My boss is unfair ... The kids take me for granted ... I dislike my appearance ... There is no money for fun things ... My parents are too demanding ... The house is too cluttered ... Traffic is too congested ..."

Now, consider the possibility that these complaints are also clues to how you feel about your current or former relationship. For example, if your boss is unfair, is that also a statement that your relationship is unfair? If you feel exhausted, are you tired about something in the relationship? If traffic is always congested, are you feeling smothered by your partner? If money is tight, might you also be saying that you and your partner have no fun together? If you dislike your appearance, do you worry your partner is no longer attracted to you? If your kids take you for granted or your parents are too demanding, is your partner also demanding and doesn't fully appreciate all you do?

Your nonrelationship complaints may or may not reflect relationship issues. You might be surprised, however, to find out that sometimes they do. Then it's a matter of addressing those concerns and making the right changes. That's what this book reveals.

The Least You Need to Know

- Fatigue is the number one obstacle to daily intimacy.

- Being unreliable and inconsistent about keeping your promises erodes trust, which makes lasting intimacy impossible.

- Addictions or abuse will prevent intimacy from growing.

- Emotional dependency or possessiveness smothers the closeness you want to achieve.

- A partner who complains (but is not attacking) is usually motivated by a desire for more closeness, not to push you away.

Chapter 4

Struggling With Intimacy and Choosing the Wrong Person

In This Chapter

- ◆ Making common mistakes when choosing a partner
- ◆ Knowing when opposites are a good match
- ◆ Learning how your childhood experiences affect intimacy
- ◆ Discovering how break-ups affect your next intimate relationship

It starts out dreamy, amazing, and fantastic. You wonder, "Can he be the one?" and before you know it all systems are go. You see each other as often as possible, eventually live together or get married, and then … it comes apart at the seams. For some, the realization that the relationship can't work comes like an unexpected whack to the side of the head. Others may have seen it coming but could do nothing to stop the downhill slide.

What gives? How do two well-intentioned people completely misjudge or mishandle their relationship? And how is it that some of those same people go on to a new relationship only to have it not work out, either? This chapter sheds substantial light on those questions and, most importantly, provides you with clear-cut strategies to keep you on the path to lasting intimacy.

The Typical Sad Scenarios

Couples file into my office every day for basically one purpose—to repair intimacy. Whatever their differences about such subjects as money, sex, communication, or parenting, I know that their foundation of intimacy has partially collapsed and is in need of rebuilding. Sometimes rebuilding intimacy is straightforward. The couple realizes they have fallen short in at least one of the intimacy categories (thought, talk, touch, or togetherness) and make a determined effort to improve matters.

But sometimes more questions must be asked. Is each person truly ready for more intimacy? If not, then trying to boost intimacy would be like trying to improve your tennis game by wearing high-heeled shoes instead of sneakers. You'd put forth a lot of wasted effort.

Just Ask!

Everyone tells me I'm a wonderful person and, frankly, I'm not bad looking. I have a good job and dream about getting married. But my last three very close relationships failed. I don't know what I'm doing wrong. Am I destined to be alone?

First of all, some relationships should fail. Some couples try to force-fit a relationship when they really need to admit it can't work. In fact, if you are feeling a bit desperate, you might have remained longer in a relationship than you should have. Second, you (or your former partners) may be weak in at least one of the four paths to intimacy. Identifying that path and then strengthening it will be essential. When you do find the right person you will be glad that your last three relationships didn't work out!

If you ever found yourself in one of the common "dances" that some couples do, intimacy building won't get very far. Let's start with one of the most common dances.

The "You Can't Live Without Me" Dance

When I see this dance I know that one person in the relationship is too controlling. Genuine intimacy is stifled when the relationship has a one up/one down quality. Intimacy can improve but only to a point. The one-down person won't feel free to say how she or he really feels for fear of displeasing the more powerful partner. And the one-up partner, although appearing to want closeness, won't risk the vulnerability that true closeness brings. So he will push the partner away at times, blaming her for that, although really needing to make space so he can feel independent and more protected.

If you recognize yourself as more controlling, therapy can help. Giving the other person room to grow adds to intimacy. And if you are the one being controlled, you'll end up feeling more lonely and dreaming about other potential lovers.

 Close Calls

Is your mate too controlling? One big clue is that there is a double standard. If he does something wrong it's either your fault or there were good reasons; if you do something wrong then it's your fault. A controlling person rarely accepts responsibility for problems. The more controlling a person is, the less intimacy there will be.

Exercise!

For about two weeks, take turns being "in charge" of the relationship regarding time spent together, talking, or physical touch. When you are in charge, you get to have final say over what you'd like to see happen. Do not use this exercise as a maneuver to get your way over a controversial or touchy subject. The goal is to do more things together without having to debate it and to demonstrate that both of you can have equal say.

The "I Can't Live Without You" Dance

Here at least one of you is too needy. Sometimes intense neediness (accompanied by poor self-esteem) masquerades as intense intimacy. But the intimacy is diluted by insecurity. Intimacy requires honesty. It's hard to be honest when you fear that saying or doing the wrong thing might cause the relationship to break.

If you are matched with a person who likes to be in charge, your neediness may fit like a glove with your mate's domineering style. But the one in charge eventually grows weary of putting up with an insecure person. Often, a very needy person craves more intimacy when in fact he or she is actually craving security. Don't confuse the two. Intimacy built on fear will collapse.

Intimacy Boosters

If you are feeling needy and insecure, it would do you a world of good to find a hobby or interest that does not involve your partner. Take a course, learn a skill, make a new friend. Do something bold that makes you feel more confident.

The "On Again, Off Again" Dance

"We've broken up several times over the past three years," Donna said. "Mike moved out two weeks ago but now he wants to come back. I'm tired of this."

Donna has a point. On again, off again relationships are exhausting. Simply trying to build more intimacy into this relationship will backfire. Why? Because one or both partners has mixed feelings about the desirability of the relationship. If you try to make yourselves get closer through more and better intimacy, one of you will get scared and pull away. But if you don't try to rebuild intimacy, one of you will get annoyed and pull away.

After the on again, off again pattern has emerged, it will likely repeat itself because you have both learned that when problems or doubts arise, the only way to cope is to run or push the other away. This is very different from the couple who never threatens to end the relationship when problems occur and who manages to mend their differences.

> **Intimacy Boosters**
>
> If intimacy is low and you are unsure you have the stamina to make improvements, try this idea: Rate your current level of commitment. Say it is 30 percent. Now ask yourself, "What would I do today to add intimacy if my commitment was 10 points higher?" After you have an answer, act that way. You can build intimacy without overwhelming you.

Over time, this pattern will reduce your trust level so low that even when your relationship is "on" one of you is waiting for the ax to fall. In fact, one of you might actually instigate an argument just to get the inevitable "I'm leaving!" over with.

Before you can rebuild intimacy, the two of you must make a pact. Tell each other you will never again threaten to end the relationship. And if one of you does leave, you both should move on.

The "Keep a Bad Relationship Going" Dance

Couples in the keep a bad relationship going dance argue a lot and claim they really can't stand the other person (yet they remain a couple) or they lead lives of quiet disconnection. They might complain that they want more intimacy but, once again, any effort to achieve it hits a brick wall.

Every couple adjusts, to some extent, to their relationship. How does one adjust to constant arguing or to the absence of any real connection? By dulling one's desire for closeness. Trying to spark some intimacy in this couple is like trying to get someone with a suppressed appetite to eat a meal. They're just not that hungry.

The goal in improving these relationships is to try to have small but sustained moments of togetherness or closeness without trying to make big inroads (yet) toward intimacy.

Exercise!

If your relationship is too hostile or barely breathing, there is an effective way to make improvements. Agree to have daily *one-sided* conversations. The person who is talking is not to accuse or blame or criticize. Instead the talker is simply to discuss past events or any relationship issue by answering the following question:

"What would I like my partner to understand that I don't think he or she understands?"

The listener is not to debate or criticize what is being said. The goal is to understand. Later (or the next day) you can switch roles. Following this exercise will eliminate the usual disputes, interruptions, or shutdowns that would ordinarily occur. Hopefully, many such one-sided discussions will lead to improved understanding and empathy. Then intimacy may be able to blossom.

Do Opposites Attract or Do They Detract?

Is it healthy for an extrovert to hook up with an introvert? Can the neat freak really learn to get along with someone whose idea of tidying up is removing the apple cores he absent-mindedly stuck underneath the sofa cushions? Can a tough as nails, unemotional type really hit it off with someone who gushes with emotion during TV commercials?

"I love my husband Ken," Alice said, "but when he insists on telling me the details of how he routed the 1,200 songs he has in his computer so that they play out of our Surround Sound television speakers, well, my eyes glaze over. I really don't care how it works. I don't mean to hurt his feelings but I can't listen when he discusses technological details."

Alice probably has no reason to worry. Inevitably there are differences between partners. But the successful couple doesn't allow differences to divide them. Statistically, couples fare better when they are similar on the following dimensions:

- Intelligence
- Educational levels
- Cultural background
- Religious background
- Values and ethics
- Future goals

A couple who is similar on those qualities can afford to have personality differences. It is fascinating to see how personality differences that are attractive in the beginning of a relationship can become unattractive over time. For example, "cute sentimentality" becomes "annoying over-emotionality"; "calm under pressure" becomes "cold and unfeeling"; "reliable" becomes "predictable and boring"; "enthusiastic and bubbly" becomes "childish"; "ambitious" becomes "a workaholic"; and so on.

Why would you be annoyed by traits that once attracted you? Your partner's traits and habits may well be qualities you yourself possess but cannot own up to. A very unemotional person, for example, is almost always attracted to a very sentimental person and vice versa. Why? The unemotional person needs emotion in his life but dislikes expressing it. So he hooks up with someone who will express it for him. The miser needs someone who can be more carefree. The spender needs someone who will refrain from spending.

Start appreciating the fact that deep down you may need your partner to be the way he or she is—even though you often object.

Happy couples see the value in their differences and don't try to eradicate their partner's annoying personality traits. Instead they try to manage their differences—in other words, be flexible about them—so that they are mildly annoying at worst.

> **Exercise!**
>
> For two weeks, encourage your partner to do something that ordinarily annoys you. Give a gift of complete acceptance. Then see what happens. By abandoning the usual tug of war, you may find that those annoying traits are not so bad after all. And your mate will be very, very appreciative.

Reason #1 for Intimacy Problems: Family Background

It is doubtful that your family of origin, no matter how wonderful, was a perfect training ground for lasting intimacy. Chances are you have at least one or two issues to resolve from your background. For example, Tina came from a loving family. But by the time she was 10 the family was hit by two hardships: bankruptcy and her mother's worsening emphysema. So Tina learned to put aside her needs and look after her younger siblings so her mom could rest and her dad could work long hours rebuilding their finances. Now an adult, Tina still puts other's needs ahead of her own and it has negatively affected her intimate relationships. She gives and gives, only to feel used and unappreciated.

The Role Your Parents Played

The impact your parents had in the development of your ability to achieve lasting intimacy could take an entire book to explain. But here are some key guidelines that may shed much light. See how many apply to you:

- An adult raised by very harsh or abusive parents has a tendency to either crave intimacy and be over-needy or fear intimacy and be detached.

- An adult who is over-involved and too close to his family of origin runs the risk of becoming less involved with his spouse and children.

- An adult who is estranged from his family of origin might become needy and possessive in his current relationship.

- An adult who was raised by an alcoholic or addicted parent probably had a chaotic home life growing up and was expected to put up a "front" to others and deny family problems. As an adult he may have difficulty trusting others and trusting his own judgment.

- An adult raised by parents or caretakers who balanced warmth with structure and discipline were given the best start to life.

Sometimes, the answer to the question *"What did I want from my childhood but did not get?"* reflects something that is still missing now in your life. If so, you might want a current friend or partner to make up for something from your past. It won't work.

Exercise!

Write down all the qualities your parents possessed. What were their values? Their strengths and weaknesses? How did they relate to one another as spouses? How did they relate to their children? Ask yourself: In what ways do I wish to be like each of my parents and in what ways do I wish to be different? You will discover that the answers you give are forces in your life. It might explain why you act and feel the way you do.

How You Coped as a Child

Think of any problems you experienced as a child. Perhaps they dealt with school, home life, friends, or self-confidence. How did you cope with those problems? There are five primary ways:

♦ **Fight.** Use aggression to deal with problems.

♦ **Flee.** Run away, escape the situation.

♦ **Freeze.** Be indecisive, unsure of yourself.

♦ **Fold.** Give up and give in. Submit to others.

♦ **Face fears.** Tackle them head on. Assert yourself.

My guess is that you tended to use one (or two) of those ways primarily. But chances are also very good that if you are going through some kind of intimacy crisis now, you are coping with it in the same way. Unless you are facing your problems head on, you will perpetuate them.

Close Calls

If you routinely complain to your parents about your partner, you must *stop*. It doesn't matter that your complaints might be valid. You will probably undermine (perhaps forever) your parents fondness for your mate and you will gain a false sense of "I'm right" because your partner's viewpoint is not being heard. If you need a good listener, talk to someone who can be more objective.

At around age 10, boys separate emotionally somewhat from their mothers. They may love their moms but they start to look toward their fathers more. What if the father is physically or emotionally absent? The boys learn to fend for themselves emotionally. If they have a problem with school or friends, they are more apt to figure it out for themselves rather than talk to Mom about it. This helps build self-sufficiency but at a price: the boys grow up to be poor communicators because talking was never the tool they used to cope. Also, these young men usually crave more intimacy because they had less of it growing up. However, after they have an opportunity for greater intimacy they pull away from it because it makes them feel too vulnerable or out of control. Their adult relationships have a "herky-jerky" look to them; closeness followed by distance followed by closeness, and so on.

Reason #2 for Intimacy Problems: The Ghost of Lovers Past

If you've been burned before you will have a firewall up. You may be particularly alert to signs that your new partner might hurt you in the way your former lover did. But you also are very likely to overreact and see signs that aren't there at all.

The following might seem like a simple exercise but it can be very effective. When you find yourself drawing negative conclusions about your partner, simply ask yourself, *"Would I bet money that these conclusions are true?"* If that question causes you to doubt your negative conclusions, perhaps you overreacted. Also, get feedback from someone who knows you and whom you trust. If several friends say your suspicions are warranted, take heed.

Just Ask!

My former fiancé was verbally and physically abusive. When I told my new boyfriend about all the abuse I received, he said "I would never do that to you." My problem is that I don't know whether to believe him.

Frankly, my radar warning sounded when I read your boyfriend's words. I believe that an appropriate response to your story of abuse would have been one of compassion, such as "That must have been awful." Your boyfriend's response was instead defensive. Proceed with caution.

Keep in mind that if you have baggage from a past relationship you are more likely to project those issues onto your new partner. For example, if your last relationship left you feeling unattractive and unappealing, you might assume that your new partner thinks that way about you, too. You may then take it a step further and accuse your partner of feeling those things. Even if your partner denies having such feelings, you may not fully believe him or her. After a while, doubting your partner's sincerity may be the reason the relationship falls apart.

You might find yourself in a new relationship with someone who has similar (negative) qualities to a parent or past lover. If your father was critical and hard to please, for instance, you might discover that your fiancé is the same way. If your former partner cheated on you, you might find that your new partner has a wandering eye or simply likes to flirt. Why would you have chosen a partner with such qualities? Because you desire to create a familiar relationship but to have it turn out positively this time. You want to heal the past by putting yourself in the same hurtful situation but with the hope of changing the ending. It's risky.

If you feel and act insecure in your new relationship and want to stop, take the following steps:

1. Identify the specific ways you act insecurely (you make false accusations, you withdraw when you feel hurt, you ask for reassurances of love, and so forth).

2. When you start to act insecure, say to your partner, "I'm sorry, that's just my insecurity acting up. It's not about you."

3. Go on to some other topic or activity. Don't wallow in that feeling.

To overcome an irrational fear, you must learn to remain in the situation long enough to trust that the feared outcome is not likely to happen. If a past relationship has left you a bit scarred or cautious, your alarm system is likely to go off more often than it needs to because it is set too sensitively. When problems or personality traits are obviously severe, that new relationship may need to end. But if you simply feel anxious and gun-shy, give the relationship more time and your partner the benefit of the doubt.

The Least You Need to Know

◆ Intimacy will be limited if you do not have a relationship of equals.

◆ If your relationship is on again, off again either end it or build it, but stop the merry-go-round.

◆ Opposites attract but you had better learn patience and tolerance.

◆ The more similar you are to your partner in background and personality, the more likely your relationship will succeed.

◆ A self-reliant child learns confidence but may need to improve his communication skills when he grows up.

Chapter 5

Making Your Intimacy Gains Last

In This Chapter

- Discovering why commonsense solutions to intimacy problems fall flat

- Testing to see if you have a hidden fear of intimacy

- Making changes by yourself in 10 ways

- Understanding your intimacy set point

- Learning to maintain your intimacy gains over time

Many people who wish to add more intimacy to their lives view the process as simple as making room on a full dinner plate for another helping of barbecued wings. Push aside the mashed potatoes and *plop* go the wings. What could be easier? If it were that simple, though, people everywhere would be creating lasting, fulfilling, intimate relationships without any advice from people like me.

The truth is that after the intimacy-building ball gets rolling, interesting and unexpected things can happen. Without some foreknowledge of what those things might be, you might end up unnecessarily frustrated.

In Chapter 3, you learned how roadblocks such as fatigue or a serious addiction might prevent you from beginning the work of improving intimacy. This chapter examines the puzzling phenomenon whereby efforts to improve intimacy might work for a while but then sputter and die. It also reveals what's really going on when someone who wants more intimacy and who has great ideas for achieving it, end ups frustrated and banging their head against a wall.

Spinning Your Wheels When Trying to Improve Intimacy

"I just want to scream!" Nicole said. "No matter what I do nothing helps. I've begged you, cajoled you, punished you, threatened you, enticed you—and you're still about as romantic as a pickle jar!"

Tom objected. "Maybe I could be more romantic. But if I'm not it's because I'm too tired from landscaping our yard the way you've been dreaming of for years. At least I kiss you when I come inside for a break … "

"No, you grope me," Nicole interrupted.

Tom sighed. "I guess that's wrong, too."

It's a common scenario: You think you have the right ideas about improving intimacy and you act on those ideas. But the actions don't help. So you blame the other person for being uncooperative, then you eventually apply the same ideas more strenuously, and once again you feel defeated. Your ideas are not necessarily the problem, but your approach might be.

> **Intimacy Boosters**
>
> If everything you've been doing to improve intimacy has failed, stop doing it. Your ideas might be valid but something more basic is interfering with your success. Possibly your mate feels put upon and misunderstood. Start there.

Why Good Ideas to Boost Intimacy Might Go Bust

There are six reasons why you bang your head against a wall in frustration when all you want is more intimacy. Recognize yourself in any of the following?

♦ Your requests for more closeness, however reasonable, come across as criticisms, and your partner gets defensive and uncooperative.

Are you willing to learn how to make requests without criticizing? Is your partner willing to take your requests less personally?

- One of you (probably the woman) is more skilled in intimacy and expects the partner to be equally skilled.

  Are you willing to teach him?

- If you are a man who wants greater intimacy, your focus has probably become more and more on sex, which makes her feel like an object.

  Are you willing to focus on thoughtful actions and nonsexual affection?

- If you are a woman who wants more affection and not just sex, you may be making your man feel rejected by cutting back on sex.

  Are you willing to be more sexual?

- You have probably read too many magazine articles that tell you—unrealistically—that intimacy can be yours in 10 easy steps.

  Are you willing to view intimacy as more profound than that?

- You are unhappy with the level and quality of intimacy in your current or past relationship and so have probably punished your partner in some way.

  Are you willing to stop retaliating?

CAUTION   **Close Calls**

When you struggle with intimacy you might punish your partner or yourself with harsh criticism (or by withdrawing). A critical response almost always backfires. The best attitude is "What can we do that will meet both of our needs most of the time?" Solutions that routinely meet only one partner's needs are not solutions; they are the reasons why the problem persists!

Improving intimacy starts with your willingness to change *your* ineffective ways of building closeness. It doesn't matter if your ideas are great in theory if they don't work in practice.

A Secret Reason Intimacy Can Stay Sluggish

In Chapter 4, you read about how your childhood experiences and memories of past failed relationships can interfere with intimacy now. Let me expand on that idea:

The more painful and unresolved your earlier experiences, the more you will desire—and at the same time feel threatened by—greater intimacy.

In other words, you will seek more intimacy with a partner, but out of fear you will also find a way to keep it from turning into high-voltage intimacy. As intimacy increases, so will your perception of psychological threat (fear of being controlled or hurt), and you will then take steps to reduce the closeness. But as distance between the two of you increases, there is a corresponding fear of abandonment and a need for connection. Thus, intimacy takes on a see-saw effect and you never feel at ease.

Sometimes each person in a relationship has a desire for, and fear of, intimacy. They are like two porcupines trying to cuddle: very tentative and cautious with a lot of complaining.

How can you tell if your struggles to achieve lasting intimacy might be undermined by a strong fear of intimacy? If two of the following apply to you, it is likely true for you. If more than two apply, it is almost a certainty:

- ❏ One or both of you has an obvious history of abuse, neglect, intensely painful rejection, or trauma.

- ❏ The two of you have a hard time staying in-sync with intimacy; one of you wants closeness while the other backs away.

- ❏ There are always excuses for why good intentions to connect and improve intimacy do not pan out.

- ❏ You want more closeness when you feel detached but you want detachment when you feel close.

- ❏ One of you is viewed as having the "problem" with intimacy. However, as that person improves, the other partner develops symptoms that impede closeness.

- ❏ You couldn't wait for your relationship to finally end. When it did end you felt devastated.

Fear of intimacy is not fatal. The first step is to admit it. Denying it will cause you to see the relationship as flawed instead of your feelings as mixed. Consequently, all attempts to fix the situation will fail. Instead of running from intimacy, better to say, *"Intimacy scares me a little. Bear with me, let's take it more slowly."* And instead of being afraid of normal separateness and fearing abandonment, better to say, *"When we're not together I feel insecure. That's MY problem and I'm working on it. I just want you to understand."*

Remember, you don't overcome a fear of intimacy by avoiding closeness, and you don't overcome a fear of abandonment by clinging. You allow a natural togetherness/separateness to emerge and you learn to trust that your deeper fears will not eventually become reality.

Exercise!

Next time you are alone, make a list of all the concerns you have about not being with a partner. And the next time you spend time together, take time to list any concerns you had about being close. For example, when you're alone you might worry that your partner prefers time away from you. When you're together, you might worry that your partner will expect more and more time with you.

Show your partner your list and have a frank talk about the reality of your concerns. You will see that most of your worries are overstated. If any fears are based on prior relationships, admit to it and don't hold your partner accountable.

What to Expect When You Start Making Changes

After you've started down the path of improving intimacy, expect to encounter a few bumps and roadblocks along the way. You might get off to a smooth start and then falter. Or it might take dynamite to spark an initial change, but then it will be clear sailing the rest of the way. If you marked your progress on a graph, most of the time it would look like the monthly stock market report—a lot of ups and downs but hopefully a trend in the right direction.

There are four other crucial things you need to know about the process of making changes: perseverance, purpose, setbacks, and mixed feelings.

Cultivate the Two "Ps": Perseverance and Purpose

Sometimes you might decide to make changes but don't persevere, especially when efforts don't bring immediate success. Without persistence, many potentially successful efforts will fail right before the finish line. Or a couple might persevere in their intimacy goals but they do not have a shared purpose. Maybe one wants to have more meaningful conversations but the other wants more sex.

One strategy that most couples overlook when trying to improve the quality of their intimacy is to ask each other how well it's going. So often, one partner thinks things are going along swimmingly and the other is secretly frustrated. But they never discuss it. Or one partner is sure he did something right in the intimacy department but his partner never noticed. Unless you are willing to participate in progress checks, you might stop persevering.

> **Intimacy Boosters**
>
> Note to men: On average, women are much better at detecting relationship flaws. If a woman wants to make improvements, don't be so quick to assume she's wrong. Better to be curious about her concerns and address them than to automatically ignore them.

Setbacks Are Inevitable

Setbacks are inevitable. Don't expect dramatic changes overnight. It takes time to incorporate new ways of behaving into your life. If an outside crisis develops, people often revert to old patterns of behavior while they are coping with the crisis. Keep that in mind.

But also keep in mind that a setback can't happen unless there has already been progress.

The hardest part about increasing intimacy usually isn't initiating changes, it is maintaining those changes. Don't assume that after a positive change has happened it will keep happening. How many times have you tried to make a personal change (such as losing weight) only to discover that your motivation is strong at first but then it decreases? Encourage one another when performance slips instead of criticizing.

Mixed Feelings Are Typical

You may have mixed feelings about making improvements in intimacy and not even know it. Routinely blaming a partner when you're feeling either smothered or abandoned might be a clue that you have underlying doubts and fears about being intimate. But in any relationship it's common for your feelings about the other person to be a little mixed, at least once in a while. You might be angry about something he did, or worried about something he might do. However, nagging, persistent doubts are more serious and should be treated as such. A good relationship isn't always perfect but neither should it make you uncomfortable or uneasy most of the time.

If the two of you have become accustomed to a routine level of intimacy, then any effort to raise that level may feel awkward or unnatural (such as sleeping on the other side of the bed; it just doesn't feel right). If you have grown accustomed to going places on your own without a partner, you might discover that having company is somewhat constraining.

The best thing to do is to accept your mixed feelings but persevere anyway. Don't first try to "get to the bottom" of your feelings. That will create delays and hesitations. Much of the time mixed feelings are a normal part of the human experience. If your mixed feelings persist and grow increasingly uncomfortable for you, then that's a sure sign something is wrong.

How One of You Can Spark Intimacy for Both of You

If you're frustrated by a lack of intimacy in your current or recent relationship, you probably have tried 10 dozen ways to jumpstart it, all to no avail. So now you're thinking, "Is this author going to tell me I should try harder to get my partner more interested? Isn't that the problem? Why do I have to be the one to get this relationship moving? Shouldn't it be a mutual effort?"

Yes, it should be mutual, at least ideally. But you might want to reread the opening of this chapter or the previous chapter to see if you have overlooked reasons for why your efforts haven't been as successful as you'd like.

A key point to remember is that the chronic, persistent, "Here we go again" effort to get your partner to change is bound to get the same results. Initial requests for change are fine. But after you've repeated the pattern with no success, more of the same "solutions" will leave you even more stuck in the mud. Your goal should be to approach being the "prime mover" with a new attitude and perhaps a few new ideas. Then see what happens.

 Just Ask!

My last three relationships all ended the same, with me pushing for more intimacy and ending up pushing the other person away. What should I do?

If you have to keep pushing for greater intimacy then either it's the wrong relationship or the wrong approach. The more you are "in charge" of intimacy, the less your partner has to pay attention to it. Sometimes it's that simple. If you cut back on your demands for closeness then your partner will either pursue closeness (which means the two of you have a chance) or your partner won't care. In the latter case, your choice is to accept the situation or move on.

Beating the Intimacy Set Point

If you want more intimacy in your relationship then your *set point*—the average amount of intimacy you feel most comfortable with—has not been reached. It takes effort to change your set point. Imagine if your partner wanted a degree of intimacy that was twice as intense as the amount you enjoy. You might be able to sustain that level for a while, but eventually you'd pull away.

When you first started to develop feelings for the person you last had a meaningful relationship with, your overall intimacy levels were probably somewhat high and sustained. Chances are those levels were inflated above your normal set point. You were intoxicated with each other, maybe had fallen in love. Intimacy, then, was like a flood, but over time the waters had to recede. Why? Because eventually the need for intimacy must be balanced by a need for separateness and individuality. You have jobs to go to, friends to see, hobbies to spend time on, and so on. The most successful couples find a way to blend closeness and togetherness with separateness. Improving intimacy doesn't always mean spending even more time together.

If a couple is enmeshed, spending less time together can actually improve the quality of their overall relationship. You have to be a "somebody" for your partner to become more intimate with. You become a "somebody" when you don't neglect your personal needs and growth. Having some separate interests can be a great thing for a couple if those interests make you a more interesting and fun person to have a relationship with.

Imagine that intimacy could be rated on a 0 to 10 scale with 10 meaning "perfect balance of intimacy and separateness," and 0 meaning "extreme separateness or extreme togetherness." If your mate has a set point of 6, efforts to get him to a 7 or 8 might be modestly successful, but you will fail if you push too strenuously. Sure, he might rise to those levels (and even higher) on any given day, but he won't stay there. However, if the two of you consistently battle over intimacy, he may well be shutting you out emotionally and functioning at a sustained level of 2 or 3, far below his own set point.

By abandoning the tug of war, your relationship is free to function at a higher degree of closeness. By not doing battle but instead gently coaxing one another to stronger levels of intimacy, you can raise your set points. One's set point is determined in

Intimacy Boosters

A form of therapy known as *EMDR (Eye Movement Desensitization and Reprocessing)* is amazingly effective at helping people *rapidly* resolve traumas and childhood emotional injuries. A handful of sessions can often achieve what months of psychotherapy usually achieve. If childhood memories are adversely affecting your current relationship, contact a therapist trained in EMDR.

large part by background factors. Resolving old childhood hurts or fears often boosts a person's intimacy set point.

If your childhood wounds make you clingy and insecure, you may appear to want more intimacy. Your set point may *appear* to be high. However, a higher set point still allows for separateness. The less you allow for separateness, the *lower* your achievement of genuine intimacy. Intimacy is not smothering possessiveness.

Ten Ways to Stop the Tug of War All by Yourself

By halting the battle of wills over intimacy, you just might discover that intimacy comes more naturally. The following ideas aren't intended to create intimacy directly. Instead, they are meant to help you let go of the resentment and the power struggle that might be preventing intimacy:

◆ Rephrase "My partner shouldn't act the way he/she does" to "It makes sense that my partner acts the way he/ she does." Think about it. Might your partner have good reasons to act the way he does? Can you imagine an objective bystander finding some merit at all to your partner's point of view?

◆ Spend the time you might ordinarily spend complaining or resenting your partner by doing something you find especially fun or interesting.

◆ Ask yourself, "What's it like for my partner to have me around right now?" If there is anything negative in your answer, start improving your ways now.

◆ Think of several things you really appreciate about your partner and find a way to express it in the next few days.

◆ When your mate does something you don't like, do something very different from your usual response. If you usually complain, find something positive to say. If you withdraw in anger, move toward your partner with interest. Try this for several weeks.

◆ When your mate does something you don't like, use it as an opportunity to do something positive for yourself. For example, Ken hated it that his wife wasn't much of a housekeeper. Every time he was upset about the house, he did 20 pushups. He turned a frustrating moment into something he benefited from. And his anger subsided, too.

◆ Repeat the following until it feels more comfortable: "I accept my partner's ways even though I don't always like or agree with them."

◆ Put your complaints in a sentence ("He should show me more tenderness … more affection … He should be more grateful," and so on). Now change the pronouns so you are talking about yourself. ("I should show more tenderness … more affection … I should be more grateful.") Now, honestly assess if those reversed statements also have any validity. If any do, work on your stuff before you complain about your partner's ways.

◆ Find a way to show your partner that he or she is cherished and respected.

◆ Do several things your partner would like without him or her asking you to do so.

The idea is to break the old pattern. After you do, it can set the stage for intimacy to flourish.

How to Maintain Intimacy Gains over the Long Haul

First, practice the Three Month Rule. Keep working at improving intimacy for three months. Don't stop even if you feel frustrated. If the two of you don't like discussing your progress, make a mark on the calendar each night. Rate that day in terms of the quality of intimacy. An "A" is above average. A "B" is fine and acceptable. A "C" is below expectations. You can see how your partner graded the day and make adjustments accordingly.

Second, anticipate setbacks. Ask, "What could realistically happen that might throw us off track?" If you come up with some ideas, can you plan around them? Can you develop a backup plan to get you back on track? Agree ahead of time that when you are off track, you will do something special together (watch a movie, have a night out, cuddle on the couch, and so forth).

The Least You Need to Know

◆ Stop punishing your partner when your intimacy needs are not being met.

◆ A repetitive tug of war over intimacy usually results in less intimacy overall than you really want.

◆ Find some merit to your partner's approach to intimacy.

◆ The amount of genuine intimacy you can achieve on a regular basis is less than what you had when you first fell in love but more than what you are probably getting now.

◆ After intimacy levels have improved, anticipate what might throw you off course and develop a plan to deal with it before it happens.

Part 2

Intimacy Through Thought

I know what's going on in your head right now. You're wondering how "thinking" can be an intimate act. Let me assure you that the way you think not only sets the stage for some luscious and profound intimate moments, but when done correctly, it is a form of intimacy itself.

Thinking your way to greater intimacy is the most overlooked form of intimacy. And it's a major reason why well-intended efforts to improve closeness in a relationship often limps along at best and perhaps fails. After you tap into the hurricane force power of "linking-by-thinking" you will make giant leaps forward in your quest for achieving lasting and life-changing intimacy.

The next four chapters reveal the key "thinking" secrets that people who enjoy genuine and lasting intimacy put into practice every day. You'll learn how to get closer to others without having to move a muscle. And you'll be taught how to think before, during, and after an argument so that true devotion will always be sustained.

Chapter 6

How Your Thinking Affects Intimacy

In This Chapter

♦ Cultivating intimacy in your mind

♦ Taking a word association test

♦ Remembering the five questions to think about if you and your partner have mismatched intimacy needs

♦ Discovering which thinking type you are

Your mind is more powerful than anything made of matter. Unleashed, even at a fraction of its potential, you can create your own heaven or your own hell. You undoubtedly have underestimated the hidden power of your mind because you are probably drugged by the routine habits and events that make up most of your everyday experiences. The morning rush to work or school; fast food lunches; absent-mindedly flipping on the TV when you get home; microwave dinners; and a host of other distractions, responsibilities, and missed opportunities that make up your typical day. That drugged feeling simply numbs you and makes you unaware of how restricted your life and your special relationship have become. You are like someone who resides in a mansion but confines herself to one or two rooms of living space.

Whether your love life seems fine, or you are currently between relationships, I doubt you have fully realized the many ways you can think yourself to better intimacy.

It is time to take a closer look at how your thoughts affect your experiences of intimacy, and to discover how linking-by-thinking can work for you.

The Powerful Role Your Innermost Thoughts Play

Kate was a thousand miles from home on a business trip when she got the news that her fiancé Roger had been in a car accident and was undergoing surgery at that moment. "It's serious," Roger's dad told her. "I'll call you the minute I hear from the doctor."

Kate collapsed on her hotel bed. She felt utterly helpless. The next flight home wasn't until the following morning. She started to pray. Her prayers were interrupted by her constant worrisome thoughts. Soon all she could think about were the countless memories she had of Roger and her together—laughing, planning their future, making love—and in her mind she placed herself by his side in the operating room. She held his hand while the surgeons worked on him. "I'm here," she said to him in her mind. "I'm with you, now and always."

> **Intimacy Boosters**
>
> Every time you have an emotional response to some action or event, it is not really the event that you are reacting to. Instead you are reacting to the thoughts you have about the event. Identify what your thoughts are so you can decide if they need to be changed or not. Positive thoughts will yield positive feelings.

The good news is that Roger survived and he and Kate were married. If you asked Kate about those hours she spent worrying about his surgery, she would tell you that she never felt closer to Roger than she did then. She literally felt she was with him during his ordeal. And those hours of fear and dread were also filled with deep, warm, loving thoughts that made her devotion to him even more profound.

"I was with him in spirit," she said. "So much so that I felt I was touching him. We were connected."

When absence makes your heart grow fonder it's because you are churning out thoughts of love, hope, and desire. Those thoughts, in turn, add to your feelings of intimacy.

Word Association Test

What do you think of when you hear the word intimacy? What words best describe your attitudes and feelings about intimacy?

First, I want you to notice your initial gut reaction to the word intimacy. Instinctively, you either recoiled, tightened up, or you felt a sense of release. Can you sense that now? Did you detect what your gut reaction was? If not, think again about the word intimacy and pay close attention to the sensations you feel in your chest and stomach area. Intimacy is either something you unconsciously move *away from* or *toward*. What makes you move in either direction? It is your attitude about intimacy. Specifically, when you think of intimacy, a cascade of words, symbols, pictures, sensations, hopes, dreams, and interpretations fill your mind—images you may not even be fully aware of.

Check off the words in columns A and B of those words that are true or mostly true for you when you think of intimacy. Check them off if they are true for you even 51 percent of the time.

A	B
❑ scared	❑ eager
❑ risky	❑ safe
❑ confining	❑ freeing
❑ difficult	❑ easy
❑ uncomfortable	❑ comfortable
❑ worried	❑ relaxed
❑ mistrusting	❑ trusting
❑ physical	❑ spiritual
❑ effortful	❑ effortless
❑ dependent	❑ interdependent
❑ giving up	❑ getting
❑ costly	❑ inexpensive
❑ sad	❑ happy
❑ unfamiliar	❑ familiar
❑ unwelcome	❑ welcome
❑ unlikely	❑ likely
❑ absorption	❑ connection

Your initial gut reaction to the word intimacy revealed that you either instinctively lean toward or away from closeness. When you examine the words you checked in the columns, you will see more precisely why you feel the way you do about intimacy.

Just Ask!

If I'm running from intimacy in a relationship, is that necessarily bad or unhealthy?

If you move away from intimacy it does not necessarily mean you are insecure. And if you move toward intimacy it does not necessarily mean you are secure. You may feel like recoiling when you think of intimacy because you are in a relationship that is overwhelming and oppressive—not at all healthy. And you might move toward intimacy because you are insecure and needy and believe that you are nothing without someone else in your life—also unhealthy.

How you think about intimacy will determine your words and actions. Those words and actions will in turn impact your life and influence your future thoughts about intimacy. Your thoughts will create your reality.

Connecting the Dots

Think about the differences you and your partner have about the meaning of intimacy. If the two of you are leaning in opposite directions, you will find yourselves in an endless tug of war unless you come up with a plan. Here are five questions to ask each other if you are on opposite sides:

♦ *Do we share the same broad goals regarding intimacy?* If your intimacy goals are not the same, think twice about continuing the relationship.

♦ *Does one of us simply want to proceed more slowly?* Slow is fine as long as there is noticeable progress. Eventually you each need to be going at the same pace or else the one pulling the intimacy-cart forward will grow weary, resentful, demanding, or depressed.

♦ *Have our intimacy differences arisen in prior relationships?* If so, you might have an unresolved childhood/historical issue that keeps you dancing the same dance. See Chapter 4.

♦ *When did our intimacy differences first arise in this relationship?* Did something happen recently to create doubt in one of your minds or have the differences always been there? Recent events can be more readily worked on. Longstanding differences might not be easily changed.

♦ *Are we willing to separate for a while and see if it changes how we feel?* Sometimes the person moving away from intimacy needs to see what he might lose if the relationship were to end. However, the longer the separation, the more you will each adapt to being apart and the greater the chance of a breakup.

Discuss your answers together. If you struggle when it comes to effective communication, make sure you read Part 3 of this book, "Intimacy Through Talk." If effective communication has always been a problem in your relationship, you should also read my other book, *How to Say It for Couples: Communicating with Tenderness, Openness, and Honesty* for hundreds of tips and strategies.

Just Ask!

My husband and I are not always on the same page when it comes to intimacy. Shouldn't we be? Are differences in desire for intimacy a bad sign?

Differences in desire for intimacy are the rule for most relationships. And even if you and your husband had the exact same intimacy needs, I doubt you would each want those needs met at exactly the same time. You'd be ready for more intimacy one day and he wouldn't. You'd be busy and preoccupied another day and he'd want all your attention. A successful relationship happens when couples learn to manage their differences, not obliterate them. A little tension in this area is okay. It allows for mutual give and take.

The Time You Spend with Your Lover in Your Mind

"We have no time for intimacy!" I hear that cry every day from couples in my office and I have just one response: "Baloney!" Intimacy starts in your mind, not on a clock or in an appointment calendar. And there are dozens of moments during the day when intimacy can be enhanced by how you think.

Simply stated, you must make room in your mind for regular, positive thoughts about your partner. The drive to work or the shopping

Close Calls

If you don't make room in your thoughts for intimacy, you won't find room in your schedule for it, either.

mall is a perfect opportunity to devote some quality thinking time to your partner. The list of things to think about is limited only by your imagination. More common things to think about include the following:

- The things that attract you physically to your mate

- Something about him or her you cherish

- The greeting at the end of the work day

- Cuddling in bed; making love

- Giving and receiving your favorite form of affection

- Having a meal together

- The kind of day your mate will likely have

- Caring that your partner is worried about something

- Planning a night out together

- How to make his or her day go more smoothly

- How you can make him or her feel more special that day

- Something you need to be more understanding about

- Something you need to apologize for

All too often partners rarely think about each other during the day when they are separated. Work and chores interfere. That's understandable, but it's not acceptable. It's simply a bad habit. Even the busiest people can make time in their hectic lives to think about their partners.

CAUTION

Close Calls

"Out of sight, out of mind" is a mindset sure to reduce intimacy. Which kind of house-plant will thrive, the one you water regularly or the one you water when you get around to it?

Have reminders planted in places you spend time. A ribbon on the passenger seat of your car serves as a fine reminder of your partner. Place a mark on wrist near your watch so that every time you check the time you will think of your partner.

One of the most important questions to consider when trying to increase intimacy is this: *"What's it like for my partner to have me around?"* (I'll remind you of that question a few more times in this book because it is so essential and easily overlooked.)

Imagine that you're driving to or from work and you contemplate that question. Answering it requires insight and empathy. If your first response is *"I'm sure my partner is perfectly happy I'm around,"* you're not digging deeply enough. You aren't perfect.

If your mate had to come up with three or four negatives about you, what would he or she say? Common complaints might be that you don't say "I love you" often enough; you take him or her for granted; you don't listen well; you're quick to criticize; you're a stick in the mud; you pay more attention to your "toys" than your mate; you don't clean up after yourself; you're not very romantic; and so on.

I only listed eight items and I bet every reader can identify with at least one of them. If any of these items refer to you, then you have a clear example of something to improve about yourself.

The Three Thinking Styles

Your thinking style is similar to your personality. You can change it, but not without some effort and practice. It has been said that your character is defined by what you do when no one is watching. Well, your thinking style is defined by how you talk to yourself when no one is listening. Your interior monologue will enhance intimacy or detract from it.

Keep reading to find out how your thinking style orients you either toward intimacy, away from intimacy, or against intimacy (by clashing).

The Approach Thinker

An approach thinker has most of these attributes:

- ◆ Tends to look on the positive side
- ◆ Expresses emotion, usually in moderation
- ◆ Is outgoing, friendly
- ◆ Dislikes conflict and seeks resolution quickly
- ◆ Is able to admit mistakes
- ◆ Can empathize with his or her partner
- ◆ Moves *toward* greater intimacy

The benefits of being an approach thinker are that you will look at ways to improve intimacy. Your manner is also easy-going which makes it easier on your partner to cooperate. If problems arise, you will look for common ground and be able to adjust to ideas that aren't ideal but are fair.

The drawbacks to being an approach thinker occur when you find partners who are more withdrawn or argumentative. You will then be consumed with ways to keep the relationship afloat and risk becoming anxious, depressed, or insecure.

The Avoidance Thinker

This person is often busy with life and uses an "out of sight, out of mind" philosophy. Such a thinker does most of the following:

- Keeps his head in the sand about potential problems
- Will shut down if emotions get too hot
- Is reserved, not likely to reveal much about himself
- Avoids conflict
- Feels misunderstood and a bit of a victim
- Is directed *away* from intimacy and closeness

Intimacy Boosters

If your partner tends to avoid dealing with issues and you don't, how you approach the topics will make a difference. Avoiders back away at the first sign of conflict or tension. Be sure you express your concerns calmly but directly. Insist that matters be discussed but be willing to have shorter, calm discussions. Avoid lengthy, "up all night" heavy-duty talks.

The benefits of being an avoidance thinker are that you are less likely to be consumed by worry when problems arise. However, by avoiding issues instead of facing them, you increase the odds that problems will worsen. You must take the time to think about matters you prefer to avoid. You must realize that your preferred mode of thinking will keep intimacy on the edge of being unsatisfying. Probably you are also a procrastinator. Procrastinators always have more stress in the long run as their problems build up and become overwhelming. An avoidance thinker must contemplate ways to tackle a problem as soon as it arises rather than hope it goes away on its own.

The Argumentative Thinker

The third style is the argumentative thinker. Such a thinker has many of the following traits:

- Emphasizes what can go wrong

- Is assertive, often to the point of being confrontational and aggressive

- Thrives on conflict; does not like to agree to disagree

- Impulsively blames others first rather than admit fault

- Believes that empathy and understanding is not the issue—being *right* is the issue

- Connects by clashing (it may or may not result in improved intimacy later on)

Argumentative thinkers make more problems for themselves. On a drive to work, for example, such people might think about something annoying in their relationship (current or past), build a case against their partners, and get angrier and angrier as they drive. Their inner monologue tends to be self-serving, with an emphasis on how they are right. And when they arrive home at the end of the day they are grumpy, self-righteous, and ready to argue the moment something goes wrong.

If you are an argumentative thinker you must make intimacy—not winning the argument—a priority. If you and your mate are both argumentative thinkers, your relationship will be very draining unless there are many, many positive moments to make up for the negative thoughts that fill your heads. You must be able to recognize what has merit in the other's point of view and be able to empathize. That can calm down the volatility and make room for more positive thoughts.

CAUTION

Close Calls

Your style of thinking is less important than who you are paired with. An approach thinker will desire greater intimacy and be gentle. But if paired with an argumentative thinker, problems will arise. Two avoidant thinkers may have lower levels of intimacy but be more accepting of that fact compared to a couple where one's style is to approach while the other's is to avoid.

The Least You Need to Know

♦ How you think about intimacy will determine how you act on it.

♦ You won't find room in your schedule for your partner if you can't even find room in your mind.

♦ Determine if most of your thoughts move you toward intimacy or away from it.

♦ Put reminders in your car, office, and home to help you think more often and more positively about your mate.

♦ If all you think about is winning the argument, end your relationship and get a law degree.

Creating More Intimacy by Building Goodwill

In This Chapter

- ◆ Taking a goodwill test
- ◆ Learning ways to build and sustain goodwill
- ◆ Achieving goodwill through common obstacles
- ◆ Improving intimacy with gratitude

Remember, positive and romantic thoughts about your mate not only set the stage for greater intimacy later on; the thoughts themselves can be a form of intimacy. How? Thoughts connect you to another person. It's that simple. Your loved one can be in the next room or the next country, but thinking about him links the two of you. Skeptics may scoff and say that such a link is pure imagination or romantic silliness but I'm telling you that linking-by-thinking is as real and at times more profound than linking by sex or touch or talk.

A great deal of evidence shows how people can psychically connect to people they care about even when that person is not physically present.

Sometimes a person "knows" that something is very wrong only to later learn that a loved one had an accident. Call it intuition or spiritual energy or vibes, the point is our minds are not localized only in our brains. Our minds are capable of extending beyond our physical bodies and connecting with others. This connection does not happen only rarely or just in a crisis. Do you believe in prayer? Prayer is an example of linking-by-thinking. How about when you pick up the phone to call your friend only to hear her say, "I was just about to call you!"

Your thoughts about a partner will create either intimacy or detachment depending on goodwill. Do your thoughts harvest goodwill? Goodwill is the fire that forges the steel of any intimate relationship. Without goodwill, intimacy disappears.

Goodwill Creates Great Relationships

When Grace and Lou sat in front of me and told me all about their relationship problems, I hunted around for signs of goodwill.

"It's her family," Lou said. "She spends all her time with them. I feel like a fifth wheel. We never have time for ourselves. If I complain she makes it sound like I'm imprisoning her, like I'm possessive. All I want is my wife back."

Grace rolled her eyes. "He's jealous. He always has been. And I'm tired of him finding fault with my family every chance he gets. They care about me. I'm not sure he does."

So far no signs of goodwill at all. They didn't look at each other when they spoke. Grace's eye rolling was a tip-off that she had lost some respect for her husband.

Intimacy Boosters

Start building goodwill by doing something together that makes you laugh hysterically or scream with excitement. Anything adventurous and heart-pounding will do: go to an amusement park; go tubing down a river; attend a favorite sporting event or compete against each other in one; or watch a really scary or funny movie. Do anything that will give you an adrenaline rush and make you say when it's over, "Wow! That was something!"

"How did you two meet?" I asked later. The couple looked at one another sheepishly, as if I had exposed an embarrassing secret. "At a resort," Lou said. "I thought I was on the "bathing suits optional" beach and started to remove my swim trunks. I had them half off when Grace came up to me and pointed to the sign. "The nude beach is way over there," she told me. "I was so embarrassed."

Grace laughed at the memory. "But you did have a fantastic tan line!"

The couple's ability to smile and laugh gave me hope. I was seeing evidence of goodwill. Now we had something to build on.

Take a Goodwill Quiz

Goodwill is an attitude, a combination of thoughts and feelings and actions that promote an overall positive outlook toward another person. It encompasses many things such as caring, concern, fondness, respect, excitement, friendship, pride, and an overriding desire to want what's best for the other person. Of course, you can have problems in your relationship and still possess goodwill. But the amount of goodwill must be greater than the amount of ill-will. If it is, you are leaning in the direction of love, growth, and lasting intimacy.

Take this short quiz to see how much goodwill is part of your relationship.

1. When I think about my partner my thoughts are generally positive.

   ❏ Most of the time   ❏ Sometimes   ❏ Not often

2. I feel proud of my partner.

   ❏ Most of the time   ❏ Sometimes   ❏ Not often

3. I take my partner's feelings and wants into consideration.

   ❏ Most of the time   ❏ Sometimes   ❏ Not often

4. I look forward to seeing my partner at the end of the day.

   ❏ Most of the time   ❏ Sometimes   ❏ Not often

5. I feel our relationship is fair.

   ❏ Most of the time   ❏ Sometimes   ❏ Not often

6. I get the kind of support I need from my partner.

   ❏ Most of the time   ❏ Sometimes   ❏ Not often

7. My partner seems genuinely interested in how my day went.

   ❏ Most of the time   ❏ Sometimes   ❏ Not often

8. We have fun together.

   ❏ Most of the time   ❏ Sometimes   ❏ Not often

9. I feel blessed that we ended up together.

   ❏ Most of the time   ❏ Sometimes   ❏ Not often

10. If it was important for my partner to change careers, I'd find a way to be supportive.

   ❏ Very probably   ❏ Maybe   ❏ Probably not

11. If I had it to do over, I'd still want to be with my partner.

   ❏ Very probably   ❏ Maybe   ❏ Probably not

12. I can easily recall many wonderful moments we shared.

   ❏ Very probably   ❏ Maybe   ❏ Probably not

If you answered "Most of the time" or "Very probably," give yourself two points.

If you answered "Sometimes" or "Maybe," give yourself one point.

If you answered "Not often" or "Probably not," give yourself zero points.

Scoring key:

21–24	Goodwill is present and rather strong
18–20	Goodwill is moderate
15–17	Goodwill is present but modest
12–14	Goodwill is shaky
9–11	Ill-will is often present
6–8	Ill-will is almost as strong as goodwill
0–5	Goodwill is almost absent

There is a magic line that divides a relationship into one of basically goodwill or of ill-will. When you are above that line, the relationship is one of friendship, problems get resolved, bad feelings don't linger, and it is easy to feel contentment and joy. A partner's flaws are easier to accept or overlook. Goodwill is self-reinforcing. The more positive you feel about your mate the more you see his good qualities and the more you treat him with love. That in turn leads to better intimacy and more goodwill.

But when goodwill falls below that magic line, watch out! Now problems linger, resentments build, and a general feeling of discontentment never quite goes away. A partner's flaws seem obnoxious and barely tolerable. Ill-will is also self-reinforcing. The more negatively you feel toward your mate the more you will see his bad qualities; and the more you will avoid him or treat him with contempt. That in turn limits any further intimacy, which leads to more ill-will.

Just Ask!

I like to think positively and have high hopes for my relationship. Isn't a positive outlook important?

A positive outlook is actually a tricky thing and can backfire. Studies show that couples who have the most stable relationships have expectations that closely match their relationship skill level. A couple with strong skills and high expectations are usually very happy together. A couple with high expectations but limited skills are usually unhappy and at risk for breaking up. Interestingly, a couple with low expectations and strong skills also tends to be unhappy. Why? Their low expectations keep them from using the skills they possess. That is a perfect example of how one's thoughts (low expectations) create a reality that need not have happened.

What Goodwill Is Not

I've listened to many people tell me that they care about their partners, that they love them, and only want what's best for them. That sentiment by itself does not reveal genuine goodwill. If you want to know if genuine goodwill exists, look at your behaviors. When there is goodwill there is kindness, consideration, and thoughtfulness. Actions are not rash, hostile, controlling, or possessive. When your partner mistreats you or you are made to feel inadequate in a relationship, goodwill is not present.

Resisting Goodwill

Couples who fall below the magic line of goodwill realize they have to improve their relationship if they are to remain together. But when I talk to them about improving

Close Calls

It's okay and normal to have mixed feelings about someone when relationship problems persist. But if you start acting on those mixed feelings, your behavior will be erratic. Your best bet is to lean in one direction and act accordingly. Even if you feel like pulling back, don't. Stick to a path until you are clear it is the right or wrong one.

goodwill as a way to improve intimacy, they often balk. They are so hurt or angry or pessimistic they don't want to try to improve their attitude. Yet they say they want their relationship to improve. They want to feel better without actually having to change how they think or act.

Three common attitudes may keep you from making an all out effort at fostering goodwill. Let's look at each of them more closely:

It Isn't Deserved!

You're probably right. Maybe your partner doesn't deserve your caring and commitment. Ask yourself two questions and be honest about your answers:

"Did I contribute in any way to our problems?" If the answer is yes, then go easy on your mate. You're both to blame to some extent. Goodwill is necessary on both sides.

"Do I want this relationship to succeed?" If the answer is yes more than no, then fostering goodwill is essential. It doesn't matter so much that goodwill may be undeserved. It's necessary for your relationship to survive.

I'm Tolerating Bad Behavior

No you're not. You can make it very clear that the things you dislike are not acceptable and need to be changed. However, you can still try to promote mutual goodwill.

> **Intimacy Boosters**
>
> A fulfilling, intimate relationship must have goodwill at its foundation. But goodwill alone is not sufficient to make a relationship thrive. It also takes persistence, mutual understanding, and a willingness to make sacrifices for one another.

I Don't *Feel* Any Goodwill to Begin With

When this happens it is not always clear whether goodwill has evaporated completely or if it's hidden under a mound of resentment. The best way to proceed is to ask yourself the following:

"If I was feeling a little more goodwill than I am feeling now, how would I act differently?"

If you can identify some specific ways you'd act, then start doing them. Put aside the fact that it feels fake or contrived. Find some quality about your partner that you care about and use that as your motivation to foster more goodwill.

Steps to Harvesting Goodwill

Goodwill is both a form of intimacy and a path toward more intimacy. Without at least some goodwill, intimacy will never get off the ground. And even if goodwill is above that magic line I discussed earlier, if it is blunted in some way then intimacy will also be blunted. You can do several things to start building up goodwill. You can do this even if you think goodwill is strong. It won't hurt and just might add even more love to the mix.

Kindling Warmth and Compassion in Your Mind and Heart

You can use your imagination to bolster warmth and compassion.

Exercise #1: Imagine Your Partner as a Child

Can you feel more warmth as you imagine your partner at age three crying for his or her mother? Imagine him opening birthday presents, skinning a knee, winning an award in school, learning how to ride a bike, or being sick with a high fever. Perhaps you already know about some real incidents from your partner's past that you know had a big influence. What would your partner have been most afraid of as a child? Most excited about? Worried about? Proud of?

Exercise #2: Imagine Your Partner Lonely

Picture him or her alone in a room on a special holiday with no one to talk to or be with. Imagine he feels sad and lonely, unsure of himself, worried about the future. What regrets does he have? What does he wish he could do over if he had the chance?

> **Intimacy Boosters**
>
> You don't have to be in a relationship currently to build goodwill. You interact with many people every day. Make interactions an opportunity to think positively about people. Look for their good qualities. Practice makes perfect.

Exercise #3: Imagine Your Partner Old and Disabled

Picture your mate sitting alone, staring out a window, feeling completely alone and without friends or family. When was the last time he or she smiled? Laughed? What preys on his mind? If he could read a comforting letter from you, what might the letter say?

Recall How You Fell in Love

Nostalgia can often rekindle the flames of warmth and compassion. There must have been some very good times together. Remember? How did you meet? Do you remember your first date? What were two or three qualities you were strongly attracted to? Have those qualities disappeared? If someone else were to be attracted to your mate, what would they see? What would that person be able to understand about how your partner feels that maybe you don't fully understand?

Create Magical Metaphors

This is a fun exercise. Try to be kind and not mean as you go along. Look around your home or office or some place outside. Choose an object. Now ask yourself, "If my partner was that object, what specific kind would he or she be?" If she were a table lamp would she be a Tiffany? If he were a couch would he be made of supple leather? If she were an animal would she be a tiger? A swan?

The point is to think of your mate in a way that is new, different, interesting, evocative, and perhaps a bit humorous. Thinking of your partner in new ways helps shake off the cobwebs that are obscuring your ability to see your mate more clearly.

 " ") Just Ask!

Whenever my last partner and I tried to improve goodwill and friendship it only lasted a little while. Then we argued about something and our goodwill slipped away. What can I do the next time?

Probably something fundamental was being overlooked. Were both of you truly committed to building goodwill? If not, one of you probably stopped putting forth effort right when cooperation was called for; perhaps because one or both of you really wanted the relationship to end. In your next relationship, make a pact with your partner to make friendship and goodwill always be at the top of your priority list. Refuse to allow the occasional disagreement to halt any goodwill efforts. Be understanding, sacrificing, and forgiving whenever possible. Most of all, pay close attention to how you think about one another when you are not together.

Here is another way to use metaphors to describe your partner. First, choose a positive description such as beautiful, tender, smart, funny, and so on. Now complete the sentence: "My partner is as beautiful as a ..." You get the idea.

You can play with the idea even further. "When my lover is at her best she reminds me of a _____. When she is tired she reminds me of _____. When she is hungry she reminds me of _____. When she is romantic she is like a _____."

Knowing Your Lover's Deepest Desires

When a couple starts to date they often have fascinating and revealing conversations about their personal dreams and longings. And each one actually takes the time to listen and encourage those dreams. After you've been together for years such discussions happen infrequently. If they do occur, practical considerations interfere with any dream building. He thinks of retiring to Bermuda, you tell him you can't afford it. You dream about starting your own business, he says the kids will have no one to look after them. He says he wants to write a novel, you tell him it takes too long and the odds are he'd never get published. See how easy it is to kill each others dreams and, in the process, kill intimacy?

Have a conversation like you did in the old days. Talk about your longings and hopes and dreams. When you're the listener, say nothing to challenge or diminish your partner's dreams.

Later, on your own, consider ways you could encourage your partner to make his or her dreams a reality.

Three Ways to Nourish Gratitude

Goodwill thrives on gratitude. It's hard to harbor ill-will toward someone when you feel thankful that he or she is part of your life.

Exercise #1: If people in your life expressed their gratitude to you, what would be 10 things they might be grateful for? Now, are any of those items things that you should also be grateful to your partner for? Chances are you have taken your partner for granted in some way. It's easy to see the sacrifices you have made for your family, but we sometimes overlook the sacrifices family members make for us.

Exercise #2: What would you miss about your mate if he or she were gone from your life? Imagine waking up and your partner is no

Intimacy Boosters

Goodwill takes root when you feel gratitude. However, goodwill starts to blossom when you show your gratitude. Don't forget to say "thanks" and to show your appreciation in ways that count.

longer there beside you. That may seem fine if it's just for a day or two, but how would you feel if that were forever? What would you miss most? What personal items would you want to hold onto and cherish? Why?

Exercise #3: At the end of the day, just before you go off to sleep, choose something about your partner that you're grateful for and think about it for awhile. It could be a character quality or it might be something he did that day that was helpful. Just pick something and meditate on it for a bit. Do this every day and see what benefit it brings.

The Least You Need to Know

- Foster goodwill in your relationship by meditating on all the things you love about your partner.

- Contempt is poisonous to a relationship and must be overcome if the relationship is to survive.

- Having high expectations for your relationship is fine as long as you possess the intimacy skills needed to meet those expectations.

- Whenever goodwill is compromised, think about what you're grateful for in the relationship.

Chapter 8

How to Think Intimate Thoughts During an Argument

In This Chapter

- Learning how pre-argument thoughts can help or hinder intimacy
- Calming down with inner talk
- Learning the four key rules about negative self-talk
- Failing despite well-intended efforts to not argue
- Winning the peace after an argument

It's time to study in slow-motion what goes on in people's heads before, during, and after an argument, and how those thoughts affect intimacy. The typical person usually focuses on the spoken words, not the unspoken-but-powerfully-important *thoughts* he or she is having. That's a mistake. No argument can ever get resolved to each person's satisfaction unless their thoughts are in the direction of peace, understanding, and goodwill.

My goal in this chapter is for you to come away with the skills of a surgeon to dissect your arguments—even the arguments that occur only in your mind—and realize, perhaps as never before, why you fight or bicker the way you do. Most importantly, I want you to learn how to argue more effectively by thinking more effectively; and in a manner that fosters intimacy rather than weakens it.

Thinking Your Way Through an Argument

The phone rang at precisely eight o'clock. Gary knew it was his sister-in-law. Now his wife, Sheila, would chat for the next 40 minutes while he cleared away the dinner dishes and horsed around with the kids. After that, he thought, she'd race around trying to get the kids ready for bed before she went on the computer to check her e-mails. He had hoped they'd have time to relax together, maybe even go to bed early and make love. Not tonight. If he complained that his wife wasted too much time talking to her sister, Sheila would blow up. She just didn't understand. He began rinsing the dishes and his resentment started to build.

Before she even answered the phone, Sheila knew how Gary would react. Couldn't he understand that her sister was going through a rough time and needed to talk? Couldn't he put the kids to bed for a change? And why would he even think that she'd want to make love when he would spend the rest of the evening pouting and acting cold. She didn't want to argue with him, again. But she had lost all her patience with his childish attitude.

Tick, tick, tick … The argument would begin soon.

Let's examine Gary and Sheila's situation more closely. Did Gary have any positive thoughts? Did any of his thoughts cut Sheila any slack? No. In fact, he had several negative beliefs even though they were not fully formed in his mind:

> **Close Calls**
>
> The more angry and upset you are with someone, the more your confidence increases about being right in the situation, however your accuracy decreases in objectively assessing the situation. In other words, you probably don't have the complete picture.

- His sister-in-law was rude to keep calling and Sheila was inconsiderate to spend so much time on the phone.

- His time with Sheila should not be interrupted.

- After the phone call, Sheila will place more of a priority on housework or e-mails than on him.

- Sheila will automatically lash out at him if he complains.

Sheila had several negative beliefs, too:

◆ Gary resents the phone call and has no compassion for her sister's plight.

◆ He wants her attention but he isn't willing to help out more and free up her time.

◆ All he ever thinks about is making love.

◆ Gary can be selfish and childish.

With all these beliefs, how can intimacy ever flourish? It can't. Does that mean that Gary and Sheila must change all their beliefs? Aren't some of their beliefs *true*? Well, maybe Gary was right when he thought that Sheila would lash out at him if he complained. And Sheila was right that Gary resented the phone call.

The easiest way to reduce anger and foster closeness would have been for each to find some merit in the other's viewpoint. If Gary thought, "Sheila will lash out if I complain. *But I know she is worried about her sister and does have a right to talk with her*," then he would automatically be less angry. If Sheila thought, "Gary resents the phone call. *But I know we don't spend much time together as a couple like we should*," then she'd be less angry and more likely to move closer to him.

Four key rules:

1. Any time you have a negative emotion (hurt, anger, guilt, anxiety, and so on) you should assume that you are thinking negative thoughts.

2. Unless you know for sure that your negative thoughts about your partner are completely true, you need to change them and make them more accurate.

3. If your negative thoughts are accurate, you need to find some way to see things from your partner's point of view, even just a little.

4. An effective argument results in mutual understanding; not in one side winning and the other losing.

From now on, I want you to pay close attention to your feelings and to the thoughts that generate them.

> **Intimacy Boosters**
>
> One way to see some merit in your partner's viewpoint is to imagine yourself doing exactly what your partner did (that you didn't like). Now try to come up with reasons that would justify your actions, had you done them. Can you imagine acting that way and having a motive that is understandable? If so, your partner may have had a similar motive.

Why You Often Fail When You Try Hard Not to Argue

Most couples are loaded with good intentions. They don't want to argue. In fact, they try hard not to argue. They may have even read books on how to communicate effectively. But eventually they do get into an argument and everything they learned to do right goes flying out the window.

That phenomenon happens for a very good reason. It happens because of something called *state dependent learning*. In other words, when you learn something new (such as how to communicate more effectively) you are more able to recall what you learned if you are in the same emotional state you were in when you first learned the information. Most people learn how to do new things in a calm state of mind. But if they have to apply those new skills at a time they are feeling stressed or angry, they are more likely to forget what they learned. This is one reason why students sometimes freeze up and have test anxiety. The test-taking conditions (stressful) are not similar to the studying conditions (calm) when they learned the material. People who work well under pressure are people who have learned to apply their knowledge to situations that are stressful.

What does this mean for you? It means that you should start applying what you are learning here in situations that might be tense. Until you can apply what you've learned under conditions of emotional arousal (anger or fear), you will limit your ability to resolve disagreements and improve intimacy.

Your Inner Announcer Giving the Pre-Game Warm-Up

Some arguments are unexpected and blind-side you. But many arguments can be anticipated. Let's begin there. You should know your partner well enough to anticipate situations that will create tension or cause an argument. You know how to push each other's buttons. That knowledge is very useful right now. It allows you to prepare for an argument, if there must be one, rather than go into an emotional skid.

Anticipate What Bugs You

There are probably one or two moments (at least) during the day when you anticipate a situation occurring that you know will annoy the heck out of you. For example, you could be driving home from work imagining that when you open your front door you will be greeted by an untidy house and a partner who is relaxing and watching a ballgame on TV. You start to get angry. You tell yourself you don't want to start an argument as soon as you get in the door but couldn't you arrive home just once to an organized household and a warm smile? Thinking along these lines shoves intimacy right out the door.

Your job now is to think ahead over the events of the next week and anticipate things that can predictably go wrong; things that you and your partner might argue over. After you have something in mind, make a running list of the negative thoughts you know you will have. Jot them down. If you are having trouble identifying such thoughts, the following sentence completions might help:

> It will bug me today if _____.
>
> I wish my partner wouldn't _____.
>
> I wish my kids wouldn't _____.
>
> I shouldn't have to put up with _____.
>
> It's unfair that _____.
>
> I hate it when _____.
>
> If I say what I really feel about _____ it will just start an argument
>
> Nobody understands how I feel about _____.
>
> I'd be happier today if only my partner would _____.

If you take the time to fill in those blanks, you might be astonished at how much stress and anger you feel; anger that eventually leaks out over many interactions and whittles away intimacy.

> **Close Calls**
>
> Emotional reasoning happens when you assume that your feelings must be valid because you feel them intensely. You believe your feelings don't lie. Keep in mind that your feelings are triggered by how you think. If your thoughts are off-base, your feelings will be distorted.

Rehearse a Positive Response

Now that you've identified your negative thoughts about a situation that you anticipate happening, you need to rehearse a positive response. Rehearsal is the key. Many people just tell themselves they will handle the upcoming annoying situation better—out of sheer willpower—but they take no time to figure out exactly how they intend to do that.

It helps to change your attitude about what's bothering you, that way you won't have to fake it when you try to act positive. How might you do that?

First, replace all "should" statements with "It would be nice if ..." statements. Look at these should statements: *"The kids should be well behaved when I get home ... My partner should greet me warmly and give me time to unwind ... The house should be fairly neat ... I should be allowed to want time for myself if I've had a bad day ..."*

The should statements are really expectations that don't fit well with day-to-day reality. They are ideals but life isn't ideal. Better to say *"It would be nice if ... my kids are well behaved when I get home,"* but to insist in your mind that things should or must be a certain way is an invitation for a letdown.

Or tell yourself, *"The kids* shouldn't *be well behaved when I get home."* Why would anyone want to say that? Because kids are kids. Too often, people get very upset when things go wrong, when "going wrong" involves situations that are ordinary and typical and impossible to eradicate. Arguing that kids should be well behaved at all times or that a lover should always greet you with joy is similar to saying it shouldn't snow in winter.

Second, honestly evaluate if you are guilty of the same thing you accuse others of. For example, are *you* a joy to behold when you arrive home? Do you always greet your family warmly? Do you help out with chores that aren't ordinarily yours to do? Do you always give your mate time to unwind when he or she gets home? If you recognize that you have faults in these areas, focus on changing your part of the equation first.

> **Intimacy Boosters**
>
> The intensity of your negative thoughts is in line with the intensity of your physical agitation. The more tense you are physically, the more likely your thoughts will be negative and hard to dispute. By physically relaxing, you make it easier to replace upsetting thoughts with positive ones.

Third, emphasize in your mind the qualities of the other person that you really enjoy, love, and appreciate. Pick two or three things and hold them in your thoughts until you notice that you are feeling more warmly toward that person.

Finally, now that your thoughts are more in line with intimacy, rehearse in your mind how you will talk and act differently. For example, if you hate coming home to a cluttered house but you know you will, anticipate walking in the door and seeing the clutter. Then imagine yourself thinking *"I'd prefer it if things were tidy but it's not awful that it looks like this. I'm sure my partner has had a busy day, too."*

Calm Yourself Before It Starts

If you have the time, try to relax. Listen to soothing music; breathe fully and in a relaxed manner; say a prayer; repeat over and over how you love your partner. Take a few minutes to physically calm down. You should rate your subjective levels of tension on a 0 to 10 scale before you try to relax. Then rate yourself again after you have relaxed. Your levels should at least be cut in half.

Your Inner Announcer Calling the Play-by-Play

Let's imagine that you've completed all your warm-ups and the discussion/argument has begun. You came into the situation with a more positive mindset. You genuinely want to handle this disagreement better than you usually do. The problem is that now there are two of you and you can't control the process by yourself. So you have to do things that increase the likelihood that your partner will want to cooperate with you and not fight with you.

Basically, your job now is to keep things from escalating or breaking down.

The situation will get worse or lead to lingering resentment if any one of the following three things happens:

◆ The conversation escalates as each person's response raises the intensity level up another notch.

◆ One of you stays there but refuses to speak much.

◆ One of you leaves the scene prematurely.

These three things occur not because of what is being said or how it is being said but because of how you are thinking. If you escalate, for example, it's because you're telling yourself that the other person's words were harsh or uncalled for. If you stop talking altogether or walk away it is because you are telling yourself it is useless to continue and that your partner will not listen. These thoughts must be changed so that the conversation can continue but be more productive.

 **Intimacy Boosters**

If you don't like what you're hearing and are about to argue, it's perfectly okay to say, "*Let me think about that for a minute.*" Then you have some time to gather your thoughts and not speak recklessly.

Inner Talk to Calm Down

Try to calm yourself down and keep the argument from escalating by saying one or more of the following statements to yourself:

◆ My goal is to understand and be understood, not to win.

◆ There is probably something about my partner's view that I have not yet understood.

◆ Is there any merit at all to what he or she is saying?

◆ Can I hold or touch my partner right now in a loving way?

◆ This is uncomfortable but we need practice learning how to manage this better.

◆ Take a deep breath and pause.

◆ God, please help.

Keep repeating one or two of these statements—or one you create for yourself— in your mind when a discussion starts to get tense or argumentative.

Just Ask!

I try to think and say the right things during an argument but I often don't. Any other suggestions?

Finding a way to touch or hold one another during a tense discussion can immediately siphon off some of the tension. Also remain seated during an argument. Standing up increases the odds of more physical agitation or premature exits. Touching or remaining seated also adds to a sense of closeness.

Inner Talk to Stay Put

Physically withdrawing from difficult conversations and arguments is predictive of relationship misery. When someone withdraws, he usually thinks he has a good reason. Typically, he thinks his partner is too harsh or critical and he hates it that they are arguing. But shutting down from an argument doesn't fix anything. If a man withdraws, he is thinking something like, *"I'll show her. I'll refuse to talk. I'll walk away. That will teach her to talk more respectfully."* Of course, such thinking is nuts. Never in the history of the world has a man's running from a conversation or argument caused the woman to think, *"I'm completely wrong to say what I'm saying. He has every right to walk away from me when I talk like that. I'm glad he brought this to my attention.*" Instead the woman is furious that he keeps running away, she views it as cowardly and immature, and it increases the odds she will start off the next argument even more harshly.

If your tendency is to run away from conversations you don't like, try thinking these thoughts:

"*I need to learn to hang in there … My partner will be less upset if I can be counted on to stay … Try to breathe properly and stay as relaxed as possible … I can ask my partner to speak more calmly … I'm just physically uncomfortable and I can handle that.*" If need be, agree ahead of time that any argument you two have will not last for more than 10 minutes without a brief time out. A time out is not an escape. It is a strategic maneuver designed to help the two of you pace yourselves and not escalate the argument.

> **CAUTION**
>
> **Close Calls**
>
> If during an argument your heart rate goes above 90 beats per minute, you are too agitated to have a successful conversation. Better to take a time out for 20 minutes or so and try to calm down before resuming the discussion. It is a mistake to continue an argument when your heart rate is too elevated.

Your Inner Announcer Giving the Post-Game Wrap-Up

One of the most problematic, resentment-inducing, intimacy-thwarting moments usually happens *after* the argument has taken place. And it takes place in your mind. Statistically, men are much more likely to fall prey to this type of deadly thinking. And it is a key reason why men tend to have more physical discomfort when arguing than do women.

> **Just Ask!**
>
> *Are all men wimps? Every guy I've dated has shut down whenever we had a disagreement or argument. They argue for awhile then they just close up shop and make me feel like I'm being ridiculous and immature by wanting to keep the argument alive. What gives?*
>
> Actually, it's biological. Research shows that when you hook up men and women to blood pressure monitors and other devices that measure distress, men's stress levels rise quickly to an uncomfortable level during arguments with their mates. (It's called *DPA* or *Diffuse Physiological Arousal.*) Women's levels also rise but not as high. That is why women, on average, can argue for longer stretches. That's why men need to learn to calm themselves during an argument and not withdraw and some women need to be less harsh.

After an argument, men think thoughts that maintain their distress. They do the equivalent of a post-game analysis and rip apart the opposing team—their partner—in the process. Their thoughts center around two themes: being victimized (treated unfairly); and how they were right and their partners were wrong. Men might still be thinking those thoughts a day or two later. And believe me, the next time an argument begins, they definitely think those thoughts. That is one reason they withdraw prematurely from arguments. They expect arguments to be destructive, illogical, or unfair. So why sit there and take it?

Nevertheless, these after-argument thoughts are destructive to intimacy and must be replaced:

♦ "She never understands" becomes "*She wants to understand, I just have to help her.*"

♦ "All she does is find fault; she never appreciates the good things I do" becomes "*Deep down she appreciates me; I'm sure there are times I take her for granted, too.*"

♦ "No matter how hard I try to be calm and rational she has to be argumentative" becomes "*If she gets argumentative it might be because she is frustrated with me.*"

♦ "I can't stand being treated that way" becomes "*I'm not a victim; I haven't always been fair to her, either.*"

♦ "She just jumps to conclusions and doesn't hear me out" becomes "*Her viewpoint isn't always wrong.*"

Knowing how best to talk to yourself before, during, and after an argument helps set you up for the next discussion. If your post-argument self-talk is more positive, you are likely to be less agitated when you anticipate future disagreements. You will think that such disagreements are more tolerable or more understandable and part of the ebb and flow of any relationship. You'll have more confidence to handle any future disagreement. And that attitude will likely serve you well.

The Least You Need to Know

♦ Unless your negative beliefs are absolutely true you need to change them to something more positive and realistic.

♦ If your negative beliefs about your partner are valid, try to think of understandable reasons your partner acts that way.

♦ You won't be able to better handle an argument without first applying your new skills in the middle of an actual argument.

♦ After an argument, stop all thoughts that make you feel like a victim or that you're always right. You aren't a true victim and you aren't always right.

Chapter 9

How to Give Your Partner the Benefit of the Doubt

In This Chapter

- ◆ Learning how giving the benefit of the doubt improves intimacy

- ◆ Discovering the four questions needed to assess blame or virtue

- ◆ Learning the three attitudes that help you give the benefit of the doubt

- ◆ Knowing when you should nit-pick and when you shouldn't

- ◆ Giving the benefit of the doubt can sometimes backfire

Hopefully, you now see more clearly how the way you think can either move you toward or away from intimacy. Chapter 7 took a broad approach about building goodwill, revealing the importance of nurturing a positive outlook toward the people you want to feel close with. The previous chapter was very specific; it showed you how to think during an argument so that intimacy still thrives.

Giving someone the benefit of the doubt is another essential skill. It is not the same as emphasizing the positive or showing goodwill, although it is an outgrowth of goodwill. When you give the benefit of the doubt, you don't turn a blind eye to hurtful or bothersome actions. But neither do you assume the worst about the other person's character or motives. Done right, it is a form of trusting; a faith in the other person's overall integrity.

The tricky part is learning when giving the benefit of the doubt will backfire. At what point do you risk excusing actions that are harmful to intimacy? Giving the benefit of the doubt is one thing—being a doormat is another.

How You Assess Blame and Virtue

Imagine coming home after a long day at work. Your partner left a note that says he's out and will be back later. You check on the cats and see that the litter box still hasn't been changed. Didn't you remind him this morning to change it? He had the afternoon off. He obviously had plenty of time. So what conclusions do you draw? Do you think, *"Gee, he must have forgotten … Maybe he had one of his headaches … Maybe he got distracted …"* or do you think *"He's so lazy … He never listens … He only does what he feels like, never what needs to get done"?*

Can you envision the domino effect that each line of thinking creates and its impact on intimacy? By thinking the worst, you get angry. Then you probably show that anger later on by criticizing your partner or giving him the cold shoulder. That leads to perhaps him getting grumpy or bringing up all the times you forgot to do something for him. By giving the benefit of the doubt, however, you still might be annoyed that the litter box wasn't changed, but that's it. If you mention it later on, you might even hear "Gee, I'm sorry. I forgot all about it." Annoying but understandable, and not fatal.

> **CAUTION**
>
> **Close Calls**
>
> The more negatively you start to view your partner, the more your memories of shared times together will also become negative. If you're not careful, you might convince yourself that happy times from the past were not that happy after all.

Giving the benefit of the doubt doesn't mean you can't complain. It means you're not going to hold it against your partner. Saying, "Stop that!" or "I don't like it when you do that" may be perfectly appropriate. But don't automatically assume the worst about your partner's motives.

When somebody does or says something you really don't like, your ability to give the benefit of the doubt depends on how you answer the following four questions:

- Was the behavior intentional or not?

- Does it represent a flaw in the person's character or a simple mistake?

- Does it affect one area of the relationship or more than one?

- Has it happened before?

How you answer these questions will lead you to both greater contentment and intimacy or to greater resentment and detachment.

Intentional or Unintentional?

If you assume the best about a partner then you will view any undesirable thing he or she does as unintended or caused by extenuating circumstances. In fact, happy couples rarely see one another as having malicious intentions when hurtful things are said or done. They think, *"You didn't really mean it."* Couples who are not getting along automatically assume the worst about a partner's intentions. *"You did that on purpose!"* is their battle cry.

It isn't always possible to know for sure what a person's intentions are. And even very nice people can get petty or malicious at times. Still, the point is that successful couples are more likely to give each other the benefit of the doubt and assume that unkind actions were caused more by situational factors (stress, a bad day at the office, physical ailments, and so on) than by malicious intent.

This doesn't mean that assuming the best of intentions will automatically make you and your partner happier and more intimate. But it usually helps. However, automatically assuming that your partner had the worst of intentions absolutely creates distance and isolation.

Character Flaw or Stylistic Preference?

Rita underwent tests for breast cancer. Her husband Phil went to one of her appointments but not the other. When she wanted to discuss her fears, Phil seemed unwilling to talk more than a few minutes before he tried to end the discussion by reassuring her all would be fine. Phil's approach made Rita feel more alone and unsupported. If she viewed him as having a character flaw she might tell herself things like, *"He's an insensitive person … He only cares about himself, not others … He has no feelings."* Or, she might view him in a bit more favorable light and tell herself, *"He rarely talks much when he's worried … He hates to think of me as ill … He doesn't want me to worry."*

Clearly, the latter way of thinking is less negative and keeps feelings of intimacy alive. The real problem with labeling a partner as having character flaws is that you then can't give credit when he or she tries to improve. You'll see the positive change as coerced, not genuine. If Rita, for example, told Phil he was selfish and insensitive and he relented and told her he would accompany her to her next medical appointment, would she view him more favorably? Unlikely. She'd tell herself that he was only coming along because she put him to shame, not because he really cared. On the other hand, if Rita viewed Phil as very worried about her, then she'd give him credit if he decided to go with her to her next appointment.

Exercise!

If you label a partner in negative ways, you'll only pay attention to evidence that supports your negative label and overlook positive evidence. By selectively attending to only those qualities that you are looking for, you will paint a very negative, distorted view of your partner. Decide instead that for two weeks you will look hard for any evidence that disputes your negative views. Be as fair as possible. If your partner does something and you are unsure if you should give him positive credit, ask yourself this question: "If my best friend did that exact same behavior, would I view it positively?" If you would, give your partner credit, too.

The truth is this:

If you get along well with your partner, you will probably view anything he does that is good as a reflection of his character; you will likely also view anything he does wrong more leniently.

If you don't get along well with your partner, you will probably view anything he does that is wrong as a reflection of his character; anything he does right you will view skeptically.

Does It Affect a Large or Small Part of the Relationship?

Bill was often grumpy when he came home from work. Carla had a hard time being sympathetic because Bill's grumpiness affected too much of their life. Dinner together was tense; he snapped at her

Close Calls

About 70 percent of all divorces occur because the couple drifted apart; not because of any major problem such as abuse or addiction. Couples drift apart when they stop thinking positively about one another and start assuming the worst.

over small things; he wanted to be left alone for stretches of the evening; and he wasn't in the mood to hear about her day. Carla wanted to give him the benefit of the doubt but couldn't.

Had Bill been able to say something like, "Bear with me, I've just had one of my usual bad days" and then at least tried to make the best of the evening, Carla would be more lenient. But until he could do that, intimacy was broken. The couple had no real connection and Carla certainly had little desire to make love after being shut out all evening.

Has It Happened Before?

It's hard to give the benefit of the doubt when your partner keeps repeating annoying behaviors. After you start to think, *"How many times have I told him not to …?"* then you won't make excuses for him anymore.

Still, some behavior patterns really are hard for people to change no matter how much you complain. Think that's a crock? Look at it this way: You want your partner to change a certain way of behaving so it fits your standard of how things should be. You get impatient that it hasn't happened. But you are unable to change, too. You can't change your standard, or you can't learn to accept the situation. See? It can be hard to make changes after all.

Sometimes it is helpful to learn acceptance (see Chapter 27 for a more detailed discussion). Intimacy stops dead in its tracks when one partner refuses to accept something about the other. If you can learn to say, "I don't like this but I can learn to live with it" you might save yourself hours of misery.

Three New Attitudes to Help You Give the Benefit of the Doubt

I once attended a show where trained dolphins performed many remarkable feats. Every time a dolphin behaved properly it received a fish as a reward. But once in a while the dolphin received a fish for no obvious reason. I asked the trainer about it because it went against the principles of reward and punishment when training an animal. The trainer said, "I know it goes against the rules, but the dolphin is also my friend." In your personal life, you might have reasons why you shouldn't reward some

Intimacy Boosters _____

Happier couples will interpret interruptions by their mates as a sign of enthusiasm and interest, rather than a sign of rudeness. Try to view it that way and see if it changes how you feel the next time you are interrupted.

behaviors on the part of your partner. But friendship is important, too. Giving the benefit of the doubt is something friends do. And it adds to a sense of closeness and overall intimacy.

If you wish to get better at giving the benefit of the doubt, try cultivating the following three different attitudes that will make it easier for you to accept your partner—and that will allow for much deeper intimacy. Let's take a look at these attitudes.

Attitude Shift #1

Start believing that your partner may do hurtful or insensitive things for reasons that have nothing to do with you or your partner's character flaws. Don't overlook the obvious.

Some situations (driving long distances with young kids; a sweltering summer day when the air conditioning isn't working) or certain hours of the day (rush hour) may simply be more stressful. If your partner is worried about a family member's health, for instance, it might be the reason why he is in a foul mood.

Poor eating habits, fatigue, and job pressures can affect one's ability to handle situations in a fair, level-headed way. If any of these situations apply, it's reason enough to cut your partner some slack. You can still tell him to shape up and stop being such a grump, but at least understand his reasons behind it.

Attitude Shift #2

Your partner may say or do inconsiderate things because he or she is hurt or simply acting out of ignorance.

It's possible your partner is hurt by something you said or did. Lashing out in retaliation isn't necessarily a smart thing or a desirable thing, but it is understandable. You may disagree that you did anything to warrant his actions, but if he thinks his actions are justified then it at least explains his behavior.

Sometimes people hurt us out of ignorance. It's helpful to consider that they have no idea they are

Intimacy Boosters _____

If your partner is hurt by something you did, but you believe he or she is overreacting or just plain wrong, it's okay to defend yourself. However, it's also a good idea to say something like, "Given your view of what happened, I can see why you'd be upset."

being offensive and to avoid jumping to negative conclusions. For example, Mary told Andy that she'd call him later. He thought "later" meant later that day. She thought it meant later in the week.

Pete spent all afternoon cleaning up a room so it would look just like Patty wanted it to look. But the first thing she said when she arrived home was that he forgot to put gas in her car as he promised he would. Pete got snippy and Patty thought he was being immature and defensive. In fact, she just didn't realize all the work he'd done for her that day. Had she known, it's unlikely she'd have made the comment about the car.

Attitude Shift #3

Your interpretations of your partner's behaviors are formed, in part, by the mood you are in at the time.

The better your mood, the easier it is to give your partner the benefit of the doubt. The more cranky or tired you are, the more likely you'll put a negative spin on things. For example, imagine you're at a party and at some point your partner leaves your side to talk with somebody else. Is that okay or is it rude? That depends on a number of things. One factor is your mood at the time. If you hate being at that party, then his actions will annoy you. If you're very shy, his actions will annoy you. If you are delighted to see that your closest friend is also at the party, you might not care what your partner does.

Just Ask!

Some of my girlfriend's traits annoy me. I've confided in my friends about this and they tell me I should break up with her. How can I tell if the advice from my friends is valid?

You can't tell for sure. I suggest you pay close attention to how accurately you're describing your girlfriend's traits. Have you exaggerated even a little? Have you left out important information? If your girlfriend spoke to your friends, would she have a somewhat different story to tell? Getting support from friends is often helpful. But if they are hearing a one-sided version of events you may get bad advice and find it hard to give your girlfriend the benefit of the doubt.

Don't Be a Fool or a Doormat

Tina's relationship lasted four years. During that time she tolerated a lot of Joe's behaviors that were really thoughtless and rude. He'd show up very late for dates without calling; he'd snap at her when he was annoyed about something at work; he'd put her down whenever she wasn't in the mood to have sex. She also discovered he was having an online relationship with a woman from a different state. He said it was no big deal. She believed him. One day he simply ended their relationship and she was devastated. She felt like a fool. Was she?

Tina made a crucial error. She tolerated some of the intimacy killers discussed in Chapter 3. Joe was verbally abusive and selfish. By tolerating his behaviors from the beginning, they became part of the landscape of their relationship and sometimes seemed normal and appropriate to her.

If you're not sure whether you should tolerate some of your partner's behaviors, ask yourself these questions:

- Do the behaviors deeply hurt me?

- Do they go against my core values?

- Have I told my partner to stop but to no avail?

- If I did those same behaviors, would my partner get upset with me?

- Do people whose opinions I trust tell me that I am right to complain?

- Are any of the behaviors insulting, hostile, dangerous, violent, addictive, possessive, or controlling?

- Am I too dependent on my partner to take a clear, forceful stand?

- Did I experience similar behaviors in a past relationship that ultimately failed?

Answering yes to just one of these questions is reason to suspect that you might be tolerating too much. Answering yes to two or more is a strong indication you are putting up with behaviors that are toxic to intimacy, your self-esteem, and the relationship.

When Making Mountains Out of Molehills Is a Good Thing

Everyone hates being nagged. But sometimes the nagger is right. We live in a society that encourages diversity and tolerance, and some people feel that they must be politically correct in their personal lives, too. But tolerating behaviors that you know are harmful or intolerable cannot be justified in your relationships. Just because you complain to your partner doesn't mean you are being intolerant. It means that you recognize some actions as difficult to put up with and as a threat to intimacy.

Do you recall as a child being told not to bring food into the room with the brand-new furniture? What happened? If your family was like most, that rule slowly became broken over time. Certain foods were tolerated "But you must be careful!" Eventually there was a spill. It created a ruckus temporarily. Then another spill, then another. Eventually the new furniture was soiled and old looking. The worse it looked the more your parents didn't care if you ate in that room. Well, relationships sometimes go down a similar path. You tell yourself that certain behaviors are not acceptable. Then you give in. Eventually you have no real standard and the relationship has degraded. There is less closeness, more aggravation; less intimacy, more detachment.

There are two particular times when having strict standards is extremely important: early in the relationship and when positive changes are followed by backsliding. If you lose sight of the ball during these times, achieving intimacy will be much more difficult.

Nip Problems Early in the Relationship

Research conducted at the University of Washington reveals that couples who maintained strong levels of intimacy and overall happiness were able to halt problems before they took root. And women were much better than men at detecting problems early on. The more the woman had a low threshold for tolerating negative behaviors, the better the relationship was years later. What might appear to some men as the women being rigid, nagging, or controlling, is really the women taking a clear stand about what is acceptable and unacceptable.

Sometimes the first stirrings that a relationship needs correcting are vague feelings of discontentment. Often there is a growing awareness of feeling sorry for yourself and maybe one or both partners prefers more time alone. Add irritability and less physical intimacy to the list and you now have good reason to believe that certain problems have been glossed over and intimacy has therefore suffered.

Just Ask! _____

I'm afraid to complain for fear it will push my partner away. Any suggestions?

Fear is the main reason people tolerate hurtful, intimacy-numbing behaviors. Defining who you are and what you'll put up with (and what you won't) is a matter of personal integrity. If a building or structure has no integrity, it collapses. If what you need to maintain your personal integrity cannot be found in your relationship, your relationship will never be a truly intimate one and it won't make you happy.

The next section of this book discusses intimacy through talk and will give you many tips on how to register complaints without it turning into an emotional rollercoaster ride.

If you're smart, you won't hesitate to point out any negativity you know you won't tolerate the first time it rears its ugly head.

Don't Tolerate Backsliding

After positive changes have been made it's vitally important to make sure those changes are more or less permanent. Backsliding is common but must be addressed as soon as it starts. Many people tolerate backsliding because they don't want to sound discouraging or unappreciative of the efforts made so far. You can be friendly and appreciative and yet remain steadfast that some behaviors aren't acceptable.

Keep in mind, there is a difference between being bossy and demanding and simply defining what you can live with and what you can't. Bossiness is an attempt to control or coerce. Defining yourself is being honest and demonstrating personal integrity.

The Least You Need to Know

- To give the benefit of the doubt is to trust that your partner's intentions are, for the most part, good and not malicious.

- You can give the benefit of the doubt and still state aloud that some behaviors are not acceptable.

- Having a low tolerance for negativity is a good thing in a relationship.

- Some of your partner's annoying traits must be accepted.

Part 3

Intimacy Through Talk

Want to get to know someone intimately? Want to add bursts of excitement to a comfortable but tired relationship? You can achieve the intimacy you desire by understanding the power of conversation.

The problem for some of you is the false belief that to improve communication you (or your partner) have to talk a lot more. Not so. Genuine intimacy requires quality talk, not quantity. Someone who is shy or reserved by nature can still create power-packed moments of intimacy—the kind of words that will open anyone's heart. The size of the conversation doesn't matter; it's how well you use it.

This section starts with intimate self-disclosure. You'll see why people who have no problem getting undressed in front of their lover have a real problem getting emotionally undressed—and what can be done to change that. You'll also learn how to gently coax a nontalkative partner to be more open, and discover how conflicts can be the stepping stone to improved intimacy. You'll discover why the most caring and devoted partners unwittingly make key listening mistakes, and why being an intimate listener is crucial to warmth, passion, and devotion.

Chapter 10

Intimate Self-Disclosure the Easy Way

In This Chapter

◆ Rating your comfort with self-disclosure

◆ Learning exercises that flex your self-disclosure muscles

◆ Knowing short, easy, and powerful intimacy phrases

◆ Understanding the key do's and don'ts when revealing yourself

Meeting someone for the first time? In a relationship that's starting to blast off? Or maybe you're one-half of a longtime married couple. It doesn't matter. Your degree and quality of self-disclosure can awaken (or re-awaken) passion and interest or it can put it to sleep. Self-disclosure is self-revelation; you reveal in a deeper way what you really think, feel, and want. In other words, you expose yourself. Self-disclosure with a partner is somewhat like sex with a partner—over time, very little happens that's new or special unless you try. And although it might be nice and stimulating, it doesn't shake your rafters as often. It's not about technique as much as it's about seeing your partner in a new light. Seeing your partner naked in a new light can be exhilarating. But "hearing" your partner naked—hearing him or her say things that are private, personal, meaningful, and heartfelt—can be a heady experience, too.

Intimate words that cause your heart to go pitter-patter need to be spoken once in awhile. You need to say them and you need to hear them. I'm not only referring to poetry or all that mushy stuff—although that certainly is both touching and intoxicating to many people. I'm referring to how certain phrases or comments, or even just a particular way of showing interest, can either breathe new life into intimacy or asphyxiate it.

Self-disclosure is an important form of shared intimacy. You open yourself up and therefore make yourself vulnerable. It's a risk, just like parachuting. And when the chute opens and you land safely, there's nothing like it in the world.

A Self-Disclosure Quiz

You might think that you express yourself often and clearly. But chances are you either withhold too much information or you reveal it too intensely—both of which can cause a reduction in intimacy. Take the following quiz to help you detect what your strong and weak points are.

1. I do my fair share of the talking in my relationship.

   Rarely __ Sometimes __ Often __

2. I say "I love you" every day.

   Rarely __ Sometimes __ Often __

3. I express all my emotions easily.

   Rarely __ Sometimes __ Often __

4. If something bothers me about my partner, I'm likely to speak up.

   Rarely __ Sometimes __ Often __

5. When someone reveals strong feelings, I'm more likely to be receptive than to want to change the topic.

   Rarely __ Sometimes __ Often __

6. When someone gets teary-eyed, I want to know more about what's bothering them.

   Rarely __ Sometimes __ Often __

7. I enjoy talking about things that make me happy.

   Rarely __ Sometimes __ Often __

8. I can talk about personal flaws or mistakes I've made when I'm with someone I really care about.

   Rarely __ Sometimes __ Often __

9. If I'm feeling close to tears during a talk, I am willing to keep talking.

   Rarely __ Sometimes __ Often __

10. In general, I don't mind revealing my deepest emotions.

   Rarely __ Sometimes __ Often __

11. The emotion I am most likely to express is anger.

   Rarely __ Sometimes __ Often __

12. I am told that I more often express dissatisfaction with something than satisfaction.

   Rarely __ Sometimes __ Often __

13. I would feel weak if I got tears in my eyes.

   Rarely __ Sometimes __ Often __

14. I prefer to keep a lot of my opinions and feelings private.

   Rarely __ Sometimes __ Often __

15. If my partner expresses how he or she feels and I don't like what I'm hearing, I'm likely to criticize or withdraw.

   Rarely __ Sometimes __ Often __

The more you checked "Often" in statements 1 through 10, the more likely you feel at ease self-disclosing and the more likely your relationships will be richer in intimacy. Statements where you checked "Rarely" are clear areas of weakness and absolutely need improvement if you want to build intimacy in your life. "Sometimes" is a typical response for the majority of people. It might be good judgment to be less revealing (such as on a first date or with people who are strangers) but when you want to build an intimate relationship "sometimes" isn't often enough.

If you checked "Often" in statements 11 through 15, intimacy through talking is not your strong suit. Your impatience and anger could damage a relationship if you're not careful, because it is too strong and your ability to show understanding and compassion is weak.

Self-Disclosure: Use It or Lose It

Common sense tells you that your attitude about someone or something—how you think and feel—dictates how you will act. For example, if you enjoy physical exertion and like to look trim, you will follow an exercise regimen. If you care about someone, you will do and say thoughtful things. The equation is simple: *attitude brings about action*.

But there is an axiom in psychology that most people ignore even though it can make a huge difference in how you treat people: *action creates attitude*. How you feel and act are two ingredients that play off of one another. You might start doing something because you have a positive attitude about doing it, but continuing to do it can increase your positive attitude. Similarly, if you enjoy something but for whatever reason stop doing it, you can lose interest in it. In that case your action (stopping an enjoyable activity) created an attitude (made you care less about it).

Self-disclosure operates on that same principle. The more you do it, the more likely you will continue to do it. That's why it is imperative that you talk more revealingly and passionately, at least some of the time, or your desire and comfort in doing so will fade and intimacy will get as stale as an old cracker.

CAUTION

Close Calls

If the person you're romantically interested in is not one to say sweet, sexy, or very revealing things, don't be so quick to accept it as "Just the way he is." Over time, he or she will become even less open. Expect self-disclosure to be a part of your relationship.

Fake It 'Til You Feel It?

If you feel uneasy about saying romantic things or revealing hard-to-talk-about facets of yourself, you're not alone. But avoiding such conversations actually increases your overall fear (yes, guys, I'm talking fear here) of self-disclosure. It isn't faking it to open up and be more tender with your words. You obviously feel those things or else you wouldn't be running from them.

I've counseled hundreds of men who've had affairs. What amazes their betrayed partners is how the guys often had heart-to-heart conversations with their mistresses—conversations they'd never have with their partner. "My wife (girlfriend, fiancée) doesn't understand me" is a common complaint from an unfaithful guy. But she doesn't understand him because he doesn't reveal himself. Why does he reveal himself to a mistress? Because she is safer. A man is more vulnerable revealing himself to someone he is close to than to someone he recently met. To keep a relationship strong and intact, each partner must be able to say heartfelt, revealing things about him- or herself.

Tips for the Self-Disclosing Faint at Heart

People who are uneasy about self-disclosure are often uncomfortable displaying physical affection publicly. They also don't like to say "I love you" when others might overhear. "That's just the way I am" is not a good excuse. Set a goal for yourself: Show at least one form of public affection in each of your next 10 outings. The more you practice, the easier it will become. Make it pay off in the end by giving yourself a special reward. Maybe you and your partner can have a weekend getaway or a nice dinner out.

Another way to enhance self-disclosure is to pick a moment from your childhood, happy or sad, that had a memorable effect on you. Now talk about it with your partner. Give details. Why was it so memorable? Did it have a lasting impact? How did it shape your personality? After you've finished, be honest: Was it really that uncomfortable talking about it? Are you willing to do it again? Pick a couple moments from your day when you had a strong emotional reaction to something and discuss them a few times a week. It can be something small, such as talking about your favorite team's win or loss. Just do it. Practice really does make perfect. The formula is simple: Mention the details of what happened and reveal how you feel about it.

Intimacy Boosters

When you say nice things, smile. At least let your eyes do the smiling if nothing else. A smile attached to a loving or romantic phrase punctuates your words and etches them into the listener's heart.

Exercise!

Some people (more women than men) are most uneasy revealing anger. In contrast, men who are reluctant to reveal their feelings usually have little problem disclosing anger but a much harder time admitting to softer feelings such as hurt, sadness, or fear. You can help. If your partner is uneasy admitting anger, say "If I were you, I'd have felt angry (irritated, annoyed) in that situation." Or ask, "Did you feel any twinge of anger? I would have." If the speaker is avoiding softer emotions, suggest them. "I know that made you angry but you sounded a little hurt (or sad), too."

Helping a person to identify and label their real emotions will add to your sense of closeness.

Short, Sweet, and Powerful Intimacy Boosting Phrases

When you're in love, say so. Periodically, say it with a few extra words. "*I love you … with all my heart … more than I ever thought imaginable … like I've never loved anyone else … with a passion that drives me crazy sometimes … and never grow tired of being with you.*" Without such added zest the routine "I love you" (followed by the predictable "I love you, too") gets, well, boring and less meaningful. Once in a while say "I love you" like you're saying it for the very first time.

Next time you have a few minutes to yourself, complete these sentences about your partner (or your hoped-for partner). Emphasize the positive:

- ◆ I love it when he/she _____.

- ◆ My favorite thing to do with him/her is to _____.

- ◆ I get so excited about him/her whenever _____.

- ◆ His/her body makes me _____.

- ◆ When I stare at him/her I can't help thinking _____.

- ◆ I smile when I think _____.

- ◆ The one thing I'd like to do sexually with him/her that I haven't done is _____.

- ◆ What I value most about him/her is _____.

That list is just for starters, but you get the idea. After you've completed each statement to your satisfaction, your job is to tell your partner those things. Don't say them all at once. Spread them out over several days. But say them. Say them when you're in bed about to fall asleep, and say them when you wake up. Call your partner up and say them on the phone or send a surprise e-mail.

Your answers should be broad and balanced. If most of your answers are sexual in nature, look for answers that talk about other aspects of your partner, too: beauty, character, achievements, and so on. If your answers say little about sex, then make them more about sex. Everyone needs to know they are sexually desirable.

How Soon Should You Self-Disclose?

Talking about the ugly details of your divorce on your first date will probably make it your last date. If you're angry at a lot of members of the opposite sex, it's best not to reveal that too soon. If you're eager to find a mate, settle down, and have kids as soon as possible, don't say that while getting to know one another; downplay it if you must mention it. Otherwise, you'll scare away potential partners who may want what you want but will be turned off by your faster-than-the-speed-of-sound approach. Dates want to feel special for who they are, not for what they will provide.

In the earliest parts of a relationship, self-disclosures should be more positive. Talk about achievements if you wish but don't boast. Be modest and give your date an opportunity to reflect on what you're saying and boast about you!

Self-Disclosure and Compatibility

Self-disclosure also succeeds or fails depending on overall levels of compatibility. The key areas of compatibility include the following:

- Intellectual/educational level
- Physical attractiveness
- Social status
- Common interests and goals
- Overall psychological health and adjustment

Think of these five areas as being similar to a school grade level. Let's say the highest grade level is a college diploma. Someone who has a college diploma in attractiveness is by this definition super-model gorgeous. Someone who has a high school diploma in attractiveness is by this definition average. Similarly, a collage graduate in the psychological adjustment category is someone who by all accounts is very secure and emotionally healthy. Someone in the third grade of psychological adjustment is immature or irresponsible. Get the idea?

Now, this next concept is very important: You will attract (or be attracted to) people who are within one or two grade levels of you in these five categories. Let's say you are a guy who is average in overall attractiveness (and most of us are average, by definition). You might be knocked out by a woman who is drop-dead-hot-off-the-cover-of-Cosmo gorgeous but will probably be somewhat intimidated by her if you get a chance to really know her. You'd end up having a more meaningful relationship with someone who is closer to your grade level in attractiveness. A woman CEO is less likely to end up with a blue-collar guy and stay happy. Someone who is not well read or educated is not likely to attract a university professor.

Keep your level of compatibility in mind when self-disclosing. Generally, the higher your grade level on any of these categories, the more you can admit flaws or put yourself down in some way without losing your appeal. A wealthy man who admits he lost money in a stock deal comes off much better than a laborer who admits the same mistake. Someone with obvious low self-esteem who repeatedly puts him- or herself down in conversation with a self-confident person is really saying, "We're not compatible."

Just Ask!

I'm not at all self-confident. I tend to put myself down publicly when I make mistakes. The man I'm dating has a high-power job and is extremely self-confident. Will he remain attracted to me if I don't improve my self-esteem?

The wider the gap in self-esteem between partners, the harder it will be for that couple to succeed. However, some people display a public mask of confidence and security but are really insecure. They might indeed be attracted to someone with obvious low esteem because that makes them appear superior. One way to tell for sure: If you have low esteem but are able to improve your confidence or are attempting some notable personal achievement, a truly secure partner will be happy for you. An insecure partner will find reasons to knock you down a few pegs after you start to feel better about yourself.

Hits and Misses of Self-Disclosure

A number of key guidelines should be followed when you or the person you're with make personal revelations. Here are some hits and misses to keep in mind:

Hit: Give the speaker room to say the wrong thing or use the wrong words when he's struggling through a revealing moment. In other words, the talker shouldn't have to worry that every word he/she says is being scrutinized for fairness and precision. Revealing difficult facets of oneself can be a sloppy process.

Hit: If the person is revealing something important about a topic you know little about (a passionate hobby or career achievement, for instance), ask questions that will help you learn more. Show an interest even if the topic is one you find boring. It's not boring to the other person and, when intimacy is at stake, that's what counts.

Hit: While listening, scan for words that carry emotional weight. Make comments that show support for those emotions such as *"That must have been hard … You must have been so pleased … What a wonderful experience … What a painful time …".*

Hit: If you are self-disclosing about a very personal topic, stay in the mid-range of emotional expression unless the other person knows you well. Otherwise you risk overwhelming that person. Don't reveal anything that is obviously painful when just starting to get to know someone.

Hit: Always show support for a person who is discussing dreams and longings no matter how far fetched.

Hit: Men especially should ask women how they feel about something they are divulging. Don't be afraid to probe.

Hit: If a man is opening up in an emotional way, use caution when asking probing questions about those feelings. He may be feeling out of control with his emotions and will use your "feeling probe" as a way to close up shop. Better to *suggest* a feeling ("That must have been difficult"). If he is very open about his emotions, take that as your cue to probe.

Miss: Don't heap so much praise on the other person that you put him/her on a pedestal. He or she will be afraid to burst your bubble by admitting personal weaknesses or flaws. Intimacy will suffer.

Intimacy Boosters

There's nothing intimate about disclosing facts. Intimacy starts when you disclose how you feel about those facts.

Miss: Don't be openly critical and hostile of others. How you speak about other people will be judged very carefully by the new person in your life. Your date/partner will soon believe that you could be just as critical of him/her.

Miss: Don't be a know-it-all when discussing personal stories or interests. If your partner has an expertise he/she is proud of, don't compete.

Miss: Don't change the subject just because the other person's self-disclosure bored you (or made you feel uneasy or bored).

Miss: If the other person admits negative feelings toward his or her family, don't agree and put his family down. Neither should you challenge his perceptions and defend his family. Simply acknowledge the other's feelings without offering an opinion.

Miss: If you learn what the other person's biggest fears, worries, or dreams are, never dismiss or minimize them. Offer an alternative way of looking at the situation if you must, but don't convey the idea that he/she is wrong to feel that way.

Miss: If a partner reveals something that was hard to say (and especially if you think he/she might be embarrassed later on), acting like it was never said will actually make him/her feel more self-conscious or ashamed. Better to let him/her know you're glad it was brought up.

The Psychology of Giving "The Silent Treatment"

Coaxing a somewhat shy person to talk more is one thing. Getting someone to open up when they're angrily claiming, "I just don't want to talk about it!" is another. Yes, intimacy goes out the window if there is no opportunity for discussing hurt feelings. But insisting that matters be talked about might not be the right thing to do either.

Linda lay on the far side of the bed, her back turned away from Dan. They had attended a holiday party earlier in the evening. Dan was on his third glass of wine when he put his arm around a female co-worker in a manner that Linda believed was obviously flirtatious. Dan disagreed. They were still arguing about it when they arrived home. Linda finally said she was fed up talking about it and went immediately to bed.

"It wasn't what you thought it was," Dan said, reaching over to touch her shoulder.

"I said I don't want to discuss it," Linda said through clenched teeth.

Dan complied. He rolled over and went to sleep. What he didn't know was that as much as Linda didn't want to talk about it, she also wanted to talk about it. And she wanted him to keep trying to get her to open up. Dan was a practical guy who took Linda's words literally. He actually thought he was doing the right thing by honoring her wish to end the discussion. It was a mistake. Had it been the other way around and Dan was the offended party who didn't want to discuss it, Linda likely would have persisted in her effort to get him to open up; and it would have been a mistake.

In times of conflict and emotional upheaval, all men and women have mixed feelings. They want to argue, they don't want to argue; they want to talk it out, they want to retreat. But the tendency is for women to lean in the direction of settling differences no matter how upset they are while men get flooded with feelings and need to retreat to calm down. So when a man says he doesn't want to talk about it, he usually means it. If a woman says it, she may or may not mean it.

The best advice? If your lover is hurt or angry and refuses to talk, don't immediately give up. But don't be pushy and demanding, either. Men especially need to push a little and show a desire to talk even if the woman is angry and silent. If repeated efforts to get the woman to talk fail, a man should honor her wishes. However, he should do so by stating clearly that he wants to talk and will approach her later. If a man is shutting down and wants to be left alone, give him 20 minutes by himself and then approach him again, gently. If he still doesn't want to talk, give him his space. A man who is flooded by emotions feels out of control and does not want to engage in more conversation.

The Least You Need to Know

- Unprotected self-disclosure is a form of intimacy; you must be willing to reveal yourself if you want a close relationship.

- The more you practice appropriate self-disclosure the easier it gets; the less you open up, the more embarrassed you'll be when expressing how you feel.

- Practice showing public displays of affection if you want to feel more at ease with private self-disclosures.

- Someone who is expressing difficult emotions needs to see you as a good listener.

- If someone is angry and doesn't want to talk, gently push for more conversation; but be willing to step back if necessary.

Chapter 11

Real Easy Talks for Real Cozy Intimacy

In This Chapter

- ◆ Uncovering the reasons some people don't talk much
- ◆ Discovering how small talk can pay big dividends
- ◆ Learning 10 things in 10 minutes about another person
- ◆ Recognizing mistakes good communicators make
- ◆ Learning how to instantly know if a talk will lead to intimacy

Talking can be more intimate than sex (even with your clothes on). The intimate nature of talk explains why many people find it frustrating. It can be such an intimate act that people literally close themselves off from it or, like a rich cheesecake, take it in only small bites. To have a truly intimate conversation is to reveal yourself. People who engage in intimate talk lose some privacy, but in return they gain closeness and sharing. When you add caring to the equation (remember that intimacy involves connecting, sharing, and caring) then bearing your soul or listening to someone else bear his soul becomes a deep, profoundly intimate act. And the shudder you experience when you are truly known and truly cared about lasts so much longer than the shudder of any orgasm.

Think that good, intimate communication involves a lot of talk time? Think again. This chapter shows how to have meaningful conversations that take very little time. Nontalkative types might discover that opening up isn't so bad after all, and talkative types will see how "less" is sometimes "more."

Why Some People Don't Like to Talk Much

On average, women derive much more satisfaction from intimate conversations than men do. And studies show that despite these enlightened times; parents speak to their daughters differently than they speak to their sons. Parents of toddlers use more emotional words and phrases when speaking to girls than boys, and they speak to girls for longer bursts of time. Another reason men tend to be less communicative is because males are raised to be competitive (and seem biologically predisposed that way, too). As such, some men view opening up much the same as giving away state secrets and thereby losing a competitive edge.

> **CAUTION**
>
> **Close Calls** _____
>
> If you are very unhappy with your partner's inability to communicate, you might be under-detecting the times he does open up by as much as 50 percent—and thereby miss a great opportunity for connection. Pay more attention. You might be surprised at what you hear.

> **Intimacy Boosters** _____
>
> Forget about long drawn-out conversations for now. Toss in a handful of brief chitchats every day. Keep them focused, noncontroversial, and light. But say something revealing and listen intently. In a month's time the quality of your overall intimacy will greatly improve.

As boys and girls get to be about age 10, they identify more with their same-sex parent. Boys drift away from their mothers at that age (they squirm when they are hugged or kissed by their moms, for example) and look to their fathers for guidance. But if a boy's dad is too busy working or otherwise unavailable; is physically present but not very talkative; or is intolerant of "weakness," that boy will learn quickly to keep his thoughts to himself and solve his problems on his own—without discussion. What the boy gains in self-sufficiency he loses when it comes to intimacy. A false mindset develops whereby being strong is equated with being silent. But the silent ones possess all the self-doubts and insecurities that anyone else has. They're just simply afraid to reveal them.

People also keep quiet because when they do try to have meaningful discussions it backfires. Maybe they feel judged, misunderstood, or disagreements ensue. Because they feel ineffective at communicating, they prefer to withdraw. Of course, withdrawing causes their partners to become more frustrated and increases the odds of future arguments, which causes more withdrawal.

The answer to these problems? Engage in quality conversations where each person feels listened to, understood, and cared about. Begin by taking advantage of those boring or uninspired conversations that take place everyday: small talk.

The Hidden Power of Small Talk

If you're like most people, you have very little free time. If you're one-half of a dual-career couple, your rest and relaxation time is at a premium. If you're a dual-career couple with kids, then you probably consider an extra-long shower like a vacation to the tropics. That's why normal, everyday small talk can actually be the kindling that lights a passionate fire later on. Couples who don't take full advantage of the small talk they engage in daily are missing an easy opportunity to create intimacy.

Small Talk with a Person You Just Met

Maybe you're having lunch for the first time. Or you just met this person at a party and you feel an attraction. Small talk is the core of your interaction. It would be inappropriate to ask deeply probing questions right away. If you're shy and not that comfortable keeping a conversation going, all you have to do is ask a number of questions and let the other person do more of the speaking. Asking questions shows that you are interested. If you focus on what's being said to you instead of judging your performance, you'll automatically come up with more comments and questions simply because you listened well.

Keep in mind that what makes conversations more intimate (or simply more interesting) are not the facts being stated ("I'm an investment banker ... I own a sheepdog ... I grew up in a large city ... I just bought a condo ...") but your feelings about those facts. An effective small-talker will share some feelings ("Sheepdogs are such fun ...") but not be over the top with emotion. A good small-talk listener will search for "feeling" words and comment on them ("Sounds like you enjoy being a dog owner ... I had a dog when I was a kid ...").

Express how you feel or what you like or dislike, and the person you're chatting with will know so much more about you. You can't start to care about someone when all you know are life facts.

Small Talk for the Established Couple

An amazing thing happens when couples know how to engage in pleasant, intimate small talk. The next time they have a disagreement their conversation goes more smoothly. In contrast, couples whose everyday chitchats are tense, dismissive, or business-like are much more likely to turn a small disagreement into a miserable argument.

Every couple needs at least 20 minutes a day of intimate connecting, of feeling like a couple, to sustain closeness and have enough stamina to get through life together. One way to achieve this is to take full advantage of everyday small talk. Every couple talks about bills, appointments, schedule of events, chores, and so on. How you chat about them can be the difference between intimacy and isolation. Here are some small talk dos and don'ts:

- ◆ DO try to sit, lie down together, or touch while engaging in small talk.

- ◆ DO limit the conversation to everyday, nonconflict issues.

- ◆ DO make it more informal by giving one another back or foot rubs, taking a walk, cuddling, having a cup of coffee, playing music, and so on.

- ◆ DO keep competing tasks (cooking, getting changed, dealing with kids or pets or telephones) to an absolute minimum while chatting.

- ◆ DON'T get aggravated or be abrupt in your small talk.

- ◆ DON'T discuss controversial topics or begin to criticize your partner.

- ◆ DON'T feel forced to keep the conversation moving; periods of silence are okay as long as you are connecting physically.

- ◆ DON'T frequently try to turn it into sex or one of you will avoid small talk when sex is not a priority.

Done right, these daily periods of connection will become a safe haven, something you look forward to. Furthermore, as events happen to you during an ordinary day, you'll be more likely to think of your partner and tell yourself "Oh, I have to talk about this later."

Exercise!

How can you learn 10 new things about your partner in 10 minutes? Easy. Make a game out of it. Whenever you want to connect but have little to say, these inquiries can help. For example, what are 10 things you can say about your past that your partner doesn't know? They need not be profound moments from your life. Recall scenes from your childhood that were fun. What was your favorite kind of present? Who was your best friend and why? Or what 10 dreams and longings do you or your partner have? (It doesn't matter if they are fanciful or unrealistic.) Who are 10 people you'd like to meet? What 10 things might you enjoy doing that you've never tried? What are 10 turn-offs and turn-ons? What were 10 exciting moments in your life? Ten scary moments? Ten favorite books or movies? Is 10 too many? Okay, four or five will do nicely. The point is to think of as many things as you can. These talks will quickly add to your sense of closeness as you share facts and feelings that maybe you never shared before.

Getting the Clam You Love to Open Up

If your partner is shy and clams up often, it might be impossible to get him or her to be as talkative and open as you are. But a 20 percent improvement is very possible. First, you have to consider what your partner's baseline level of communication is. In other words, what did he or she come in with before this relationship? The more you are trying to change your partner's personality the less successful you'll be. But many people start out as good conversationalists and dry up over time. That baseline level is where you have the opportunity for the most improvement.

Ask yourself the following questions before you try to get your partner to be more talkative:

+ *Am I craving more talk or more intimacy?* If you really want more intimacy, make sure you focus on the three other intimacy paths (thought, touch, and togetherness) as well. You might tolerate less conversation if intimacy improves elsewhere.

+ *Do I tend to turn conversations into bitch sessions?* If so, you might be turning off your mate. Making complaints now and then is fine but minimize harsh criticisms and keep the volume down.

+ *Am I choosing an inopportune time?* Sure, an avoider will always tell you it's not the right time to talk. But don't insist on talking when it's time to sleep or during some other activity that has your partner's rapt attention.

♦ *Have I shown appreciation for times we did converse?* You might be reluctant to give the nontalker a pat on the back for talking because you think that regular conversations *should* happen. Still, let him know it meant a lot.

If you're willing to meet your partner halfway in the conversation department, he or she might be willing to lean in your direction a bit more.

What to Say

The idea is to respectfully acknowledge your differences in desire for conversation but to suggest options that might make each of you feel better. As much as you don't like having to pester him to talk, he doesn't like being pestered. You must turn it into a win-win situation where each of you benefits.

First preface your request, and then make a request for change. Examples might include the following:

I know you're not much of a talker and I don't expect you to want to have as many conversations as I do, but it means a great deal to me when we do talk. Can we agree to have more time for conversation?"

"I know we have different preferences when it comes to carrying on a conversation. Is there something I can do that would make you feel more comfortable talking?"

Intimacy Boosters

Sometimes, simply having a regular connection-time together (coffee in the morning, a walk after dinner, a night out once a week, and so on) allows conversations to develop more naturally and effortlessly without self-consciousness.

"I like to talk more than you do. For me to get what I want, I need your cooperation. For you to get the privacy you want, you don't need my cooperation. Can we come up with a way to make this fairer?

It's easy to focus on the nontalker as the one with the problem. However, although fundamental differences might exist in your desire for conversation, those differences may well be inflamed due to the tug-of-war between the two of you. Focus on what you might be doing to keep this issue stuck.

What Not to Say

Don't label your partner as defective because he or she doesn't want to talk as much as you do. It will only create resentment and defensiveness. Don't threaten. Don't bring up your complaint in a harsh way, no matter how justified you feel. Harsh start-ups almost always cause a conversation to deteriorate. Finally, don't criticize your partner if he finally does open up. Don't say things such as, *"Is that all you have to say? … It's about time you said something!"*

When You're the Clam Being Pried

If you're not much of a talker, you've probably been told many times that you need to open up more. And you're tired of hearing it. What I'd like you to do is aim for a 20 percent improvement. That's doable. It isn't fair for your partner to fully accept your silent ways if you're not accepting his or her talkative ways. And more than that, your partner is probably right. Intimacy is missing in your relationship, and one reason it's missing is because you don't reveal yourself more and you don't ask enough personal questions about your mate.

Think of it this way. Do you have a hobby or interest that is not just an interest but a passion? For example, do you really love music? Or sports? Or hunting? Or gardening? If you really love something, you don't simply partake of it casually, do you? No, you probably learn all you can about it and get involved in it as often as possible. When you love something, you move toward it. You don't wait for it to come to you. You seek it out. Well, your partner wants you to seek her out. To learn everything about your partner you can't sit back and expect that knowledge to just appear. You have to investigate and take the time to learn more. That's where conversation comes in.

Nontalkers get defensive easily when asked to talk more. They blame the other person for being too demanding, needy, or for not quickly getting to the bottom line. Nontalkers don't listen intently. Instead they scan for the key points; much like a speed reader scans a page for the essential information and overlooks everything else. The problem with such a method is that it reduces the purpose of any conversation to a simple exchange of facts or ideas, not as an opportunity to connect or share feelings.

Here are some tips for nontalkers:

◆ Don't immediately offer quick-fix answers unless specifically asked. Ask more questions and find ways to enable your partner to divulge more of how he or she feels.

◆ Be patient. Remind yourself that the conversation is not a race. It's okay to take more time to understand all that's being said to you.

◆ When you're at a loss for words, use pitch-back phrases that show you are listening and trying to understand. Such phrases include *"That's interesting … That must have made you feel … Tell me more … Can you say that another way? … Uh huh …"*.

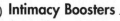

Intimacy Boosters

If you're trying to be a better talker, tell your partner that you're aiming for a 10 to 20 percent improvement as a start. By keeping expectations modest at first, neither of you will become discouraged.

♦ Don't sigh, roll your eyes, or use body language that shows disinterest or impatience.

♦ It's okay to preface your conversation by saying, "Bear with me. Talking is not my strong suit."

♦ If you're losing focus no matter how hard you try, say that. Then say that you want to continue the talk in a little while. If you need a prop while talking (something to fidget with), that's okay as long as you explain that it helps your concentration and that you really are paying attention.

Not-So-Obvious Mistakes Good Communicators Make

Some people consider themselves to be good communicators. They might actually be better than the people they talk to on a daily basis, but they may also have a lot to learn. Sometimes, conversations that should be short, sweet, and easy go haywire because the talkers make mistakes that are not obvious and therefore hard to correct. And sometimes the mistakes are obvious to the listener but the talker refuses to admit to them.

Communication is tricky in large part because it is highly subjective. Have you ever known someone to be offended by a remark you would have laughed off? Has someone ever distorted the meaning of something you said? Despite subjectivity, certain comments and phrases are almost guaranteed to be taken the wrong way.

Unintended Dismissals

A poorly spoken remark can come off as a dismissal. The listener feels disregarded and unimportant. "Not now, I'm busy" may be a true statement, but it can sound off-putting. It's so much nicer to say something such as, "I'm sorry but I can't right now, I'm too busy. Would later be okay?" The difference is small but important: recognizing that the other person has feelings.

"I didn't hear you" can also be a turn-off. Some people don't hear well because they don't pay attention. They give the impression they are listening but they're really thinking about something else. The other person gets annoyed, not because you didn't hear, but because it's the tenth time you didn't hear. Similarly, saying "Oh, I forgot" is understandable, unless you have a history of forgetting. Then no matter how sweetly or compassionately you say it, it will go over like a lead balloon.

"What do you want!" or "What do you want now?" will also be heard as dismissive. The other person may likely respond, "Forget it, nevermind!" and go storming off.

" " Just Ask! _____

I'm always putting my foot in my mouth. The other day my girlfriend was applying make-up and I asked if it would take long. She felt insulted. Am I a clod or is she taking things too personally?

If you admittedly have a history of being overly critical (even good-natured teasing) then you run the risk that neutral comments you make will be heard as criticisms. In that case, work on being kinder and cut out the wisecracks. If you honestly believe that your comments are well-intended and not mean spirited, then it's possible that your girl-friend has past experiences that make her overly sensitive to criticism. You might want to ask her about that.

Unintended Pressure Phrases

"We make a nice couple, don't we?" At the early stages of a relationship, comments such as this might frighten away your date. Don't talk about being a couple until it's very clear you are one. At the early stages of a relationship, simple inquisitive comments might be taken as too possessive or controlling. For example, "Where were you? … What took you so long? … I called you at work and you didn't answer. How come?" It's not that those phrases should go unspoken, but be aware that they might be a turn-off because they suggest a level of commitment, obligation, or intimacy that the other person might not feel. Similarly, frequent requests for reassurance such as, "Do you really love me? … Can I count on you to be different from all the rest? … Will you eventually leave, too? …" suggest an insecurity that can be off-putting. If you ask these questions and get a defensive response, your partner thinks you're pushy, too needy, or both.

Confusing Validation with Agreement

Helen was fed up. It seemed to her that whenever she expressed an opinion Peter found a way to make her wrong. "You always have to be right," she complained. "You can't just accept what I'm saying without challenging it in some way." Peter, of course, disagreed. Helen turned away, angry and hurt. "Why can't you show me support? Why won't you validate my feelings?"

What does Helen really want when she asks for validation? She wants to know that her feelings make sense to Peter and that she is not foolish for having them. Peter believes that validating feelings is the equivalent to agreeing with them. It's not. Peter could say, "It would bother me, too, if I felt that someone always challenged what I say. I don't agree that's what I'm doing, but I can understand how you feel." That shows understanding and support while maintaining his viewpoint.

Hidden Criticisms

"This floor is so dirty! … The checkbook isn't balanced … The kids are bored … I need a break … Another rainy weekend …" Anything wrong with these phrases? Not unless they are disguised criticisms. Does "The floor is so dirty" really mean "Why won't you wash it for a change?" Does "Another rainy weekend" really mean "You bore me"? Hidden criticisms suggest the speaker is uncomfortable being openly assertive and probably has a build up of resentments. Usually, the listener feels the sting even though the attack was subtle. A more direct and polite request is better: "The floor needs washing. Would you do it?" or "I'm bored. Let's do something enjoyable this weekend."

Sometimes the speaker is criticizing him- or herself. "The checkbook isn't balanced" might not be intended as a criticism of the partner. But when a partner hears a critical tone with no specific reference as to who is being criticized, the partner often assumes he's being attacked. That can lead to an unnecessary argument.

Failing to Preface Touchy Remarks

If you intend to criticize, a softer start-up is usually a good idea. "I'm angry about something and I'd like to talk about it" is a better opening than "You ignored me at the party last night!" Other ways to preface touchy remarks might be …

- ◆ "Bear with me, this isn't easy to say."

- ◆ "I know we've talked about this before but I need to bring it up again. I'll try to be brief."

- ◆ "You might not like what I'm about to say but I need you to listen and see if there is anything that has merit."

◆ "I know that you see things differently than me about this topic but I want to see if we can find some common ground."

◆ "This isn't easy for me. If I twist my words, give me a chance to get it right."

Some people dislike "cushioning the blow" by having a soft approach. They view it as being unassertive or "walking on tip-toes" around the person. Such beliefs are wrong. If you intend to criticize someone they will probably get defensive and may never be willing to see your point. By prefacing your remarks you improve the chances that defensiveness will be held to a minimum.

Short Power Phrases That Mean a Lot

A power phrase is really just a brief show of love and attention that makes the other person know you care and are thinking of him or her. It's not pushy. Your partner might not be receptive to what you say but that's okay. Maybe he or she wants time alone or is busy. The idea is to take an interest in a small way without going into a full-court press; to have brief verbal encounters that mean something.

A terrific use of power phrasing is to first pay attention to any sign of emotion the other displays: happiness, frustration, boredom, anger, and so on. Then comment about it in a friendly way. "Anything wrong? … You seem preoccupied. Are you? … You seem tired. Can I get you anything? … You really seem to be enjoying that book … You look worried ever since that phone call …" All these comments show you are paying attention—and that means a lot. Don't push too hard, however. If the other person really doesn't feel like talking, back away with a smile.

Compliments are perfect power phrases: "You look handsome in that suit … I love it when you laugh like that …" Even ordinary conversations can be spiced up with a power phrase now and then. If you ask, "What's the weather like today?" wouldn't you occasionally like to hear something like "Hot, you sexy thing! And getting hotter!"?

Think of your lover's heart as a rose. Often, even in loving relationships, the rose is somewhat closed on any given day. You want your lover's heart to open to you. The best way is not by high praise but by humility. A smile followed by "Thanks for putting up with me. I know I can be an idiot at times," can cause a closed flower to blossom. Any time you admit fault or weakness in a sincere, nondefensive way, your lover's heart is more likely to open up. "I'm sorry. I know I haven't been attentive lately. You deserve better than that."

Finally, ask your partner's opinion (especially you men out there!). "What are your thoughts about …? What ideas do you have about …?" Such remarks show that you value your lover's views. Asking for an opinion when the outcome doesn't matter to you (such as what restaurant to go to) is not what I'm getting at. Be sure you ask for opinions on important topics.

By using power phrases to give snazzy compliments, to open your lover's heart, and to make your partner feel needed and valued, intimacy will follow as day follows night.

Power phrases connect you with the other person when otherwise there might be no connection. They're brief, but like a shooting star, they can be just as fascinating.

> **Intimacy Boosters**
>
> Compliment people one additional time every day. In a month's time not only will they will feel better about you but you will feel better about them. The magic of compliments is that it also makes the one doing the complimenting feel good.

How to Instantly Know If a Conversation Will Succeed

Some conversational clues are like seismographic indicators. They predict whether a talk will turn into an earthquake or not. Paying attention to these clues will help you take immediate steps to change the course of the conversation. If you are in a relationship, it's best that you are each aware of these indicators and have a pre-agreement that if these signs show up, the conversation must go in a different direction. Without mutual cooperation you will be able to do very little to halt the outcome other than withdraw from the conversation—which is not a helpful long-term strategy.

The "Be Still My Beating Heart" Test

Research from the University of Washington reveals that after anyone's heart rate rises 15 or more beats per minute during a discussion or conflict, the discussion may well deteriorate. Take your pulse when you are calm. During a tense discussion, take your pulse again. If it's 15 points higher, it's a good idea to briefly stop the discussion and try to relax. Belly breathing is a fast way to relax. Simply allow your stomach to puff out as you inhale. This allows the lower part of your lungs to expand. A few minutes of this breathing will lower your heart rate. Certainly, a pulse of 90 or above is too high to have a productive discussion.

The "How Old Do I Feel?" Test

Some discussions get crazy because one or both of you is either talking like a child or being spoken to as if you are a child. Talking down to another is the same as treating them like a child. If you are feeling talked down to or, in contrast, you have an "I know best" attitude and speak to your partner like a child—stop. Parent-child dialogues will never work or make you happy. After you realize it's happening, put a halt to it. Each of you should then speak on an Adult-Adult level: respectful, assertive, and willing to seek common ground.

The "Yield" Test

Are you willing to go along with some of what your partner has to say or are you unyielding? Can you find some merit in what's being said or do you always disagree? Can you give in on some points, even if you don't always agree? The more you can each yield, the better the conversation. Stubbornness will get you nowhere.

The Least You Need to Know

- How much you say is not as important as how well you say it.
- Pleasant, focused, and brief exchanges of small talk can help sustain intimacy as long as you listen well and show interest.
- If you crave more conversation, you might really be craving more intimacy.
- You can validate how someone feels without always agreeing with them.

Chapter 12

How to Make a Positive, Lasting Impression

In This Chapter

- Knowing the importance of body language in creating intimacy
- Learning the rules for luscious eye contact
- Knowing the best rule for dressing to impress
- Avoiding bursting another's bubble accidentally
- Discovering creative ways to give compliments and stoke intimacy

Some of the most intimacy-packed (or the most damaging) words can be spoken without much forethought. "I can't believe you said that!" is an often-heard complaint that is almost always followed by the reply, "Said what?" In other words, people shove their feet in their mouths and blow a hole in intimacy without ever knowing what the heck they did wrong. The problem is that where intimacy and relationships are concerned, the cameras are always rolling. You're always "on" even when you think the stage lights are off. In your relaxed, "I'm just being myself" moments you are still adding to a sense of intimacy or detracting from it—you usually just aren't paying attention one way or the other.

This chapter helps you identify the small, overlooked, often unconscious ways you communicate. This includes nonverbal body language. Your body language speaks volumes even when you're mute. If you want to achieve more intimacy, it pays to notice what your body is saying to those you want to be close with.

Intimate Body Language

It was a rare night out. Meg and Ron had such hectic work schedules, and the new baby added to hours of no-sleep, no-sex, and not much intimate conversation. The restaurant was classy. Nice, romantic touches added to the décor: elegant oil paintings, mahogany walls, even a river view. Meg's bubble started to burst as soon as the appetizer arrived. Ron chowed down on it like it was his first meal in a week. She stared at him, amazed he could eat so much so fast without even looking at her. She tried to talk about something, anything except their fast-paced lives. "Funny," she said, "a lot of people can't watch their spouses chew food without getting a bit put off. But somehow your chewing doesn't bother me at all." She smiled, hoping her light humor would shake him into some kind of person-to-person awareness. Instead, Ron looked at her quizzically. "What are you talking about?" he asked. Before she could respond, he was plunging his fork back into his sea scallops. Meg looked away and spotted a man at another table. He was smartly dressed, handsome, his hands clasped in front of him as he stared intently into some lucky woman's eyes while she spoke. Meg sipped her wine and sighed. She was glad that sea scallops didn't make a crunching noise. Otherwise, Ron would be a real turn-off.

All Ron had to do was pay more attention to Meg and act like he hadn't just entered a hot dog eating contest. What might have been an intimate, enjoyable evening turned out to be just a frustrating getaway from home. A night out with her girlfriends would have been so much more enjoyable. Body language starts with a few essentials. Read on.

Intimacy Boosters

If possible, pay attention to the size of the other person's pupils at the start of a conversation. Do they expand or close up as the conversation continues? Expanding pupils are a clear sign of interest.

The Eyes Have It

Intimacy can rise or fall depending on eye contact. Imagine that you're revealing something very personal, very important, very heartfelt, and not easy to speak about. It took some courage to say what you're starting to say. After several sentences you glance up at the person you're speaking to. Her eyes are turned away. How do you feel now? If you're like most people, you feel a twinge of hurt or embarrassment. You wonder if you're saying something silly or inappropriate. If you are not one to speak openly to begin with, you probably start to think you made a horrible mistake.

Now imagine the same scenario except this time when you look up, you meet the other person's gaze. She's listening carefully, intently, and there's a look of caring on her face. You breathe a sigh of relief. You don't feel as uncomfortable being so open. You divulge even more than you imagined you would. That's the power of eye contact.

Here are some rules for intimate eye contact:

◆ Show a lot of eye contact when listening to someone speak.

◆ Looking away is normal and appropriate from time to time; be more conscious of when your eyes meet and when they don't.

◆ If you are looking at the speaker and he/she does not make eye contact, it's a sign of discomfort. Look away a bit more to put them at ease.

◆ If someone really cares about you, you need to meet their gaze, especially when talking about important feelings.

◆ An intense gaze coupled with a slight smile is a way of saying, "Wow, I think you're amazing."

◆ It can be sexy to stare at your lover's face and slowly work your way down the body. However, looking into the other's eyes as if you are trying to see his or her soul can be even sexier.

◆ If you are speaking and the other person hardly looks at you, he or she is disinterested.

◆ Constant staring is a turn-off.

◆ The first time you see your partner naked, spend as much time staring at the face and eyes as any other part of the body.

◆ When your partner isn't watching, stare at a part of his or her face or body that you might ordinarily ignore. Imagine kissing it. Keep staring until you feel some tingle of passion.

The bottom line is that when you make hard-core intense eye contact, you are communicating that you want to know the other person better and that you want to be better known. Intimacy, in its broadest sense, is unprotected knowing.

Dress to Undress

You don't have to dress to kill to impress someone, although once in a while it can be exciting. Casual dress is fine. However, you want to look your best in whatever you wear. You want to accentuate the positive. If jeans and a tee shirt make you look irresistible, by all means wear them often. The key to intimate dressing is to dress in a manner that makes the other person want to undress you. Tight, revealing clothes aren't at all necessary. Just wear what you look and feel good in. If sweat pants and shirt make you look frumpy, then only wear them when you're exercising, not when trying to impress someone.

People in an established relationship often get used to dressing down. They wear old favorites that don't fit properly or they dress in whatever feels comfortable without considering overall appearance. Wearing clothes that are primarily comfy means that your relationship is probably comfy, too. But comfy is not necessarily passionate. And sometimes a comfortable relationship means you're taking one another for granted. Not good.

Close Calls

Intimate eye contact or way of dressing that is all about having sex will not turn on someone you just met who is interested in a more mature relationship. Body language needs to say "I like you ... I'm interested in you ... You fascinate me ... I want to know you better." If it's just a come-on for sex, deeper intimacy may never happen.

Overall Physical Appearance

If you're overweight you're like the majority of Americans. Don't worry so much about being unattractive if you're overweight. Instead, do your best to exercise and eat right. Trying to look your best appeals to many partners, even if your efforts don't get the results you want. When Tim gained 40 pounds in six years, his wife didn't mind the weight gain so much. What annoyed her was that he seemed to not care how he looked. That bothered her more than his weight. His not caring about his appearance made her think he didn't care about her.

Good personal hygiene should be an obvious thing to maintain. Still, many people get lazy when they have an established relationship. They wash up less often, are less concerned about the smell of their breath when kissing, or they don't stay well groomed. If you want intimacy to stay alive, personal hygiene and grooming should be at the level it was when you first dated your partner. Anything less is taking your relationship for granted and blunting intimacy.

Match Each Other Move for Move

Couples who are totally enchanted with one another tend to do something naturally that nonconnecting couples don't do: they move in sync. They don't do this in an extreme way, but if you watch a couple in love while they're having dinner or talking, many of their movements and gestures are synchronous or nearly so. They reach for their wine or lean in at the same time. They each start to take the other's hand. If they are watching something of interest such as a play or movie, they instinctively look at each other or squeeze hands when they see or hear something that reminds them of their life together. In a group of people, in-sync couples who are not standing near one another still find a way to look at one another at the precise moment, as if they are psychic.

If you are not yet close to someone but would like to be, pay attention to ways you can synchronize some of your actions. It has a subconscious effect on the other person. It is a way of saying that you two are a "we."

Just Ask!

I'm never quite sure if someone is flirting with me or not. Any clues?

Flirting, by definition, is a bit ambiguous and subtle. It's designed to convey interest but not so openly that a turn-down would be embarrassing. Someone who flirts will almost always make more eye contact. Or perhaps there will be some slight touching, a brush on the hand or shoulder, a broad smile, and so on. The flirt then will pull back just long enough for you to wonder if it was sincere. That will be followed by yet another connecting gesture. After you receive the second message you can bet that the other person is interested in you.

Recognize the Other's Bubble and Don't Burst It

Tammi was an accomplished painter. She only sold a few of her pieces but she loved painting and often received rave reviews from friends and family. She wanted to set up a special room in her house just for painting. She asked her boyfriend Carl to help her move things around. After moving out some furniture to clear away space, Carl stared at about a dozen oil canvases that had to be carried into the new room. "Okay, let's pick up all this crap and then we'll be done," Carl said. Tammi was shocked.

"It's not crap," she said. Carl tried to defend himself, saying it was just an offhanded comment and that he didn't mean it the way it sounded. Tammi didn't see it that way. Maybe he didn't intend to hurt her feelings but it was obvious he didn't understand the importance that painting and art had in her life. Their relationship ended soon after.

Sam had gained 20 pounds in five years. His spare tire bothered him but nothing he did seemed to get rid of it. His wife Ariel didn't seem to mind, or so he believed. One day at the beach Ariel pointed to a young male hard-body walking by. Then she poked Sam in his belly and sighed. "In my dreams," she said, all the while staring at the sexy guy. Sam felt hurt. He knew he didn't have a perfect physique, but in his heart he always believed that Ariel thought he was still hot. Now he no longer believed that. His bubble was burst. From that moment on he pulled away sexually from Ariel. He couldn't get it out of his mind that she was tolerating his appearance but pining away for some younger stud.

> **CAUTION**
>
> ### Close Calls
>
> Good natured teasing is risky. Being thin skinned may have nothing to do with it. If you tease someone about something they are secretly insecure about, they might laugh with you but then pull away from you.

All of us have a certain view of ourselves where we try to accentuate the positive. Maybe we take pride in a certain ability or accomplishment. It is really part of our personal legend. If anyone throws dirt on that legend, even in a joking or teasing manner, it can be the death of intimacy. If you see yourself in a positive light, regardless of how accurate it is, you will want others to see you in that light, too. If someone you love and care about exposes you and reveals that maybe you're not as special as you think, it can be a wound that will never fully heal.

How would you feel if you viewed yourself as an expert in car mechanics but your partner mocked your ability?

How would you feel if you are an esteemed professional but when you join in on a group conversation and say hello, your spouse says, "Be quiet! Sheila's talking. Don't be so rude!"?

How would you feel if you worked hard painting a room or repairing something in your house only to be told that a professional could have done it better?

You can tease a lover about some things and he or she won't mind. But never put down the legend. Never. Unsure what your partner's personal legends are? Complete the following sentences to find out.

My partner is very proud of _____.

Whenever my partner talks about _____ he/she gets very animated and excited.

My partner has worked hard to overcome _____.

It would hurt my partner's feelings if I teased him/her about _____.

My partner will probably most want to be remembered for _____.

My partner secretly wishes he/she could _____.

My partner's favorite hobby is _____.

My partner has a thin skin when I talk about _____.

When your bubble has been burst by someone close to you, it's like being naked and having people snicker. You feel exposed, vulnerable, ashamed, or humiliated. You also get angry and very hurt. Intimacy will rapidly deteriorate, and for good reason. Why should you get close to a person who will be mocking or ridiculing or not encouraging your positive self-image?

Intimacy Boosters _____

If someone else teases your mate unkindly, don't stand idly by. Let your partner know that you think he or she is still wonderful and talented in your eyes. Never agree with a bubble-burster.

Uncommon Compliments for Uncommon Intimacy

When you first meet someone and like them, it's natural to want to say something complimentary. And of course, compliments are important all throughout a relationship. But too often the compliments you give and receive are ordinary, predictable, and uninspired. That's still fine. A nice word is a nice word. But if you want to achieve greater intimacy or if you really want to impress someone, you have to think outside the box.

Aaron was a talented musician who played at local clubs. When Michelle wanted to get to know him better she complimented his musical talent. "You play fantastic!" she said. It was thoughtful but it didn't show up on Aaron's radar. He'd heard those compliments many

Intimacy Boosters _____

Compliment your sweetheart in front of family and friends. Say it with a gleam in your eye and packed with pride. It will add immeasurably to intimacy and commitment.

times. He appreciated Michelle's words but Michelle did nothing to stand apart from the hundreds of other people who liked Aaron's music. Celebrities hear the same compliments all the time. It grows tiresome for them. If you ever have a chance to meet a celebrity and want to make an impression, saying how wonderful and talented the person is will go in one ear and out the other. Imagine if Michelle complimented Aaron this way: "I was spellbound by the way you played that difficult middle to your last song. Not many musicians could do that. You really take extra care refining your craft." Such a compliment, especially if understated and not over the top with exuberance, achieves two important things: it reveals a bit of a working knowledge of musicianship (and therefore a common interest); and it offers very specific (not general) praise. Those two ingredients can help build an attraction where none might have existed.

People in established relationships often make compliments that are dull as dishwater. Telling your mate she looks "nice" in her new outfit or that he did a "great job" on the lawn is pleasant but that's all. It's time to get creative and put intimacy back on track.

Exercise!

Think of some ordinary, everyday compliment you might give your partner. Now imagine that a person of the opposite sex, a stranger, met your mate and wanted to posses him or her in every way imaginable. How would that person give a compliment? If you tell your wife she looks nice in her dress, can you imagine the other guy saying, "My God! I can't take my eyes off of you! You look fabulous! I could stare at you for hours and never get bored." Talk to the one you love like you would if you were trying to win him or her over. Ask yourself, "What would someone else who is attracted to my partner say to entice them into a relationship?" You needn't make things up. Your partner probably does deserve more compliments than you've been providing.

Giving compliments has a magical consequence for the giver: The more you do it with sincerity and exuberance, the more excited and passionate you feel toward the person you're complimenting. The reverse is also true: The less complimentary you are, the more boring the other person becomes to you. Intimacy and boredom never go together.

Follow these guidelines to give fantastic compliments:

◆ Compliment what is important to the other person, not what's important to you.

◆ Listen for the positive emotion (excitement, pride, eagerness, and so on) that the other person expresses. Those are areas that are most important to that person and where a compliment will be well received.

◆ Dig deeper. Don't compliment the obvious. If complimenting someone on a job promotion, for example, look for ways to compliment the hard work that led to the promotion. Pick a specific detail that others might overlook and hone in on that. General praise is always less meaningful than providing specific examples of what impressed you.

◆ Don't use well-worn words and phrases such as "You were wonderful … That was great … How beautiful … You must be so excited … Nice job … Good for you." Instead, give specific examples of how you were affected: "I was blown away by your performance; I never felt so moved."

◆ Praise ordinary things that usually go unappreciated. "I love the way you entertain the kids. They're always so happy with you."

◆ Choose a certain virtue you admire (kindness, compassion, generosity, and so on) and hunt for ways that the other person displays that virtue. Then praise it.

◆ After you give a compliment, ask a probing question. People usually enjoy discussing details of something they are proud of or happy about. ("Your new bathroom is stunning. How did you ever think of such a design?")

Close Calls

If you're being complimented by someone special, be careful not to be so modest. Saying, "Oh, it was nothing" is actually a slight putdown of the other person's praise. A sincere "Thank you" is more appropriate.

The way you compliment someone can make a lasting impression or none at all. When intimacy is at stake, a well-intended but uncreative compliment can keep intimacy blunted and stale.

Oops! Handling Embarrassing Moments

It happens at some point in every relationship, often when you first meet. You try so hard to make a good impression but then something goes wrong and you feel embarrassed. Or maybe you're just fine but the other person does something humiliating. Or maybe you've been a couple for years and when socializing your partner makes a bit of a fool of himself. What should you do?

If the embarrassing moment was clearly accidental your best bet is to respond with little fanfare, as if what happened was not a very big deal. Your date will appreciate it.

If practicalities are involved (the car broke down, a pair of pants was badly torn, a wallet was misplaced, and so on) focus on fixing the situation and not on the fact that you might have to abandon your dinner plans or be late for the movie. Handling it gracefully and without making the other person feel even worse will pay huge dividends. Your kindness will be greatly appreciated.

When the dust settles and the immediate crisis has passed, try to find some positive benefit to what happened. It's okay to make a small joke but don't make fun of the person, even good-naturedly.

If you're the one who made the embarrassing mistake (you spilled coffee all over someone, you made a social faux pas) don't let it consume you. It's normal to feel bad. Don't put yourself down if you can help it ("I'm such an idiot!") especially repeatedly. If you're angry and upset, your job is to make the best of a bad situation. Remember, you're not alone. You're with a date or your partner and their evening has taken a hit. Don't add to the misery by being impossible to be with. Stomping around angrily just shows immaturity. Nice going. Now you can forget intimacy.

When the event has passed, express appreciation for the other's patience or helpfulness. Don't make a huge deal out of what went wrong. Embarrassing moments have a way of being fondly remembered years later and can add to a couple's story of their relationship. Intimacy is an adventure and embarrassing moments can be an adventure, too.

The Least You Need to Know

- Make eye contact a lot when you are talking to the one you love.

- When you dress in a manner that makes the other person want to undress you, you're probably looking your best.

- Never make wisecracks about something very important to the other person.

- Giving nice, sincere compliments makes you like the person you're complimenting even more.

- Don't dismiss a compliment in the name of modesty; say "Thank you" instead.

Transforming Complaints into Intimate Encounters

In This Chapter

- ◆ Discovering that every problem has an intimate solution
- ◆ Learning to cope with problems that keep recurring
- ◆ Knowing how to be less defensive
- ◆ Detecting hidden underlying problems

Complaints within a relationship aren't especially fun. But they don't have to squash intimacy. Done right, making or receiving complaints can result in even better intimacy. In fact, complaints are intimate moments in disguise: you just have to undress the complaints to get to the intimacy.

Intimacy happens when there is connection, caring, and sharing. Complaints can mess up intimacy when they're made with little display of caring or if the people involved don't make a mutual effort (sharing) to resolve the situation.

It's easy to feel intimate when you're having a positive, loving, tender, gosh-no-matter-what-I-say-it's-completely-accepted-and-respected conversation. But it's necessary to do the harder work of a relationship, too. That's the stuff that doesn't come easy or look very pretty but happens anyway and needs to be better managed. Sure you can feel intimate when you're feeling nothing but love, but you can also feel intimate when you're angry and not being understood. It depends on how you handle it. This chapter shows you how.

The Two Types of Problems Intimate Partners Complain About

Todd was always a sports enthusiast. He played pick-up basketball at the local YMCA whenever he could, liked to rollerblade, golf, and play tennis. He had an athletic physique and competitive nature. Holly loved him but grew tired of his "love affair" with sports, as she called it. Some days she wasn't sure whether sports was his mistress or whether she was the mistress and sports was his first true love.

Jennifer and John had a different problem. Jenn disliked doing laundry and going food shopping. John had no problem doing those chores but he hated doing them all the time. When Jenn should have been helping with those tasks she'd often procrastinate, and that would eventually lead to an argument.

These two scenarios represent the two basic types of problems people encounter in their relationship. Some problems, such as the laundry/shopping issue, are fixable. Other problems, such as Todd's love for sports and its impact on his schedule can only be managed, not permanently fixed.

> **CAUTION**
>
> **Close Calls** _____
>
> The worst mistake a couple can make is to try to permanently solve a problem or personality difference that, by its nature, can never really go away.

Problems That Never Go Away Completely

Personality traits and core values are part of a person's hard-wiring and unlikely to change much. Are you extroverted or introverted? A talker or close-mouthed? Adventurous or timid? A neat freak or control freak? Do you love the arts or find them boring? Are you inquisitive by nature? Does religion and spirituality play an important role in your life or are you agnostic or an atheist? All these qualities and attitudes are fairly permanent. If any of them annoy you, trying to get the other person to change them will be next to impossible.

Still, intimacy can succeed despite personality differences. In fact, about 70 percent of all disagreements couples have are about nonfixable problems. Trying to fix them once and for all only makes the relationship worse.

Just Ask!

I want to marry Brian but we have different religious faiths. And I can tell we have different ideas about raising children. Should we get married?

Couples from different religions have slightly higher divorce rates than same-faith couples but it's a small difference. It is most problematic when one person is very religious and the partner is nonreligious. Every couple has at least three areas of disagreement that will never change. Disagreements about childrearing, spending habits, and desire for sex are the most common. Success is not predicted by how well a couple resolves their differences but rather by how well they *manage* their differences.

The key is to find a way to learn to live with differences. In a way it's like having a trick knee or some chronic medical problem that never goes away completely. It can be bothersome but need not ruin your life. Every couple must do three things to keep permanent differences from causing turmoil:

◆ Be willing to have regular, repeated talks about the issue when it comes up. There is no such thing as a once and for all discussion when dealing with repetitive, personality-based differences.

◆ Be willing to be flexible and accommodating. "How would you like to handle it this time?" is a good question and a good approach. Sometimes it works your way, sometimes it doesn't, sometimes you compromise. That's what friends do.

◆ Find a way to laugh, joke, or chuckle about it. This is the best way to make what otherwise might be an aggravating, "Here we go again!" talk into a playful, intimate encounter.

In the beginning of this chapter you read about Todd, the sports enthusiast, and Holly. Todd's love for sports wasn't just a hobby, it was his passion. As much a part of him as his fingerprints. Unless Holly could accept that, they would never survive as a couple. However, the solution is not for Holly to keep quiet while Todd plays in all the athletic events he wants. Every week they need to talk about his plans or wishes when it comes to sports, and her wishes for togetherness. He needs to carve out space for her in his schedule and she needs to let him do his thing. On some weeks, one of them might completely give in to the other. Sure, they might get creative (she might take up tennis or rollerblading, for example, or he might learn to enjoy one of her nonathletic hobbies) but mostly they need to learn how to tolerate their differences.

It will never work if Holly insists he gives up most sports or if Todd insists he can do what he wants whenever he pleases.

They also need to learn to joke about their differences. "How about you be Michael Jordon next weekend," Holly would say, "because this weekend I want you all to myself." Todd even had tee shirts specially made for them. His said "Crazy Sports Man!" and hers said "I'm in Love with a Crazy Sports Man!" Light-heartedness helps when personality differences get annoying.

Fixable Problems

Fixable problems make up only about 30 percent of the problems couples face. Fixable problems are not based on personality differences or core values. They have to do with convenience, personal preference, and situational demands. When Jennifer disliked going food shopping and doing laundry, John was willing to do his share to help. When she procrastinated or didn't do her part, it caused a rift. However, these problems are fixable. Jenn may prefer not to shop but she does anyway. Or the couple might decide that John can do all the laundry and shopping if Jenn would do some of the chores that he hates such as cooking meals, cleaning the bathroom, or tending the garden.

> **Intimacy Boosters**
>
> Solving a problem by mutual cooperation adds to a sense of teamwork and friendship, and that adds to intimacy. Lack of cooperation causes resentment and intimacy breakdown.

Solving fixable problems can still be complicated. But the point is that they are fixable, once and for all, if the couple is willing to cooperate and compromise.

How to Complain and Simultaneously Boost Intimacy

Intimacy requires caring. If you complain in an uncaring fashion you might ruin intimacy even if your complaint is valid.

To avoid quashing intimacy while making a complaint, follow these five steps:

1. Keep it simple.
2. State what you'd like to have happen.
3. Ask for an opinion.
4. Brainstorm win-win solutions.
5. Show thanks and affection.

A long-winded complaint creates tension. Just state your complaint succinctly. "I want us to save more money … We don't spend enough time together … I'm tired and need a vacation … There's too much to do when we get home from work." Practice stating your complaint in one sentence, two at most.

Then offer a possible solution. Keep it tentative, after all it's just a suggestion. "I'd like to stop going to restaurants and save the money instead … Maybe we can plan a regular date night … I was thinking we might go on a weekend getaway … Maybe we can hire a maid to do some of the mundane chores we both hate."

Ask for an opinion. "What do you think?" Ask if he or she has any similar concerns or competing concerns. For example, you might suggest a weekend getaway but be told that a major office project is due in a few weeks and it will take up all his free time. You might suggest ways to cut costs and save money but your partner may have different suggestions.

Intimacy Boosters

You don't have to make a complaint immediately. It's okay to wait and think things over; you might change your mind. But if you're still annoyed or concerned a week later, it's time to speak up.

Next, try to come up with a plan that meets each of your concerns for the most part. This is not the time to insist that your way be the only way. Remember, cooperation is key.

If you're on the receiving end of a complaint, your response is crucial. Keep intimacy at the forefront of your mind. Will your reaction enhance intimacy or diminish it? Giving in is not necessarily an intimacy-enhancing act if you resent it later on.

Try following these steps if your partner registers a complaint about you or the relationship:

Close Calls

If your partner is usually unassertive but chooses to make a complaint about you, give him or her room to misspeak because it's unlikely the words will flow smoothly anyway. Pouncing on the other's words will add to his or her anxiety and lead to a "Why bother?" attitude.

1. Don't automatically react negatively. Scan what you hear for any legitimate and valid point. At a minimum, let it matter to you that your partner feels that way.

2. Don't dismiss any proposed solution. Be willing to think matters through and get creative.

3. Offer alternative solutions if you wish.

4. Agree to take some steps to address the complaint.

So many people have had bad experiences with former partners (or their parents) whereby complaints turned into arguments with no cooperation and no resolution. Demonstrate that you can cooperate and that your partner's complaints matter to you and you will stoke the fires of intimacy.

Tips for Taking It on the Chin Like a Champ

Defensiveness is normal but it's also problematic. It rarely sheds light on a problem and often leads to more bickering, frustration, and conversation breakdown. It is an attempt to dismiss what the other person says by defending yourself and making the other person wrong. It fits with a competitive, winner-loser mentality that is not consistent with intimacy.

When you're defensive, it makes it hard to look for solutions. To the defensive person, the real problem is the fact that a complaint is being made in the first place!

Maggie was dog-tired. She took care of a sick infant all day and her husband Ed was late getting home. He arrived home sweaty and filthy and in need of a shower. Maggie just wanted to hand-off the baby to him and hibernate. Now she had to wait. Ten minutes into his shower Maggie stormed into the bathroom, pulled back the shower curtain, and demanded he hurry up. "I've had a long day," Ed shot back. Maggie went into a diatribe about how miserable her day had been and that 10 minutes in the shower was more than enough time. Anything more was selfish. "Be reasonable," Ed said. "You be reasonable!" she shouted back.

Intimacy Boosters

If you criticize, don't be shocked when you get a defensive response. If you want to sidestep defensiveness, keep your complaints polite, don't make it a personal attack, and if possible make a sincere affectionate gesture.

Later, Ed was still miffed. "Wanting 15 minutes in the shower isn't asking much," he said. Maggie wouldn't hear of it and the argument re-ignited. Who was defensive? Actually, both were but Maggie won the prize for being the most defensive and the most hostile. Their defensiveness impeded any talk about solutions. Had they each been more aware and more kind, their conversation might have gone like this:

Maggie: *"I know you've had a hard day and want to relax in the shower but I'm at my wit's end. Would you mind being quick and giving me time to myself?"*

Ed: *"I'm exhausted, too. Can I have 15 minutes?"*

Maggie: *"If you do it in 10 I'll make it up to you later …"*

Ed: *"Sounds like a good deal to me."*

How could Maggie and Ed have gotten from complaining and criticizing to non-defensiveness and problem-solving? It's a four stage process:

1. Cooperate, don't compete. Remind yourself you are a team. If one of you must lose for the other to win then you both lose in the long run.

2. Downshift your emotions from angry or hurt to mildly impatient at worst. Pause before answering, take a few breaths, tell yourself that your partner is upset, not character-flawed, and that the complaint is worth being heard.

3. Begin your first comment with the words "You're right about …" or "I know what you mean …" Search for something to agree with.

4. If the complaint really is off-base, don't take it personally. Tell yourself, "It's not about me." Ask, "What can I do to help?"

Intimacy Boosters

Whenever you discuss a complaint, follow the conversation with some positive connection (such as a hug) or thoughtful gesture. Convey a "No hard feelings" attitude.

Reduced defensiveness almost always adds to a feeling of intimacy. And greater intimacy leads to nondefensive conversations.

Are You Still Angry?

One way to increase intimacy is to explore the hidden, unspoken issue that often underlies most complaints. It's safe to say that the majority of complaints are not just about the topic being discussed. Hidden agendas lurk when the complaints go unfixed or when a partner still isn't happy even though a problem has supposedly been solved. Here are some other clues that hidden issues exist:

♦ Anger over little things

♦ Agreements that never get acted on

♦ An increasing desire to be alone

♦ Flash-fire anger

- Use of strong, inflammatory language (especially if it isn't typical of your partner)
- Debates over things you should be able to easily agree on
- Someone routinely withdrawing from arguments

> **Just Ask!**
>
> *I compromise—a lot. But I'm starting to resent it. I'm sure my wife feels that she compromises all the time, too. Why aren't we happy? Isn't compromising a good thing?*
>
> Compromising works when you also get your own way once in a while. Always meeting in the middle gets boring and annoying. Furthermore, most people make many silent compromises and their partners have no idea that a sacrifice is being made. When those hidden sacrifices start adding up, you will feel entitled to get your way on certain issues and are angry if you have to give in or compromise again.

If you're still angry after you and your partner have said all the right things to fix a complaint, then you need to dig deeper. You're not upset for the reasons you think you are.

Loss of Love

If you are feeling unloved or unlovable, you might complain about a lot of small things. Everything your partner does or doesn't do will be analyzed through the lens of "Does he really care?" You might actually insist that some things go your way and be unwilling to compromise—not because you're inflexible, but because you want evidence you are loved. If you've been hurt in a prior relationship, you might be more sensitive to this issue and question your partner's depth of caring. It's dangerous to start thinking "If you loved me you would …" Your partner will view that as unfair or manipulative and resent having to pass whatever test you decide to give on any given day.

Your best bet is to simply state that you question your partner's depth of love and to have a mature discussion about it. Maybe your partner isn't in love with you or maybe you're too sensitive. Focus on the specific things you can each do to regain a sense of closeness and put aside your doubts about whether love exists for now.

Loss of Esteem

If you feel inadequate in any way or if your self-esteem has taken a hit lately, you might have more arguments with your partner. Maybe you don't feel attractive anymore or you got laid off from a job. Maybe you feel inadequate in some important endeavor such as parenting, money management, making new friends, or household repairs. If so, you will take complaints from a partner much more personally and find yourself either withdrawing or picking fights.

Unhappiness with one's appearance is often a culprit. It can lead to reduced sexual intimacy. People who dislike their looks don't always want a partner to pay attention to their bodies by showing sexual affection. They feel too self-conscious.

It's best to simply talk about your self-esteem concerns and explain why they might be causing some arguments. Your partner may have sympathy for you and cut you some slack. Then talk about specific ideas that will help improve your esteem.

> **Intimacy Boosters**
>
> When figuring out solutions to complaints, make sure you use the word "we" at least as much as you use the word "I."

Loss of Control

Does the relationship seem fair? Do you feel you have enough influence? If not, you might argue over who does the food shopping or who takes out the garbage. Relationships get balanced eventually, but not necessarily in a healthy way. For example, it's not unusual that if one person controls the purse strings, the other controls sex. If one person feels in a one-down position, he or she will withdraw from, punish, or otherwise make the partner pay in some way. It might not be a conscious attempt to get even. A person who feels controlled or treated unfairly might become depressed or develop many disabling physical symptoms, all of which impact the controlling partner.

When the relationship is unfair, intimacy starts to disintegrate. You simply cannot be open and vulnerable to someone you believe is too controlling.

> **CAUTION**
>
> **Close Calls**
>
> When you have a complaint, don't get overly attached to one solution. Be open to other possibilities, otherwise you might end up in yet another debate.

The Least You Need to Know

◆ A complaint is an intimate moment in disguise.

◆ Stop arguing about personality differences; those differences must be managed, not solved once and for all.

◆ Learn to be less defensive by first finding some truth in any complaint your partner has.

◆ Unless the relationship feels fair to both, problems will be inevitable and intimacy will crumble.

Chapter 14

How Great Listening Creates Unheard of Intimacy

In This Chapter

- ◆ Comparing good listening vs. intimate listening
- ◆ Discovering the mechanics of intimate listening
- ◆ Recognizing emotional triggers that short-circuit intimate listening
- ◆ Learning the top 10 snafus listeners make

Talented stage actors possess one skill that most audiences never realize is important in acting: being a sensitive listener. Actors who are comfortable on stage but less adept at acting might know their lines well and even say them well when alone. But if they don't really listen to the words and tones of the other actors, they miss the subtleties of dialogue and are no longer reacting to the rest of the cast but simply repeating words from a script. The final product is sub-par. In contrast, a less-experienced actor who takes the time to really listen to what's being said to him or her on stage can turn in a fine performance.

As a psychologist I've counseled thousands of people. In the first interview when I'm primarily gathering information, it's not uncommon for people to tell me how much the initial session helped. Why? Because I was the first person who really listened. Actually, I'm one of many who listened; but I'm one of the few who heard what the people really meant, not just what they said.

Effective listening is at the heart of verbal intimacy. It is a direct path to understanding the people in your lives and being understood. In these times where protected sex is valued, intimacy at its utmost is unprotected. Genuine listening, without distractions and judgments, is a form of unprotected intimacy.

Not All Good Listeners Are Intimate Listeners

A good listener understands. An intimate listener understands in a heartfelt way. A poor listener acts as if he or she is the center of the world. The focus is on what he or she is thinking and feeling, not what the speaker is trying to convey. A good listener puts aside personal opinions to understand. An intimate listener combines understanding with complete acceptance and a depth of caring.

Close Calls

If you cry, "You're not listening to me!" and you really mean "You're not doing what I want you to do!" then listening is not the issue. The issue is that you want control.

Understanding is not necessarily agreement, and that's where many couples mess up and intimacy takes a tumble. When you listen to understand and accept rather than listen to challenge, you'll discover that disagreements don't need to make a difference as far as intimacy is concerned. Insisting that someone agree with you is a way of not listening to that person; of not understanding why that person doesn't agree with you.

When you feel understood you are also more open to changing ways about yourself that others don't particularly like. It's a bit of a paradox. The more accepted and understood you feel, the more willing you are to accommodate other people's needs and make changes. Couples or friends who are gridlocked on some emotional, divisive issue, do not feel understood or cared about—and that is the main reason they remain gridlocked.

There is another side to the paradox: the more you listen to and understand your partner, the more you can tolerate his or her ways and have less of a need for change. Mutual understanding is a great peacemaker.

Intimate listening takes a bit of extra work. Simply caring about someone doesn't guarantee you'll listen well. In fact, the more caring you are the more you may cut off listening when you hear something you don't like or that worries you. In the opening chapter of this book, I revealed that genuine intimacy requires three ingredients: connecting, sharing, and caring. Many well-intended listeners care about the other person and are sharing in conversations, but they aren't fully connecting. Connection is more than a verbal hand-off during a conversation. It's like two wires connecting to complete an electrical circuit. True connecting has an energy and a focus to it. An intimate listener is focused intently on the speaker and pays attention to all aspects of the communication.

Intimacy Boosters

If your partner likes to get to the bottom line during conversations and you like to expand on details, give the bottom line sooner and then go back and fill the story in. Similarly, if your partner likes to expand on details, he/she probably wants to hear more details when you're describing something.

Just Ask!

I want my partner to get to the point when she talks. She gives me lots of unnecessary details. How can I get her to be concise?

You view conversation as a means to an end, a way of giving and receiving pertinent information. I suspect that your partner views conversations as ends in themselves. She probably sees talking as a way to connect to you, not just a way to inform you. Do you see affection as a means to an end (sex?) or do you see inherent value in it? Have you ever enjoyed a sporting contest even though your team lost? Your partner has the right idea. Ask her to get to the point only when you are in a rush and need an immediate answer. Otherwise, think of her detailed conversations as a kind of foreplay warm-up. It makes her feel closer to you.

The Mechanics of Intimate (Not Just Good) Listening

There isn't a surefire formula to follow when it comes to being an effective, intimate listener. What works for you may not work for someone else. But there are some general guidelines that will help. Keep in mind that listening is interactive. How a person talks (tone of voice, words used, and so on) can make it easier or harder for others to listen. And a very good listener can make it easier for an anxious person to talk. Intimate listening is as much about the right attitude as it is about technique. Someone who really has no interest in hearing you out but who complains, "Okay, okay, I'm listening!" won't score any brownie points no matter how technically skilled he is.

The Right Attitude

The verb "to know" has in hundreds of years past implied a sexual knowing. "He knew her … " meant he had sex with her. But it also meant more than that. It meant that he *really* knew her—in more ways than one. Intimate knowledge of one's partner goes far beyond sexual knowledge. Only an effective listener will know his or her partner better than anyone else. The right attitude has the following characteristics:

- To always want to learn more about one another, to recognize that people grow and change, and that one's partner and one's relationships either evolve or stagnate.

- To welcome negative emotions as well as positive ones during intimate conversations. Intimacy allows for diversity.

- To be receptive to honesty, even if you don't like what you are hearing. A punishing response to a partner's attempt to speak openly and honestly can kill future attempts at honesty.

- To be honest in what you say but to say it with compassion, understanding, or kindness.

- To realize that an honest comment is not necessarily objectively true but it represents what the other person believes to be true. You can disagree without being disagreeable.

Being an effective listener doesn't mean you must have daily heart-to-heart talks. Unfortunately, however, many people regard focused listening as similar to stopping at a red light: It's a temporary delay when you'd rather be moving along to some place else.

Close Calls

Be honest about what's bothering you in your relationship but be kind in your expression. Honesty without kindness is like surgery without anesthesia.

You don't have to possess an advanced degree in listening to be effective. In fact, even when you make mistakes (and you will), what counts is effort and a desire to listen well. A heartfelt, "I don't understand but I want to. Would you mind explaining that to me again?" can be very effective. Even saying, "I don't think I understand completely, but I can see how important this is to you" also shows an uncommon level of listening and empathy.

The Right Place and Time

It's harder to be an intimate listener when you're tired, ill, or preoccupied with your own problems. Everyone has heard the advice not to engage in heartfelt talks when the other person is ready to fall asleep. But there's another side to this issue: Sometimes a person opens up in a very important way when the timing isn't right and the place isn't ideal. What then? Must the speaker always have an exquisite sense of timing? Can't the listener make accommodations, too? The truth is that very bad listeners are very good at making excuses about why now is never a good time to talk.

When you dismiss a comment by asking, "Why are you bringing this up *now?*" realize that the other person probably had a hard time mentioning it in the first place. By not discussing it when it's being raised, you run the risk it won't be discussed at all.

Intimacy through effective listening is not about convenience, good timing, and "fitting someone in." It's about caring, putting aside one's own wishes for the moment, and not missing golden opportunities for closeness and understanding.

> ### Exercise!
>
> Make a pact with yourself that the next five times your partner talks to you in a bid for attention you will stop whatever you are doing and listen. View that person as the only other living being on the planet at that moment.

The Right Body Language

Make eye contact and try to have your body positioned so it's facing the other person. Looking away is a sign of disinterest. Don't perform some other task at the same time if it can be helped. Hearing someone say, "Don't worry, I'm listening" while they are brushing their teeth or sweeping a floor is a turn-off, especially when you have something important to say.

Sometimes intimate, heart-to-heart talks occur in bed with the lights off. There is no eye contact then. At such times let your physical movements speak for your eyes. Show that you are listening by a timely physical gesture (avoid blatant sexual acts if the topic is serious or if one of you is upset). A properly timed gentle squeeze or hug shows you care and that you're listening. The same is true if you are trying to be a good listener while driving. You can't engage in regular eye contact while you're driving, but you can reach over to hold hands or caress the other person gently as a way of showing interest.

The Right Verbal Response

It's difficult to listen well if you're being attacked or yelled at. Chapter 15 explains in detail how to cope with such a situation. For now, your job as a listener is to let the other person know that you're "getting it." Even a simple "Uh huh" conveys interest. Other short phrases you should say are: "Tell me more … Keep going … Is there anything else?" If you ask questions, your job is to try to understand not challenge. "You can't be serious?" doesn't convey a desire to understand and it makes the speaker defensive. If there is something you don't understand, say so. Say it without a critical tone, more as a wish to understand better.

Don't interrupt with stories of your own. Don't contradict, at least not right away. Don't lecture. Don't sigh or roll your eyes.

If you have really listened carefully and do understand, you should be able to express in your own words the speaker's point of view. And the other person should nod and agree that you do in fact understand.

Emotional Triggers That Shut-Off Intimate Listening

Listening is easy when you're calm, focused, and interested in what's being said. But in intimate relationships all it takes is one of these three factors to be out of whack and listening will falter.

> ### Exercise!
>
> A good opportunity to practice your intimate-listening skills is when your partner is complaining about someone else. (When the complaint is about you, it's difficult not to get defensive.) Avoid giving immediate advice or challenging what you hear. Ask questions that help the speaker clarify his or her view. Show empathy. Comments such as "That must have been hard for you … I can see why you'd be upset … You went through a lot … I see what you mean …" demonstrate that you are listening and caring.

Certain emotional triggers will throw you off track when you are trying hard to be a good listener. Your job is to recognize the following triggers and plan a counter-strategy so good, intimate listening can flourish.

When the Speaker Is Critical of You

Always remember that anger and criticism is just a front for feelings of hurt or fear. Asking "How did I hurt you?" lets the speaker know that you "get it." That isn't always easy to do because people automatically get defensive when criticized. The problem with defensiveness is that it makes the other person feel that their emotions—hurt, anger, pain—are being dismissed. You want to accept the emotions even if you disagree with the criticisms. When you act less defensively, the speaker feels heard and their anger starts to diminish. When the anger continues to rise, it usually means you've stopped listening and have started getting defensive.

When the Speaker Is in Pain

Sometimes caring too much can short-circuit listening. You might want to shut down the conversation because you don't want to hear your lover's pain. Hasty reassurances such as, "Don't worry, it'll be alright" are cues that the way you are feeling has taken priority over how your lover is feeling.

If you are a rescuer-caretaker by nature, you also might be a mediocre listener (much to your surprise). Rescuers and caretakers feel another person's pain intensely so they automatically assume they are listening well, too. The fact is that people tend to stop listening after they think they understand the problem. Rescuers-caretakers are "fire"fighters, those who rush to put out the flames of another's pain. Very good listeners are not firefighters. Instead, they take their time to hear all that needs to be said, no matter how painful. An effective listener very often does not need to fix the problem with advice. The listening itself has healing properties.

Symbolic Reminders

If what you're listening to reminds you of some past, emotional experience in your life, your ability to hear what's being said can be compromised. A critical remark from a partner might send your mind reeling if your parents were critical, too. When you were a child you may have been unable to effectively argue against your parents. But now you're old enough to argue back and you might take it out on your partner. Or maybe you hold a job where many people complain every day. You're tired of hearing it. So when you arrive home only to hear your partner's complaints, you have no patience.

The best thing to do is recognize situations when your listening is impeded by some reminder of past hurt. It might not be possible to untangle those memories from your present conversation, but recognizing they're there can keep you from overreacting. A good thing to say might be, "It's hard to listen well now because I'm reminded of the time when …"

When You've Heard It Before

The moment you realize you've heard it all before, you'll stop listening. However, in an intimate relationship, something else is taking place, too. When partners repeat themselves, chances are it's because they didn't feel heard the first time around. You might think that you did listen well, but take my word for it, you didn't. You missed at least one point. Your best bet is to acknowledge the situation. "If you're repeating yourself, I must have misunderstood something the last time you spoke about it. What is it you want me to understand?" Such an attitude shows patience, humility, and a desire to have things work out. Your partner will love you for it.

> **Just Ask!** _____
>
> *When my girlfriend tells me I'm not listening and I know that I am, I get frustrated. How can I prove that I am listening?*
>
> Repeating words you hear shows you listened, but it doesn't necessarily show that you listened intimately. An intimate listener hears the leading-edge emotion (joy, hurt, concern, fear) behind the words and reacts to them. Take the time to ask yourself what her leading-edge emotion is and respond accordingly. For example, if she is complaining that you spend too much time with your male friends, her leading-edge emotion might be fear of losing you or hurt that you take her for granted.

Top 10 Listening Blunders

Perhaps the best way to listen well is to refrain from making the kinds of blunders that well-intended people often make. Good listening is often more about not doing something wrong than it is about doing something right.

Which of these top blunders do you make?

1. **"Don't worry about it" and other reassurances.** Better to keep your lips zipped and continue listening. Reassurances are usually given too quickly and the speaker feels cut-off.

2. **"That reminds me of the time ..."** Listening is not about your story, it's about the other person's story. Wait until the other person is completely finished before you jump in with your tale.

3. **"I know exactly how you feel ..."** The listener won't take your word for it. Show that you know by using empathic phrases such as, "That must have been hard ... No wonder you feel that way ..." and so on.

> **CAUTION**
>
> **Close Calls**
>
> Think your mate is too emotional? Chances are you are using that as an excuse to hide from the fact that you aren't emotional (or sensitive) enough. Patiently listen to his or her emotions and your mate will feel heard and cared about and become less emotional in the process.

4. **Speaking in clichés.** "That's life ... There's always a silver lining ... Make lemonade out of lemons ..." has the effect of minimizing what a person is saying. Clichés are universal. The other person wants to be heard as an individual.

5. **"I'm sorry you feel that way."** Nothing heartfelt there. You're really saying, "You shouldn't feel the way you do."

6. **"Can you hurry up?"** Say that and the other person's heart closes up immediately. If you really haven't the time, say so. But show a sincere desire to hear about it as soon as possible.

7. **"Why are you crying?"** Sounds like a criticism. Just recognize that the other person must really be upset or saying something that is hard to say. Respect that, don't judge it.

8. **"Why didn't you tell me this before?"** This is off-topic. Save it for later—after you have listened long enough to understand what the other person is trying to say.

9. **"Have you tried ..."** Don't offer suggestions until you are sure you really understand the problem. Premature solutions are a downer for intimacy.

10. **Silence.** Say something that acknowledges the other person!

No one ever outgrows the need to be listened to. People who live alone often talk out loud to themselves just so it seems that somebody is listening. Intimacy blossoms when you feel that the other person cares enough about you to want to hear what you have to say, regardless of how it makes them feel. Intimacy requires a sense of safety. Good listeners demonstrate over and over that they can be trusted.

The Least You Need to Know

- If you don't understand, you haven't been listening.

- No one wants to make personal changes if they don't feel listened to and understood.

- After hearing the other person out, be honest in your response but also be kind.

- Be willing to drop what you're doing once in a while to listen; intimacy and caring does not happen on a convenient schedule.

- If you're a caretaker and rescuer, you don't listen as well as you think you do.

Chapter 15

The Conversation Repair Shop

In This Chapter

- ◆ Learning how conversational blunders can still add to intimacy
- ◆ Taking a quiz to see if you're good at making conversational repairs
- ◆ Automatically squashing intimacy by using so-called "innocent" phrases
- ◆ Knowing what to say and do when a conversation starts to get crazy
- ◆ Saying the special words a man and a woman really need to hear

So many people (men, listen up) believe that the best way to keep arguments to a minimum is to shut down conversation at the first sign of trouble. People, who would otherwise rush into a burning building to save an animal, will run for the hills when their partner is burning mad. What's lacking is the know-how to repair a broken conversation. Repairing a conversation is easier than you think. Moreover, a successful repair always adds to a sense of intimacy. Withdrawing from conversation always adds to a sense of incompatibility.

Repairs are not just meant for arguments. Everyday conversation is filled with examples of innocent yet poorly thought-out remarks that make the person you're talking to feel misunderstood or disrespected. Anytime you have to defend yourself by saying, "That's not what I meant!" you have entered the world of unintended miscommunication. It's normal to go there. It helps a lot if you know how to wiggle out of it without causing any damage.

This chapter reveals the phrases you should avoid saying because they inevitably diminish goodwill and intimacy. You also learn how to effectively mend conversations that have started to tear apart at the seams.

The "Walking on Tip-Toes" Conversation

"Think before you speak" is a useful guideline. But when you must be so careful not to say the slightest thing the wrong way because it will be interpreted in the worst possible light, intimacy has flown out the window. You shouldn't have to walk on tip-toes as you maneuver through a conversation. Say what's on your mind without being intentionally harsh or unkind. And if you're the listener, give the speaker some elbow room. Don't pounce on the first word that sounds imprecise or unfair while missing the spirit of what's being said.

The more cautious you are during a conversation, the more likely you will mess up. And the more over-sensitive you are, the more you will react harshly to what's being said when patience is called for.

Mary and Steve were arguing about finances—again. The argument began with their usual debate over how money should be spent but it quickly escalated into a conflict about the way they were arguing. Steve resented her sharp tone of voice. Mary resented his constant interruptions. Steve complained that Mary kept bringing up unrelated issues into the discussion, such as the fact that her parents agreed with her about finances. Mary charged that Steve's voice was loud and patronizing.

Mary and Steve were unrealistic. They somehow expected that they should discuss a hotly divided issue without making any conversation errors whatsoever. And after the errors were made, they pounced on them, indignant that the rules of polite conversation were so rudely tossed aside.

CAUTION

Close Calls

Preventing conversational errors is not always possible, especially because a well-intended comment might still be heard the wrong way. The more you try to make conversations run perfectly, the more you will fail—and the more you will avoid talking altogether. Focus on repairing conversations instead.

Mary and Steve desperately needed to do three things: expect that conversational no-no's will happen; not get up in arms about it; and be willing to repair the mistakes as soon as possible. People who have problems with intimacy do just the opposite: They believe that something is terribly wrong if conversations don't run smoothly; and they complain, blame, or run (rather than make repairs) when conversations get ugly.

The "Are You a Plumber or a Perfectionist?" Quiz

Every homeowner needs a plumber now and then. Things break down. That's life. Relationships need periodic repairs, too. It's not a problem if things go wrong in a relationship. It's a problem if repairs cannot be made. The more of a perfectionist you are about your relationship, the more unhappy you will be because problems are inevitable. Take this quiz to see where you stand. Answer True or False:

1. I choose my words carefully during conversations.   T___ F___

2. If I say, "I didn't mean it that way," my partner usually accepts it.   T___ F___

3. Some topics are best left alone.   T___ F___

4. If a discussion escalates into an argument, one of us can de-escalate and calm us down.   T___ F___

5. There is no excuse for being unkind during an argument.   T___ F___

6. If one of us says the wrong thing we apologize.   T___ F___

7. It's better to keep conversations light, otherwise it just ends up in an argument.   T___ F___

8. Even if one of us gets too emotional, we can carry out a discussion.   T___ F___

9. We can never come to an agreement, so we shouldn't bother discussing it.   T___ F___

10. If I'm not feeling heard during a discussion, my partner tries to listen better.   T___ F___

11. At the first sign of conflict, I prefer to end the discussion.   T___ F___

12. Sometimes we use humor during a stressful discussion to break the tension.   T___ F___

If you answered True three or more times on the odd-numbered statements, you are more of a perfectionist where communication is concerned. You unrealistically expect discussions to run smoothly and you withdraw from them prematurely when they don't. If you answered True four or more times to the even-numbered statements, you are a "plumber": good at making repairs during conversations.

Think of your relationship as buying a house. If you are good at home repairs, you can purchase a fixer-upper and get a great value for your money. If you have no skill in making repairs, you'll spend more money on outside help. Your best bet is to learn to fix as many things by yourself as possible.

Entering the Bermuda Triangle of Conversation

Some comments are obviously hurtful or insensitive and would be a problem in any relationship (such as abusive name-calling or vicious language and tone). But all too often in relationships we say well-worn phrases that we have no idea annoy our partners. When you hear yourself saying, "What are you so upset about? All I said was …" you have entered the Bermuda Triangle of Conversation. There, for inexplicable reasons, friendly chitchat disappears and horrible things start to happen to dialogue and intimacy. Here are the top dirty-dozen:

"There's no sense in getting so upset."

You might intend to sound sympathetic and helpful but you're really patronizing. If the other person truly is upset, don't say it makes no sense. A more caring and helpful thing to say would be something such as, "This really bothers you."

"Does this make me look fat?"

Most guys would never ask such a question. And most guys hate being asked such a question. They can't win. If they answer yes, they can expect no romp in the hay for at least a fortnight. If they answer no, their partner won't believe them. My advice to ladies is to say what's really on your mind. "I think I look fat and you won't find me attractive." The guy can then tell you he finds you attractive (and he probably does) without having to utter anything about being fat.

"Didn't we discuss this already?"

You probably did discuss it but your partner didn't think it was resolved. Drumming your fingers and showing impatience won't win you any awards right now. In your previous conversation you probably arrived at some conclusion (which is why you think the topic is off the table), but you overlooked your partner's feelings about the conclusion (which is why she is putting it back on the table). Your partner is unhappy about something. Find out what it is and see if it can be fixed.

"I can't think that far ahead."

Your partner wants to plan something (maybe a wedding???). Planning a vacation or even a night out can be almost as fun as actually doing it. By not thinking far ahead you remove a source of enjoyment for your partner. Also, it might be viewed as a cop-out on your part, a way to avoid making a commitment.

"It's up to you."

How thoughtful. Done once in a while it might be viewed as generous. Done routinely it means the other person has to do all the thinking and decision-making for the two of you. A partner who is upset with this comment believes you don't care enough to have an opinion. Show interest. Get involved.

"Why won't you talk about it?"

Insisting that your partner talk and explain himself when he clearly isn't interested won't help your cause (even though I agree that he probably should open up). Better to say, "I know you'd rather not talk but I'm hoping you'll change your mind later. This is important to me."

"I don't want to talk about it!"

But she does want you to talk. Who wins? Neither of you win if one of you doesn't show flexibility. Refusing to talk is the same as saying "I don't care what you think." Is that what you want to convey? Better to say, "I need time to mull it over. I'll talk later." Uncomfortable conversations won't kill you.

"It's only a ballgame!"

Anytime you minimize the importance of a sporting event to an enthusiast, he or she will come away thinking "You just don't get it." It will cut away one more slice from the intimacy pie. An enthusiast loves the sport or loves the team. The devotion has gone on for years and probably has its source in childhood. It's like saying that your wedding anniversary is "Just a day" or that the Declaration of Independence is "Just a piece of paper."

"You're not validating my feelings!"

Your right, your partner probably isn't. But telling him that will upset him on a number of levels. First, he hates psychological jargon. Second, if he thinks that your feelings are wrong (invalid) he doesn't understand why he should validate them. When you tell him that feelings aren't wrong or right they just "are," he thinks you're insane. Better to say "I know you disagree with my view but I need you to understand how strongly I feel. If I don't get my way, I at least want to think that my feelings matter to you."

"What do you want now?"

You're trivializing the other person's concern. You might as well say that you can't be bothered with such unimportant topics. A friendly "What's up?" works nicely.

"If you don't like it you can leave."

That's like saying "My way or the highway." If you're sincere, the relationship is on shaky ground and perhaps it should end. If you're just frustrated, say that instead.

"I told you I'd take care of it!"

Hmmm. Sounds like you're tall on making promises but short on providing essential details such as when and how you'll follow through. You're probably feeling nagged. And you're being nagged because you've left your partner out of the loop. Be more specific about the details without painting yourself into a corner.

The preceding statements are worth avoiding because they inevitably require you to make a repair. If you're not fortunate enough to know how to make repairs, such comments will pop the intimacy bubble faster than you can say, "I put my foot in my mouth."

Regulating Your Intimacy Thermostat

Your home thermostat is a small marvel. It detects when the temperature is getting too cold, signals the furnace to turn on, and turns off the furnace when the temperature is in the comfort zone. A good relationship has a similar quality. Successful couples detect when the emotional temperature is getting cold, discuss a problem, and end the conversation before things get too hot. Sometimes couples escalate conflict and things get uncomfortably hot. Happy couples know how to "lower the thermostat."

A successful repair involves a number of steps. First, someone has to notice that matters are getting out of hand and that a repair is needed. Next, each person must want the conversation to be mended. Someone must then initiate a fix-it attempt. Finally, that attempt must be accepted by the other person. If any one of these steps is missing, the intimacy thermostat is broken and the relationship will get very cold or miserably hot.

> **CAUTION**
>
> **Close Calls**
>
> You can make a beautiful attempt to repair a broken conversation but the outcome depends less on your sense of timing and the words you use than it does on the other person's willingness to cooperate.

The longer you wait to repair an escalating conversation the more damage will occur. How many times have you said something in anger that you regretted later? It's important to pay attention to your body during a tense discussion. Feel the tension in your chest, stomach, hands, and arms. As that physical pressure builds, it's a sign that matters may get out of control and one of you will either get too angry or will withdraw from the conversation. Imagine that your body is like an automobile engine and you are accelerating. You can feel the engine race as you shift into higher and higher gears. Your job is to notice when your engine is racing and immediately downshift. You can downshift by repairing your perceptions, your language, or your physical agitation.

Repairing Perceptions

A perception is not simply what you saw or heard or felt, it includes your interpretations. If your partner says something unkind, what exactly does that mean? Does it mean he or she is an unkind person who cares nothing about how you feel? Perhaps. Or does it mean he or she is frustrated and overreacting? Review Chapter 9 on how to give the benefit of the doubt. Repairs are so much easier to make when you are able to see your partner in a more favorable light.

Perhaps the most helpful perception has to do with interpreting anger. When your partner (or anyone you have a relationship with) gets angry, do you view that negatively? If so, you will likely make at least one mistake: You will complain about the other's anger and ignore the content of what's being said; or you will withdraw. But imagine if you interpreted the anger as a sign that what was being said was very important to that person? Chances are you would show interest and take that person seriously. And that would have a powerful impact on the course of the conversation. You would have effectively made a repair, just by showing interest.

Intimacy Boosters

Mending a broken conversation is not about being right or winning the argument. It is simply, and only, about making repairs.

Repairing Language

The following might be the most immediate and effective way to put a derailed conversation back on track. When you try to fix matters using helpful words, you have three effective options:

- ◆ Admit your own verbal mistakes and try to correct them.
- ◆ Request that the other person modify the way he or she is talking.

◆ Point out something the other person said that you liked, agreed with, or found helpful.

Admit your mistakes by saying something such as, "I shouldn't have said that ... I didn't mean it that way ... Let me rephrase that ... Can I start again? ... Bear with me ... I know I'm coming on too strong ... I'm doing my best to calm down ... I'm sorry ..." and so on.

Ideally you will recognize your own mistakes and correct them as soon as possible. However, your partner might be the one to point them out to you. That gets tricky. You might disagree with the other's perception. For example, if your partner complains that you are too harsh in your tone you might respond, "No I'm not!" That isn't help-ful. Your best bet is to state that you weren't aware of it and then make the changes that the other person wants. This is not the time to nit-pick. Neither do you want to make the changes grudgingly. Think of it as similar to driving with your partner and you dis-agree on how best to get to a destination. Rather than debate over whose idea is the best, agree to disagree. The main goal is to get to where you want to go even if it isn't the quickest route. Be willing to go along with some points you don't agree with if it means you will ultimately make a successful repair.

Use tact when you request that the other person make changes in the manner he or she is speaking. Otherwise, by being belligerent in your tone you are making the same kind of mistake you want your partner to stop making. Start by saying, "Would you mind ... I'd appreciate it if you would ... It would help me a lot if you would ... Please ..." and so forth. Always show appreciation when the changes you request are made.

Just Ask!

I can say "I'm sorry" when I make a blunder during a conversation but my boyfriend seems incapable of admitting any mistakes. Any suggestions?

If he is receptive to your apologies then you might be able to have fairly productive dis-cussions. However, intimacy will still be blunted if he won't admit to his own flaws. You will resent him and not feel as close to him as you would if he were able to make apologies, too. In general, is he kind to you? If so, his defensiveness might be some-thing you can learn to live with. If he tends to be angry, demanding, accusing, and gen-erally selfish, then you should move on. Intimacy cannot happen with self-centeredness.

Finally, a great way to make a repair when the conversation is heating up is to agree with something the other person is saying. Even if you disagree with most of it, select something that makes sense and point it out. "I see what you mean ... That makes sense ... No wonder you feel the way you do ... I like what you said about ... I agree with you about ... You're right about ..." and so on. The tension between you will immediately downshift the moment you find some merit in what the other person is saying.

Repairing Agitation

Intense physical agitation will cause you to escalate an argument or to withdraw in a huff. Men are especially prone to feeling overwhelmed when conversations get too intense, and they often leave the room and end the discussion in a poor way to calm down. Premature exits reduce agitation in the short term but add to a couple's sense of detachment and incompatibility. Intimacy is connection, not disconnection.

Pausing from an intense discussion is fine and perfectly appropriate as long as the conversation resumes. During the break it's a good idea to physically relax or to do some activity that takes your mind off of the frustrating aspects of the discussion. It's also a good time to find some merit in the other's viewpoint. That way, when the talk resumes, cooperation is more likely.

The One-Two Double-Play Combination

Fixing conversations is a two-person operation. One of you cannot succeed without cooperation. The most common blunder occurs when one person tries to de-escalate an intense discussion and the other refuses to oblige. Statistically, men are more likely than women to be uncooperative, but some women can be just as stubborn.

People who don't cooperate with a repair attempt underestimate the value of a repair for improving communication and intimacy. Put off by a partner's unkind comment, the person feels entitled to be angry and stubborn. But it's a huge gamble. It's gambling that the one who offered the olive branch and tried to mend the conversation will still be gracious after their attempt has been rebuffed. It can be difficult to have the humility and presence of mind to make a repair. That task becomes more difficult when one's partner is being uncooperative.

Intimacy Boosters

If you are so hurt or angry that you can't accept the olive branch when it's offered, at least acknowledge the other's attempt to make amends. Say "I know what you're trying to do and I appreciate it, but I'm still too upset right now."

Sometimes a repair attempt isn't made during a discussion but later. And it might even be a bit disguised. "Can I make you a cup of tea?" could easily be one person's way of reconnecting after a tense or divisive discussion. Be alert for small words or gestures that are really efforts to make a connection. Cooperation is necessary then, too. Imagine a scene where one partner places a hand affectionately on the other's shoulder and there is no response. Or one person asks a simple question only to be met with an impossible to understand grumble. Such attempts to connect, if not met with some positive response or acknowledgement, can create more divisiveness and hurt feelings. Intimacy will suffer.

A Phrase Every Woman Wants to Hear

Every woman wants to know she is loved, needed, and respected. She wants to know she is attractive to the man in her life; that he desires her. Just as importantly, women need to hear a sentiment that men may feel but don't often express. It might show up indirectly in how a man acts toward the woman he loves, but it needs to show up clearly in his words: *"I cherish you."*

A woman who feels cherished feels desired not merely on a physical/sexual level but on a deeper, almost spiritual level. She feels deeply loved and desirable for all of who she is, despite her flaws (which she probably knows too well). A woman who feels cherished feels safe in the arms of her man. She feels not just loved but beloved. Even a small kiss from her man, if done with a deep sense of cherishing her, can make her sway; make her feel like time has stopped and there is no other person in the world but her lover. And a woman who feels cherished will love her man like he wants to be loved. Sex will be passionate, at times fierce, but always beyond sex. When he enters her she will feel as if he has entered her very soul.

A Phrase Every Man Wants to Hear

Men want to be loved and respected, too. But there is one sentiment that is not often expressed directly although it might be conveyed indirectly. And it's a phrase that gives courage and a burst of self-confidence to the average man when he hears it from the woman he loves: *"I have faith in you."*

The words "I have faith in you" tap into a man's deep-seated, hard-wired need to provide for and protect the people he loves. It indicates that he is trustworthy and that he can be counted on to do the right thing. The average guy doesn't want much from the woman he loves. Telling him that you have faith in him makes him feel confident, needed, and well, more like a man. And if he is not struggling with any addiction or any severe personality disorder, it will awaken or supercharge his feelings of love and passion. He will crave more intimacy. Of course, he might show it in his most natural way by wanting sex. But it won't be sex for the sake of sex. It will be sex for the sake of *you*, the woman; sex where he wants to melt into you and never let you go. Sex where he wants to enter your soul.

The Least You Need to Know

- Expect that communication gaffs and thoughtless remarks will happen; don't get bent out of shape over them.

- If you inflame a conversation with unkind words or stubborn refusal to hear the other person's view, apologize and try again.

- If your partner tries to repair a conversation that's gotten out of hand, don't be stubborn or indignant. Cooperate.

- Give your partner the benefit of the doubt if he or she says, "That's not what I meant!"

- Whenever possible, view your partner's anger not as something negative but as a sign that the issue is important to him or her.

- If you're a woman, find a way to tell your man that you have faith in him; if you're a man, tell your woman that you cherish her.

Part 4

Intimacy Through Touch

Many people, even loving couples who've been together a while, can have sex without really being intimate. Intimacy is not just about being naked or applying a new technique. Intimate lovers speak from the heart as well as the body. They connect at a deeper level of energy and emotion. They caress each other not just with their hands but with their eyes; they kiss not just with their lips but with their souls. Sexual penetration comes after a penetration of their spirits, of their vital force.

The next five chapters reveal how intimacy can blossom and become more profound through physical connection. You'll learn what sexual intimacy means to men and women and how you can use these differences to improve passion and closeness. You'll read about ways to add playfulness to your intimate moments so that you not only feel aroused and excited by one another, but delighted. You'll also learn about some common obstacles to sexual intimacy, as well as the powerful role of affection as a driving force in physical closeness.

Chapter 16

Sex and Intimacy

In This Chapter

◆ Knowing when to make your relationship sexual

◆ Recognizing the three motivations for sex

◆ Uncovering what sexual intimacy really means to men and women

◆ Quizzing yourself on how well you understand the opposite sex

Sex is not the primary pathway to intimacy. That's why the chapters on sex arrive halfway through this book. The more genitally focused you are, the less intimate overall you will be in your relationships. That's the bottom line. And that's the main reason many people fail to cultivate genuine intimacy—they confuse having sex with true closeness.

Still, although sex isn't everything, it comes pretty darn close. And that's another reason why many people fall short in the intimacy department—they underplay the importance of sex as a way to maintain and nurture a healthy, intimate relationship. When you place either too much or too little importance on sex, your relationship might continue but intimacy will suffer.

When you are in a monogamous relationship, sex becomes the primary way to connect and express love that is not found in any of your other relationships. It is a form of intimacy that you share exclusively with your partner. That makes it special indeed. If that aspect of your relationship suffers in any way, then your relationship loses a big part of its uniqueness. Of course, other aspects of your relationship may be distinctive. Perhaps you have children together or you went through some difficult period of life together and feel particularly bonded. Still, sexual intimacy is very precious to couples in love. And it must never be taken for granted.

How Soon After Dating Do You Have Sex?

The "Wait until you're married" philosophy of sex is not at all popular in our culture. And that opens up a host of questions for many people. Is there a right time to start having sex? How soon is too soon? Is there a benefit to delaying sex?

The answers depend on your values and goals. Are you interested in a permanent, committed relationship or just some fun? In other words, are you interested in finding a mate or in mating who you find? Research findings are clear; couples who delayed having sex for at least several months were more likely to get married. When couples had sex within the first month of dating, only about 10 percent ended up getting married.

Exercise!
Keep track of the number of times you made love over several weeks (assuming you and your partner are of normal health). Subtract the number of times you either argued or believed that your partner was uncooperative during that same stretch of time. If the resulting difference is a positive number, your relationship is probably happy. If the difference is a negative number, you are probably not as happy as you would like.

Of course these numbers are somewhat misleading. Many people have sex within a month of dating who never have any intention of getting married or remaining committed, which is a big reason they break-up so soon. Still, it's safe to say that anyone who is in a relationship and is willing to delay having sex, probably has some deeper feelings for their partner. It is the nature of those feelings, not the absence of sex per se, that improves the odds the couple will eventually marry.

Where sex and intimacy are concerned, sex is best used as a way to reflect and deepen an already intimate relationship. Delaying sex in a new relationship improves the odds that you will have taken the time to know one another better on both an intellectual and heartfelt level. It is not at all a good idea to use sex as the primary method for obtaining intimacy. In other words, if achieving maximum levels of intimacy is your goal, sex should come later rather than sooner. How much later? Only you can decide. But you will know you timed it right when the relationship continues to grow and blossom after the sexual relationship has begun. Sex too soon has a higher risk of short-circuiting the relationship. In the following sections, I describe the three motivations for sexual behavior. The first two are more basic but quite normal. The last one is more profound. A healthy and happy person who has achieved a strong level of intimacy in his or her relationships will incorporate all three motivations, with the third one predominating. When intimacy and happiness levels are lower, people use the first or second motivation most of the time.

Motivation One: Sex as Immediate Gratification

There is nothing wrong per se with wanting immediate gratification. We are built with drives and instincts to want to fulfill urges as soon as possible. Of course, an emotionally healthy person learns patience. Knowing how to delay gratification is a sign of maturity. Still, everyone has given into the urge to eat something they shouldn't or to impulsively buy something or to have ravenous sex for the sake of ravenous sex.

Key attributes of this approach to sexual fulfillment include the following:

- Hot, passionate, unbridled sex

- Fervor at the expense of tenderness

- Heat at the expense of warmth

- Creative sex or uncreative sex

- Self-absorbed sensuality

- The sense of satisfaction is short lived and must be repeated

- Pregnancy is not typically a motivator

When you tap into the raw power of immediate gratification, it can reap some benefits for your sex life. Sex for pleasure only can be quite hot and spontaneous. Couples who occasionally engage in spontaneous acts of sexual abandon can be very happy together and easily get fired up over one another. The drawbacks to sex-for-pleasure-only come when the relationship is superficial and true intimacy is low or absent. You begin to realize that while sex may be amazing you are more of an object of pleasure than a person with inherent value. You are fulfilling someone's physical need, and he or she is fulfilling your need. Who you are as a person is secondary. People who get stuck at Motivation One are usually less happy in life because happiness is equated with pleasure and sensual pleasure is always time-limited and fleeting.

Even in the middle of a sexual act that is deeply heartfelt, moments can occur when all you think about is yourself. All you feel are the physical sensations of sex and you do what you can to make it more intense. Or you fall back and allow your partner to completely take over while you luxuriate in complete self-centered, sensual pleasure. That selfishness is absolutely normal and a wonderful way to experience pleasure. But in intimate relationships, there is also a give and take. You should engage in self-centered pleasure but not all the time. With true intimacy, pleasuring the other is as important as being pleasured.

> **Intimacy Boosters**
>
> If your relationship is already loving and tender, add zest with occasional bursts of unrestrained passion. Rip off each others clothes and make love anywhere but the bedroom. Try to say or do one thing you haven't done before (or not in a very long time).

When instant gratification is the prime motive, sex can be adventurous and creative or urgent yet predictable. It depends on the people involved.

When immediate gratification is the main reason for having sex with a new partner, genuine intimacy will probably fall short. That's because the level of caring is naturally low because you don't know the other person well enough to feel a depth of caring.

Motivation Two: Sex for Ego Gratification

Everyone likes to have their ego (not just their body) stroked. A job promotion, an award, a compliment on an achievement can make you feel good about yourself. There is nothing wrong with ego gratification. We all need boosts to our esteem that come from some form of achievement or recognition. But some people get stuck there. All they care about are accomplishments, winning the next game, and being "better than."

Ego gratification is closely connected to sexual gratification.

People usually feel good about themselves when they have sex—when they feel wanted. They might feel attractive, desirable, sexy, or even powerful. On the other hand, not having sex can have the opposite effect—they might feel unattractive, undesirable, or weak.

People who are divorced or widowed (or anyone of any age who has been out of the dating scene for some time) sometimes discover that having sex with a new partner is a tremendous boost to their self-esteem. Feeling perhaps out of shape and less than desirable, it's a wonderful feeling to know that someone wants you and can't keep their hands off of you.

Key attributes of the sex-as-ego-gratification approach are as follows:

♦ Sometimes sizzling, usually technically effective sex

♦ Sex can be spontaneous, but only if it boosts the ego; planned sex is desirable

♦ Precision about "what works" sometimes comes at the expense of adventurous creativity

♦ Pride and possessiveness can interfere with sexual compatibility

♦ Its effect on self-esteem is limited and conditional

♦ Pregnancy may be desirable if it fulfills an egotistic need

If your relationship is new, the choice to have sex will less likely be motivated by love and devotion than by a desire for physical pleasure or an ego trip. Don't kid yourself about the reason if you don't want either you or your partner to get hurt. Relationships where sex comes very soon have the highest break-up rates.

Sex for ego-gratification-only has its obvious drawbacks but it has its benefits, too. There is nothing like feeling desirable and attractive to boost your self-esteem. The more self-confident you are, the more adventurous you might become in bed or the more creative at work. When sex feeds your ego, chances are you will be focused on pleasuring your partner, too. You will want to make your partner feel the most pleasure he or she can feel—thanks to you.

> **Intimacy Boosters**
>
> Find a book on sexual techniques and become a *sexpert*-a skilled and knowledgeable expert about sex. Use your new knowledge (everybody can learn something new) to bring your partner pleasure in ways he or she hasn't experienced before.

Motivation Three: Real Love

Sex for the sake of genuine love incorporates the best of all worlds. Combining sex and love involves the three elements of genuine intimacy: connecting, sharing, and caring.

Sex for the sake of love is symbolized by the heart and soul and represents a higher developmental stage. It says, "I want you—not to fulfill a need or to stroke my ego—but because you mean the world to me and I cannot live without you." Whereas sex for pleasure or for ego gratification is by definition very superficial, sex for love has depth and breadth. Sex for love has these key attributes:

- It is both hot and passionate as well as warm and tender.

- It is as much about the other person as it is about yourself.

- It is not dependent on "new and different" to sustain itself.

- It surpasses physical appearance as the source of happiness and fulfillment.

- Pleasure and happiness during sex is based on both sexual satisfaction as well as devotion and commitment.

- Its effect transcends time; love can go on forever.

- Pregnancy may well be desired as a reflection and an outgrowth of the couple's love.

Close Calls _____

A little wine or a drink before making love might seem romantic now and then. Done too often, it gives the impression that alcohol is necessary before love-making can happen. Alcohol can lessen a man's staying power, too.

When people's motivations for sex is based on love, they might also be motivated by pleasure or ego gratification. Research indicates that the happiest and most devoted of couples also have fantastic sex lives. That includes not just tenderness and warmth but hot, sizzling passion, too. Surrendering to pure, sensual pleasure while in a loving relationship is perfectly normal and is one reason why a happy couple's sex life is so rewarding.

What Sexual Intimacy Means to Men

Exceptions obviously exist, but for the most part the average male does have a different attitude about sex and intimacy than the average female.

If you're a female, take the following brief quiz about men's sexual attitudes. Don't answer according to how you *should* answer (forget political correctness) but according to how you usually think and feel. If you think the statement is true even 51 percent of the time, score it as True. Otherwise, score it as False.

1. Men usually want to have sex just to "get their rocks off."   T___ F___

2. When a man shows sexual affection, he is really after one thing.   T___ F___

3. Quickies for a man are almost always about sexual release only.   T___ F___

4. Most men would have sex with any number of women if they knew they could get away with it.   T___ F___

5. If a man feels owed because his woman hasn't had sex with him in a while, it shows that he is immature.   T___ F___

6. A man who keeps pushing for sex, despite hints by his partner that she's not interested, is being selfish.   T___ F___

The more you answered True to these statements, the more you misunderstand men's attitudes about sex and intimacy. (See Appendix A for a more complete elaboration of these answers.) Men's emotions when it comes to sex are more complicated than a mere instinctive drive. Sure, plenty of men fit the bill as sex-crazed, ego-centric, horny-as-all-get-out, stuck-in-adolescence tomcats. But I'm referring to the typical guy, perhaps your guy, or the guy you recently dated. To him, sex and intimacy are very intertwined. What often appears as the guy pushing for sex is really the guy pushing for closeness. (It gets confusing because sometimes *he* doesn't realize that's what he's doing.)

Of course, men's sex drives are partially governed by biological cravings. Once activated, it can be uncomfortable for a man not to get relief. But women have a physical need, too. Sex drives are not gender-specific.

> ### Exercise!
>
> For all you women out there, the next time your man is "only after one thing," give him the benefit of the doubt and assume that the one thing he's after is greater closeness with you. Give in to his sexual wishes. He will definitely feel more connected to you.

What many women fail to fully appreciate is that for men in an important relationship, sex is a means to an end. The end is intimacy and closeness. (The newer the relationship, the more likely that having sex is the goal, not closeness.) Most men are not fantastic talkers so they communicate love and a need for intimacy by using physical, not verbal, methods. For men, sex is a form of intimacy that leads to greater intimacy.

Joe's Story

What happens to a man when he feels sexually rejected by someone he loves? He experiences it as a reduction in love and desire for him. Yes, he might have to use his intellect and remind himself that the woman he's with is "tired" or "just not interested tonight." But those reasons don't always soothe the underlying feelings of rejection. Listen to Joe, a typical guy. I've heard stories like his a thousand times:

> Last night was like so many others. It had been about 10 days since we made love. We were in bed, both of us were tired. I started caressing her body. Next my fingers started probing. At first I thought she liked it because she let me keep going. Then she flinched. It was a polite way of saying, "Not now." But I wanted to feel closer to her. And I guess I wanted her to want me even when she didn't want me, if that makes any sense. I feel like a kid when she's not interested, like a little boy who's being told by his mother that he's had enough candy for one week. I don't want to go to sleep feeling that way so I continue to press for sex. But that usually makes her annoyed, like I should have gotten the hint by then. So I roll over; aggravated and feeling undesirable. The next night I go at it again, Charlie Brown running to kick the football and hoping Lucy won't pull it away at the last minute and make him feel like a fool. She thinks I push for sex too often and that I only want sex to fill a need. She's right in a way. But what I need is her.

Ironically, the more a man feels rejected the more likely he will pursue sex more rigorously (at least for a while) and risk coming across as "only wanting one thing" or acting as if he's "entitled" to sex. More often than not he's feeling a tad insecure and seeking confirmation that he is loved and desirable.

Roger's Story

What about men who show a lot of sexual affection or who enjoy quickies. Are they just sex maniacs? Or could their actions, however unromantic or hurried, be a way of seeking closeness? Listen to Roger:

> I do enjoy grabbing my wife sexually when we're alone. Nothing has to come from it. I'm not expecting sex. But I like slipping my hands under her bra or down her pants. Same thing with having a quickie. It makes me feel really special and desirable. I love that she seems to enjoy it. If she pushed me away a lot just because I got a bit grabby I'd really feel offended. I think couples should

always be that playful. What's nice is that after I fondle her or caress her or we hurriedly make love in about three minutes right before one of us has to leave somewhere, I think about her long after we're apart. It reminds me of when we first started dating and she was constantly on my mind. I liked that phase, that infatuation phase, the falling-in-love phase. And that's how I feel when we show sexual affection. It brings it all back. It's all about connection. It's not just about sex.

The best way to tell if your sex-focused man is just a self-centered, pleasure-seeking-at-all-costs Neanderthal or a loving guy is to watch how he treats you when sex is not the issue. Is he kind? Thoughtful? Does he take an interest in you in other ways? If so, give him the benefit of the doubt when he gets grabby.

" " Just Ask! _____

What's the best way to convince my girlfriend that having sex at least once or twice a week is normal? She thinks I'm sex crazed.

First, mismatched desire is quite common. Second, my guess is she'd rather "make love" than "have sex." You probably think you show her a lot of thoughtfulness, but she doesn't think that way. She probably feels somewhat used and taken for granted. Third, there might be other aspects of your relationship where you are more concerned about getting what you want than in meeting her desires. If so, she will not be that sexually interested in you. Improve intimacy in the nonsexual areas of your relationship. Show her love and consideration on her terms, not just yours, and your sex life might improve.

What Sexual Intimacy Means to Women

For most women, making love isn't purely a physical act and doesn't always have to do with sexual release. For women, making love involves making one another feel loved not just when cuddling or having sex but at various small moments during the day. A lover who caresses a woman deeply, tenderly, and nonsexually for many, many long minutes in bed (or elsewhere)—not just for 10 seconds or not just until he senses she is lubricated and ready for penetration—demonstrates that he has at least some notion of what making love really means to a woman.

A woman certainly can (and does) make love quickly without much foreplay and fanfare just for the sake of pleasuring her partner or relieving her own sexual urges. But that isn't the way she ultimately wants to make love. For her, it goes beyond sexual pleasure. It involves a deeper connection, a sharing of energies, of feelings, a penetration not just of bodies but of souls. A man who stares at his woman's naked body and tells her tenderly with just his eyes that she is gorgeous, sexy, and the most beautiful thing in the world; and tells her with his mouth that he is so in love with her and wants her; and tells her by the way he breathes, by the way his chest rises and falls as he contemplates her and soaks her all in that he wishes this moment would last forever; has made love to her without ever having touched her.

If you're a man, take the following quiz. Don't answer according to what you think all the textbooks say is true, but answer according to how you think and feel on a daily basis. If you think the statement is true even 51 percent of the time, score it as True. Otherwise score it as False.

1. When a woman fondles her man sexually, gets him aroused, and then leaves him high and dry, she is being an insensitive tease.   T___ F___

2. If a man wakes up aroused and rolls over to press against his woman, she should (much of the time, anyway) follow his lead and want to have sex.   T___ F___

3. Foreplay typically means caressing the woman's breasts and genitals and kissing her until she seems ready for intercourse.   T___ F___

4. Helping your woman out with daily chores and responsibilities and freeing her up so she has time for herself should have little to do with her level of sexual desire and passion.   T___ F___

5. There's no need to flirt with a woman you already have a steady relationship with.   T___ F___

6. A man is ready to make love when he has a full erection; a woman is ready to make love when she is lubricated.   T___ F___

Okay, guys. The more you answered True the more you haven't a clue as to what's really going on with your woman when it comes to sex and intimacy. The correct answers to the quiz will be explored in greater detail in Appendix A. For now, it's important to understand that women don't equate making love purely with sexual arousal and release. Got it? If you want to have sex on a Friday night, foreplay starts Friday morning at the very latest—and it has nothing to do with stimulating her manually. It has everything to do with stimulating her lovingly, soulfully, and with genuine thoughtfulness and tenderness. It means telling her whenever you can that you love her dearly and that you think she is beautiful. It means being thoughtful enough to anticipate when she will have a hectic day and taking steps to make her feel relaxed and pampered when she comes home. It means easing her burdens even if it is inconvenient for you. And yes, it means the occasional card or love note or phone call in the middle of the day just to say "Hi."

Intimacy Boosters

After achieving a climax, intimacy can linger if a man holds his woman close for a while and doesn't just roll over and go to sleep. She'll love it.

One main reason guys have trouble understanding a woman's sexual intimacy needs is because men's brains are organized into compartments. Think of a man's brain as a bedroom dresser and all the drawers represent his varied interests and preoccupations. He has a work drawer, a sports drawer, a lawn mowing drawer, a something's-wrong-with-the-car-and-I-can't-figure-it-out drawer, and so on. And yes, there is a sex drawer. When he opens that drawer he sees all his tools of the trade and makes sure they're all in working order. "Let's see, tongue? Yep. Fingers? Yep. Penis? Yep. Whiskers too scratchy? Oh, I'm sure she won't mind. Okay, it's a go." After that drawer is opened, that becomes his focus. Sex means … well, going all the way. It doesn't mean just cuddling. It certainly doesn't mean getting aroused, about to explode, and stopping just because she's not in the mood, it's time to go to work, or the kids have just woken up.

A woman doesn't have a sex drawer. She has a huge walk-in closet. And it contains things that a man would never associate with having sex because it involves activities that happen hours and days before a sexual act ever starts (such as him giving her a sincere, heartfelt compliment or leaving a love note under the pillow). A woman has the ability to make love passionately with a man and still feel it was worthwhile even if she doesn't reach an orgasm. Not typically a man. After he gets an erection, an orgasm must follow, otherwise it's like inserting a dollar in the candy machine and getting nothing in return. Why bother? Sexual release is part of a man's wiring when he thinks about sex and intimacy. But if he wants to make love to a woman on a woman's terms, he needs to make sexual release secondary to showing her that he loves her in ways that are meaningful to her.

Kate's Story

What goes on in a woman's mind when her man wants sex and she doesn't? What would she love for him to understand? Listen to Kate:

For Brad it usually happens in the mornings. He snuggles up against me and starts caressing me just enough to let me know he's awake. When he presses closer I can feel that he's hard and I know what he wants. But not only am I not aroused, and not only is foreplay out of the question because we have so little time before we have to get out of bed, but I'm still half-asleep! So I get a little aggravated. Then I feel guilty. So I reach down and start touching him you know where. I want him to feel pleasure but I don't really want to go all the way. Can't he just enjoy some stimulation and leave it at that? No. Once my hands get involved he's wide awake and wanting more. So on other mornings when I know he's all excited and ready for action I keep my eyes closed and act like I'm still asleep. I refuse to touch him anywhere because he'll assume I mean business and I don't mean that at all.

What I wish he understood is that sex doesn't have to be all or nothing. I know he gets physically uncomfortable when he's aroused and has no release but is that so bad at least once in a while? If we could just caress each other and cuddle most mornings, I'm sure there'd be days when I would get aroused and want to have sex.

Rachel's Story

What's the difference to a woman, between having sex and making love? A world of difference. Listen to Rachel:

Just last week I had one of those really wonderful sexual experiences with Ed. The days were long and hectic and we had little time together. One night he just held me in his arms for an extra long time as we stood in the kitchen. He told me he missed me and how much he loved me. He kissed my mouth so tenderly, like he hadn't done in a while. Then he said in his most romantic voice, "Friday night. Ten o'clock. If I don't have you then I think I'll die." The next day he left me several notes, little reminders, that he was thinking ahead about Friday night and couldn't wait. Later when he came home from work and kissed me he started to get a little grabby. I didn't mind at all. I wanted him to. But he stopped himself. "No," he said. 'I'm saving it all for tomorrow night.' By the time Friday night arrived I was more than ready for him. I wanted him so much. He undressed me slowly and took several minutes kissing my entire body before I fell back onto the bed. He kept kissing me starting with my legs and working his way up and he wouldn't let me touch him right away. I was his. It still gives me goose bumps.

The Least You Need to Know

♦ To a woman, making love is not just about sexual release.

♦ If you want to establish a loving, committed relationship, delay having sex for at least several months.

♦ It's okay to have selfish moments during sex; it can add to the passion and intimacy as your partner focuses fully on pleasing you.

♦ A woman who is lubricated is sexually aroused but not necessarily ready to make love unless it has been preceded by a lot of tenderness and warmth.

♦ If a man who has an erection is sometimes willing to be sexual and sensual without it always resulting in an orgasm, his woman will be happier and more likely to be sexually playful.

Chapter 17

Hot Intimacy

In This Chapter

- How intimacy can go from warm to hot in mere seconds
- How to make sensual connections when time is at a premium
- How a man can increase his sexual pleasure every time
- How an unusual exercise can create incredible pleasure

There's routine sex (predictable and a bit bland) and then there's hot, sizzling sex (carnivorous, impassioned, and all too infrequent for the average person). Many people miss out on the great sensual stuff that lies halfway between humdrum and scorching. Hot intimacy can fill the gap for very busy or tired people who want to make a zesty connection with someone special but don't have the time or opportunity for a full-court press.

Hot intimacy isn't always about sex (though it often is) but it's always about intimacy. Hot intimacy is body-to-body closeness but with extra spice; it's warmth and caring but with a delectable, playful edge; it's one-on-one connection but with an added hormonal oomph. And it doesn't have to take much time. You know you've succeeded at hot intimacy when you and your partner giggle or have great big smiles. Hot intimacy is fun.

This chapter also discusses a special technique a man can use to heighten his sexual pleasure and release, and also reveals an unusual but effective technique couples can use to turn sex into real, hungry passion.

The Hot Intimacy Formula

Adam opened the door to his apartment to find his fiancée Amanda up to her neck in paperwork. She was behind schedule on an important project and her patience had run thin. She barely acknowledged him when he came over to her. "Rough day?" he asked, rubbing her shoulders. "The worst," she replied, still not looking at him. He massaged her neck for a while. Then he bent down and kissed her for an extra long moment. He paused, then kissed her again, this time even more tenderly; his tongue gently tracing the inside edge of her lips. "Not now," Amanda said. "I have too much work to do." He cradled her face in his hands. "I know you do. But I just wanted to tell you how much I love you and how happy I am that I have you in my life." He kissed her again, this time his mouth barely brushing against hers as his lips lingered there. She felt his warm breath mix with hers. He stroked her hair as he stood up and left to fix her a cup of tea. She watched him for a few moments before she rose, went over to him, and kissed him fiercely. "Thank you for that," she said. "I love you, too."

It had taken all of a minute but Adam's actions hit Amanda like Cupid's arrow. Later that night she forgot how tired she was and they made love as passionately as they ever had.

That's an example of hot intimacy. There are dozens of others, and many more will be listed here. What Adam did was not that difficult to do. It didn't require planning or creative thinking. It took what he already had in his possession—his love for Amanda and his willingness to focus on her needs while putting aside his ego. He took a routine moment, a happy-to-see-you kiss, and transformed it into hot intimacy. And he did it when Amanda wasn't even that receptive. You can achieve the same results in your life.

The formula is simple: Take a routine act that has "warmth" to it and add an extra dose of passion, love, or playfulness and voilà!—you have hot intimacy. The following list gives more suggestions on how to turn the ordinary into the extraordinary and warm into hot:

- Do something together that usually only one of you might do; add a loving word or act.

- Take the ordinary "I love you" and make it more special with a note or an intensely tender physical gesture.

> **CAUTION**
>
> **Close Calls** _____
>
> Hot intimate moments are not always supposed to be an immediate invitation to have sex. They might suggest sex and may inspire sex later on, but should not be done as a way to lead immediately to sex in all cases. Otherwise, your partner won't be receptive to any hot intimacy ideas if she isn't ready to make love.

- Slow down what might otherwise be a hurried, mutual activity and add more touching.

- Add to any encounter with a long, long look into the other's eyes. Let your eyes smile.

- Do something playfully sexual where it is least expected (but not embarrassing!).

- Do or say something sweet in public that you never did or said before.

- Do something silly or goofy during sex; something that will bring out a chuckle or a smile.

- Remind your partner about some special, heartfelt (or funny) moment you two shared. Give a hug and a squeeze as you talk about it.

- Create a quick, sensual/sexual ritual that only the two of you know about; perform it before you leave for work in the morning or whenever you might think it appropriate.

- If you walk side by side in public, hold hands; if you hold hands in public, put your arms around one another; then add a kiss or two or three or four …

Got the idea? Any act or interaction that has become routine and predictable deserves a thorough going over with hot intimacy in mind. Think about all your usual, mundane rituals: getting out of bed in the morning, fixing breakfast, showering and getting dressed, watching television, preparing a favorite food, and so on. Can you think of any way to tweak these moments so that you add a little zest and a little intimacy?

Temperature's Rising—Warm to Hot!

I've included 20 examples of how you can improve your ordinary interactions and make intimate moments go up in temperature from warm to hot. You might add your own twist to these ideas and hopefully will also create a number of your own.

- Warm: Getting routinely dressed or undressed in front of your partner.

  Hot: Put on a show, do a little striptease, or help your mate get undressed. Help him or her button or zip up, all the while finding ways to kiss various parts of his or her body.

- Warm: Catching a quick peek of your partner when he's stepping out of the shower.

Hot: Obviously, showering together is hot stuff but isn't always practical. How about taking showers right after the other? You step out as he steps in. Meet somewhere in the middle for a kiss, a cuddle, and a squeeze. Or step into the shower when your partner is almost finished with his. Do some quick soap rubs and whatever else tickles your fancy before he steps out.

Intimacy Boosters

Showering together is often logistically impossible for parents with kids who need attention or who are inquisitive. Not ready for back-to-back showers? Sneak in when the kids aren't looking, open up the curtain, and gaze admiringly at your partner. A grab, a kiss, a stroke, even just a wink can add lust and desire to what otherwise would be an ordinary time apart.

◆ Warm: Having a "quickie."

Hot: On a day where you have a lot of time together, have a quickie but *do not* reach orgasm (guys, that means you). Pull out just in time. Thirty minutes later, have another quickie. Once again, no orgasm. Wait 20 minutes, have another quickie and again don't reach a climax. (This can get fun especially if you have to hide from kids or family members who might be around.) By the fourth (or fifth or sixth …) time you'll be so hot for one another you won't be able to stand it. Go ahead, have your orgasm and try to recall the last time it felt that good.

◆ Warm: Giving a peck on the cheek when you arrive home for dinner.

Hot: Slowly back your partner up against a wall, raise his or her hands up, and hold them to the wall while you kiss as passionately as you can his or her lips, neck, chest, and so on. Then ask what's cooking.

◆ Warm: Having a little affection while putting groceries away.

Hot: Dip your finger in the softened half-gallon of ice cream and place it sensuously into your lover's mouth. Or place it somewhere on your lover's body and lick it off. No ice cream? Any finger food will do.

◆ Warm: Going for a walk and holding hands.

Hot: Get behind a tree or rock and have a one-minute tongue kiss and (if you think you won't be arrested) a minute of groping. No need to be an exhibitionist. Keep it between the two of you.

◆ Warm: Getting away for a romantic daytrip or weekend vacation.

Hot: Find an activity that revs up your adrenaline; something adventurous or spine tingling. A rollercoaster ride can do the trick or even a movie (an adventure movie or a chick flick works well). Ever try a balloon ride? Surges of adrenaline create an urgent sense of closeness, and activities that make you laugh riotously will bring you closer together. Don't forget a lot of holding and affection.

- Warm: Brushing her hair.

  Hot: Brush her hair, nibble on her ear, massage her temples. Get a soft, soft brush and gently use it on her back or legs. This is not sex time. Keep it sensual.

- Warm: Drawing a bath for your partner.

  Hot: Sit on the edge of the tub by his or her feet. Use some warmed up, perfumed oil and massage the feet slowly for the next 20 minutes.

- Warm: Rubbing your partner's aching back.

  Hot: Make it a 20-minute body rub that never gets sexual (although it might get close). Tantalize, tease, but don't make sex the endgame. Only got five minutes to spare? Fine, do the body rub for five. Too many family members around and need privacy? Lock a door. A few minutes is all you need to make it short and sweet.

Intimacy Boosters

It's a paradox: The more you make hot intimacy about closeness and sensuality (but not sex), the more likely your sex life will improve in leaps and bounds.

- Warm: Making a date for lovemaking.

  Hot: Choose a timeframe (a weekend, a week, two weeks) where you will try to set a record for the number of lovemaking sessions. The catch? You can't make love in the same place twice. Extra points for creative locations! If going all the way so often in a short time frame seems a bit much, select some other sensual or sexual act.

- Warm: Reading a sexy novel to stir your interests.

  Hot: Read passages from a sexy novel to your partner.

- Warm: Massaging his or her feet.

  Hot: Lie down together on opposite sides of the couch so that your partner's feet are in your lap. Each of you remove one of your partner's socks very slowly. Now massage each other's foot. Then remove the next sock and start on the other foot. (Do this naked and you will have a great view.)

◆ Warm: Writing a love note.

Hot: Make a sexy or romantic screensaver for your lover.

◆ Warm: Cuddling and affection during the course of an afternoon.

Hot: On a lazy day, neither of you wear any underwear. Sweatpants and tee shirts might be all you need. Do lots of grabbing and cuddling.

◆ Warm: Relaxing for an hour together after one or both of you comes home from work.

Hot: Meet each other at a nice bar, restaurant, beach, or park. If you're outdoors, bring a small snack or jug of wine.

◆ Warm: Having a nice dinner for two at a romantic restaurant.

Hot: Make it a progressive dinner at many restaurants. Have a drink in one place, an appetizer in another, and so on. Get a little touchy-feely at each place. Adventurous? Try to get a little more touchy-feely at each successive place. How much can you get away with without anyone noticing?

◆ Warm: Sharing a kiss as he or she gets out of the shower.

Hot: Have a large bath towel waiting that has been toasting in the dryer for 10 minutes. The heat from the towel will be exhilarating.

◆ Warm: Loving cuddling and stroking.

Hot: Have your partner lie down naked. Lightly scratch his or her body with your fingernails. Never get sexual. Keep it tantalizing and cover every square inch of his or her body. Your partner will have chills!

◆ Warm: Drinking a cup of cocoa on a wintry night.

Hot: Take the cocoa outdoors. Sit and watch the snowfall together. If the mood strikes, use your partner's inner thighs as a hand warmer.

Intimacy Boosters

As your lifestyle, interests, or habits change, so should your moments of hot intimacy. Always be on the lookout for new ways to add hot intimacy to warm moments. Variety helps keep what's hot from cooling off.

Remember what it was like when you first fell in love and couldn't keep your hands off of one another? The tips for hot intimacy will absolutely re-create those feelings. And if your relationship is new and already exhilarating, these tips will be a sure way to keep those fires burning.

Fireworks Without the Final Boom!

Manny and Gloria thought their sex life was fine. At times it was amazing. Most often it was fun and warm. But it was also repetitive.

"I can pretty much write the script from memory," Manny said. "First we kiss. No, wait. First, I usually grab hold of her bottom and pull her toward me. Then we kiss. Kissing doesn't go on for very long before it's a hand-fingers kind of deal. As soon as she touches me down there we're off and running. We may or may not have oral sex. Usually within 20 minutes at most it's all over. We enjoy it. But it does seem predictable."

"It's highly choreographed," Gloria chimed in. "Like synchronized swimming. After witnessing a hundred performances you know what comes next. It's nice, don't get me wrong. But maybe we could use some ideas on how to make it more interesting."

When people want new ideas on how to make love they think breadth, not depth. In other words, ideas that are new or different become the focus. But making the old and familiar work even better is another way of looking at it. Sometimes adding depth, not just breadth, to the same routine makes it a different routine. Besides, every new idea eventually becomes an old idea. There are only so many positions (unless you are a contortionist).

Exercise!

This is for men. Before a man ejaculates he has a sensation in his groin that tells him it won't be long before he explodes. It is a very pleasurable sensation that feels like an erotic tingle. If the man stops thrusting at that first moment of tingling, the ejaculation process will cease. He will remain erect and after a few seconds or so can resume lovemaking without automatically ejaculating. If he keeps thrusting after the erotic tingle starts, he soon reaches a moment of inevitability whereby even if he stops thrusting he will still ejaculate. As any man knows, stopping the act right when the moment of inevitability has happened leads to a rather blunted orgasm. However, a man can increase his physical pleasure by thrusting after the erotic tingle begins but ceasing before the moment of inevitability happens. This pattern can continue as often as he wishes. Also if he times it right, he can enjoy a more drawn-out erotic tingle and still stop thrusting before the ejaculation is inevitable. If he keeps halting the process in the manner I just described, his level of pleasure will rise. And when he does finally climax, it will feel several times more intense.

But there is one technique that I strongly urge couples to try now and then. At first glance it seems completely the opposite of what you think you should aim for— have sex but don't have an orgasm. Don't abandon this idea just yet. It can give you some of the greatest sensations you've experienced. And yes, eventually it does lead to orgasm but just not right away.

Imagine having an hour of lovemaking time but the rule is there can be no orgasm. That doesn't mean you can't do things that might lead to orgasm but it does mean you have to stop before it gets to that climax. If the No Orgasm rule applied, what would you do? You'd use your imagination. You'd also linger in places you might otherwise move quickly past. And you would tease your partner by stimulating him or her to *near* orgasm. You would just have to rely on your partner to stop you in time. This rule forces you to add both breadth (new ideas) and depth (improving the old methods).

Listen to Gloria again. "I don't always achieve a climax, so this exercise didn't bother me at all. In fact, it was wonderful. Manny had to rely on other facets of his "craft" to please me and he certainly did. Maybe the biggest change was the way he kissed me. We kissed for long stretches. His kisses were tender and sensual and it was as if time had stopped. I don't remember the last time we kissed in such a stimulating way. Ironically, he got me so excited that I knew I could have multiple orgasms if we went with it. But we followed the rule. The next morning we did it all over again but this time we broke the rule. When I finally came, it was breathtaking."

Just Ask!

The No Orgasm rule sounds great but I know that the man in my life won't want to go along with it. Any suggestions?

First, tell him that it's also an issue of fairness. If you are like most women, you achieve orgasm about 50 percent of the time, on average. That means you rely on other aspects of lovemaking to fulfill you. Extra time, tenderness, and imagination on his part can fill that gap. Or you can try a Delayed Orgasm rule. Tease one another to near orgasm a few times but make the process more drawn out. His orgasm will ultimately be more intense as will yours.

This is a good exercise for those times when a man is excited and raring to go and the woman is not (perhaps in the morning before you have to get up and go to work?). She might be reluctant to start any sexual activity because he will expect her to go all the way. But if the couple views those times as opportunities to have sex without orgasm, then she can give him a little playful something and he won't think she's disinterested. For example, a lot of manual or oral stimulation without orgasm may make the man feel like he's about to burst. But if it's followed with a promise to finish things up later (she can pick the day and time), it can turn a frustrating moment into an "exquisitely frustrating" one.

The idea behind the No Orgasm rule is simple: the journey is often more important than the final destination.

The Least You Need to Know

- There is a large expanse of tingly sensuality that takes little time and that many couples overlook.

- Hot intimacy is about playful, imaginative, and fun sensuality.

- Make hot intimacy about sex one-quarter of the time and about sensuality and connection the rest of the time. Ironically, it will lead to more sex in the future!

- Delaying orgasm or having sex without orgasm on occasion can actually increase your pleasure of sex.

Chapter 18

Overcoming Obstacles to Sexual Intimacy

In This Chapter

- Knowing what's normal when it comes to sexual satisfaction
- Overcoming personal and relationship roadblocks to sexual intimacy
- Learning how to communicate your sex needs
- Knowing what to do when one of you doesn't initiate sex as often as the other

Physical intimacy can carry a great deal of emotional power. So when it isn't working right, one's emotions can get out of whack. You don't think that sex can pack an emotional wallop? Wait until it's withdrawn from you and then tell me how you feel.

There are many ways that sexual intimacy can take a nosedive and thereby affect how you feel about yourself. If it's been a long time since you've had a regular, physical connection with someone, your body becomes something you try to ignore or not feel. You might go through your days trying to relate to others as a person without physical needs for closeness. Or you do the opposite. You seek greater physical connections with people, but in ways that might sometimes be inappropriate. When your physical needs are not getting met, your judgment of yourself and others can get distorted.

Sexual intimacy can grow flat in any relationship even when the couple reports they are pretty happy. Humdrum happens. But if your relationship is a committed one, you can't let humdrum become routine. This chapter will help you identify some of the common obstacles to sexual intimacy and show you steps to overcome them.

What's Normal?

Although the range of sexual activities is quite wide, most adult experiences are fairly commonplace when it comes to sex. In other words, if you and your neighbors are physically healthy, your neighbors are probably having sexual experiences pretty similar to yours. They are also having similar frustrations.

In a major study of 100 educated, married couples (average age was 33) who reported having a satisfying relationship, about one in five wives and one in three husbands were dissatisfied with their sexual relationship. Forty percent of the men reported having occasional erectile problems. Half of the men and three-quarters of the women reported occasional disinterest in sex. Over half of the couples had sex about once a week. One-third had sex less than that, and about 10 percent had sex once a month. All of this is normal. (However, so is getting sick, but most of us prefer to avoid illness whenever possible.)

CAUTION

Close Calls

If you must always be right and if you tend to judge others easily, intimacy of any kind is not really possible. Intimacy comes to you when others trust you. It is difficult to relax, trust, and be vulnerable with anyone who is judgmental. Others might have sex with you but they will never feel safe.

The good news about that study is that you're not alone if you aren't completely satisfied with your sex life, and it doesn't mean you can't have a happy relationship if your sex life is a bit sub-par. The bad news is that a relationship that is satisfying might be comfortable but not necessarily strong. Comfortable can sometimes lead to complacency. Complacency can lead to wandering eyes, the "I love you but I'm not in love with you" sentiment, and feelings of low self-worth, irritability, and depression.

The bottom line is this: Aim for above-average physical intimacy. Intimacy, in all its forms, is too important to take for granted.

Common Roadblocks to Physical Intimacy

If your car was just not running right and you worried that one day it might fail altogether, you'd probably take it to a mechanic and get it fixed. But when people's sexual engines don't have the same old zip that they used to, there is a tendency to ignore it, pretend it's nothing serious, and hope the problem goes away. And because sexual energy has an ebb and flow (it comes in waves), people eventually notice that the old horny feeling eventually comes back like the swallows to Capistrano.

But sometimes desire remains flat. Or maybe your desire is just fine but other distractions keep your levels of physical intimacy from soaring. Don't take an "I'll get around to it" attitude. Physical intimacy is a living, breathing spirit. If you ignore it, mistreat it, or don't give it room to fully live, it might disappear in you or in your relationship.

The most common obstacles to physical intimacy fall into two categories: inner obstacles and relationship obstacles. Let's examine both.

Inner Obstacles

Inner obstacles to physical intimacy have to do with your past experiences and your current view of yourself.

- A dislike or self-consciousness about aspects of your body

- Performance concerns

- History of trauma or sexual shame

- Low desire

Almost half of all American adults are displeased with their weight and therefore their appearance. People who are older and divorced or widowed are even more likely to be uneasy about the idea of sharing their (older) body with a new person. They fear being viewed as unattractive. Some of these anxieties can be alleviated somewhat if the person is able to lose weight or modify their appearance in some way. But much of what needs modifying is in the head. Attitudes that downgrade oneself will lead to avoidance of sexual intimacy. And avoidance usually perpetuates the underlying belief that there is a good reason to keep avoiding ("I'm unattractive … No one will like what I look like …").

How you feel about your body (the judgments you make about it) are often changing. For example, Kathy weighed 280 pounds and had no desire to be sexual with her husband. When she lost 50 pounds, her sexual desire skyrocketed. She weighed 230 pounds—a weight that would have made her feel unattractive years earlier, but now she feels attractive. It's all about how you look at it.

The key to overcoming self-consciousness about your body is to get physical anyway (affection-only can be fine) with someone you trust. You have to face your fear to overcome it. Worrying about it and hoping it goes away with some form of intellectual pep-talk might work but probably not for long. The more physical you are, the more you will realize that many of your concerns do not really matter to the person you're with.

It's also crucially important to accept your body. Acceptance doesn't mean you like it. It means you will no longer emotionally oppose the reality of what is. "I accept the way my body looks even though I wish I was more attractive" is a healthier attitude than either condemning your appearance or trying to convince yourself you look ravishing when you don't believe that is true.

> ### Intimacy Boosters
>
> Much of your comfort with yourself, your partner, and your sexuality lies in acceptance. Accept yourself and your partner as you might a young, insecure child who just wants to be loved.

People with performance concerns (usually a man who worries about his ability to get or maintain an erection) also avoid physical intimacy to avoid embarrassment. However, no matter what the underlying fear is (such as a fear of heights, flying, or physical intimacy), avoidance always causes the problem to intensify. When the problem is worse, you'll be even more likely to avoid it, thereby making the situation doubly worse. By consulting a physician or a qualified therapist, a man with performance issues can get help for his situation.

People who have been sexually abused might have sexual intimacy issues as an adult. They might also have issues with trust. If their partner is more highly sexed, it might be interpreted as the partner being forceful, demanding, and abusive. A qualified therapist can help. EMDR (Eye Movement Desensitization and Reprocessing) is a wonderful and highly effective technique.

Low sexual desire can have many causes, not the least of which is ordinary fatigue and letdowns in life (loss of a job, for example). A physician should be consulted because hormones might also be playing a role. Unfortunately, people with low desire avoid sex, which adds to their self-consciousness about it. For many people, desire doesn't come first but it comes about after the sex act has begun. Cuddling, closeness, petting, and warm hearts can often jumpstart low desire into high desire. You have to be willing to act sexual at times when you don't feel like it.

Exercise!

When performance anxiety is the problem, this strategy helps:

The man and his partner must commit to at least five to ten physical encounters that last about an hour each. The goal is not to have intercourse or to get aroused. In fact, if the man gets aroused, he is not to try to have intercourse or reach a climax. Instead, the couple must work in stages over the course of many encounters.

1. In the first stage, the couple might hold and caress one another and not even be naked. The idea is to get comfortable being physical with no pressure to perform.
2. In the next encounter, the couple might be in some state of undress and caressing and petting is allowed, but no breast or genital contact. The couple advances to stage three when they both feel at ease during this stage.
3. In this stage there is genital contact but no effort to make each other aroused.
4. In stage four there is genital contact with brief efforts to get the other aroused.
5. Finally, all the stages lead to this one with arousal and climax.

This is helpful because the man learns to accept not being aroused while in a sexual situation because the goal of the early stages is to not get aroused. After he feels at ease with that, his anxiety lowers and his ability to get an erection is not interfered with.

Relationship Obstacles

Physical intimacy problems almost always contain some psychological element. Anger, anxiety, and shame are the three big emotions that can knock sexual intimacy flat. It's always a good idea to evaluate the relationship when physical intimacy is not up to snuff. Common psychological obstacles to physical intimacy include …

- Feeling disconnected or uncared for by your mate
- Neglecting daily hygiene
- Having a sloppy or insensitive approach to sex
- Feeling controlled by a partner

Sexual desire usually shrinks when you're not feeling particularly loved by your mate. Although many men might seek sexual closeness as a way to improve the overall connection, those same men may shut down sexually when they feel routinely neglected, disrespected, or unloved. Then it becomes a vicious circle: the more you pull away from your mate the angrier he or she gets, which makes you pull away even more. Your best bet is for each of you to focus on your role in the perpetuation of this problem. Are you willing to show less anger and more warmth? Are you willing to show more affection even when you have reason to hold back?

Hygiene concerns are more common than you might think. Many people start getting sexual without a thought to having showered or brushed their teeth or freshened their breath. Are the sheets clean and fresh? Do you need a shave? Many people have told me over the years how their partner's teeth have yellowed or gone bad and it was a complete turn-off. When sex has been sluggish, make sure you've taken that extra step to be clean and well groomed.

Any physical approach that routinely conveys the attitude "I want sex" and not "I want you" will also be a turn-off. When affection is almost always about sex, a partner can feel used. People want to feel desired for who they are, not just for the sex they can provide. Tender, nonsexual affection shows that.

Finally, if you think that your partner is too controlling in the relationship, your physical desires will almost always go up in smoke. If a relationship is unbalanced because one person is controlling, the other person will consciously or subconsciously try to correct that imbalance. One way to do that is to control the physical relationship and say no to sex and affection. Aim for fairness in the relationship. It will pay dividends in the sexual intimacy department.

Having Sex: What Men and Women Must Try to Do

Are you irritated, even a little bit, about your sex life? Do you think your sexual relationship is fair? Do you get back the kind of satisfaction that you try to give? The more unfair you think it is, the more you will either withdraw from sexual encounters or you will get in a tug of war about them—making complaints and demands and feeling entitled to have things go your way. Take the following quiz to find out where you stand.

1. Sex tends to go more hurriedly than I'd like.   T___ F___

2. I wouldn't mind having more quickies.   T___ F___

3. There is an over-emphasis on genital stimulation when we have sex and not enough caressing.   T____ F____

4. I'm more highly sexed than my partner.   T____ F____

5. I prefer more tenderness and petting during sex.   T____ F____

6. If I had to choose between a romantic encounter and a sexual one, I'd choose sex.   T____ F____

7. Nobody's perfect, but I satisfy my partner just about 100 percent of the time.   T____ F____

8. By now I'm convinced I know what turns my partner on sexually.   T____ F____

9. We can easily talk about our sexual relationship and needs.   T____ F____

10. There are some sexual things I wish my partner did more often.   T____ F____

If you answered True to numbers one, three, and five, you want a more romantic edge to your sex life. Probably, you are a woman (or man with a greater capacity for tenderness and romance). If you answered True to numbers two, four, and six, you like your sex to be focused more on the physical/genital aspects than on the emotional.

Numbers seven through ten address your ability to communicate about sexual needs to your mate. If you answered True to numbers seven and eight, don't be surprised if your partner disagrees with you. You might be fantastic in bed but the chances are still good you haven't figured it all out yet. That is especially true if you answered False to number nine. If you can't easily talk about your sexual desires and preferences, you're probably missing something. That goes double if you answered True to number 10. If you want something more, sexually speaking, the odds are you're not asking for it. Of course, it might be something your partner finds completely displeasing, in which case you'll probably have to learn to live without it.

Just Ask!

If my boyfriend wants me to do something sexually that I find offensive, must I try anyway? He says I should. But I want him to be more romantic and he says he's just not that kind of person.

He's operating under a double standard: you change for him but he won't change for you. Not a good sign. Consider getting out of this relationship. By the way, it is not that hard to learn to be more romantic. But it is very difficult to learn to enjoy certain sexual activities that you find distasteful. You're better off finding a guy who is more in sync with you sexually.

Typically, men want their sex a little quicker and with less foreplay than women. Men enjoy quickies for that reason. After a man is erect he often assumes his partner is just as aroused and interested in climaxing as he is—or that she will be very shortly.

The key is that each partner must be willing to have sex the way the other person wants it. Otherwise it will be either a tug of war or one person will be routinely dissatisfied. And when you have sex your partner's way, do your best to enjoy it and not see it as an annoyance. That means you guys out there need to show more romance. Hold her and kiss her tenderly without making it a sexual grab. Help her out with things she is busy with. And be willing to have longer lovemaking sessions so she has plenty of time to warm up to you sexually. And you ladies out there should try to enjoy sex even when it's quicker. Make it playful even if you can't make it as deeply passionate as you would like. Let him know that you enjoy pleasing him in ways that he really likes.

Intimacy Boosters

Make a distinction between physical foreplay and emotional foreplay. Emotional foreplay (tender, thoughtful words and gestures, warmth, giving compliments, nonsexual affection, and so forth) is as arousing to many people, especially women, as sexual foreplay is.

Talking About Your Sexual Needs

If talking about sex makes you uneasy, keep in mind that for a few minutes of clear talk, you can reap sexual rewards for years to come. Chances are you won't find the conversation as bad as you might think. Here are some key ideas to keep in mind:

◆ Never make harsh criticisms about sex. Emphasize what you want to have happen, not what you don't like.

◆ Never, ever use broad, negative judgments such as "You're frigid … You're a sex maniac … You're perverted …".

◆ Don't bring up the topic of sex at inopportune moments.

◆ Think of three things you'd like to see happen during sex. Choose one of them. In the middle of being sexual just blurt it out. "I want you to _____." The less you say and the more urgently you say it, the more likely it will happen with little discussion.

◆ If you're uncomfortable discussing your sexual turn-ons, say so. You'll feel better and your mate might cut you some slack and be open to what you want to say.

- Odds are high that if you have turn-ons you haven't talked about before, so does your partner. Don't be surprised if opening up causes him or her to open up, too.

- If your mate goes along with your wishes, give immediate positive feedback. ("That was fantastic!") If it didn't go the way you wanted, talk about what went well and what you'd still like to see happen.

Talking gets easier if you each foster goodwill.

Let Your Fingers Do the Talking

If you can't speak up during sex, let your fingers do the talking for you. Felicia loved receiving oral sex but always thought that Ned spent a lot less time on it than she wanted. So when he was about to come up for air and try some other position, she gently guided his head back to where she wanted it. When he finished she once again applied a little pressure to his head and he got the message. Actually, he was delighted to do it for her because all he wanted was to please her. He never knew it meant that much.

> **CAUTION**
>
> **Close Calls**
>
> When you communicate about sex, be nice. But don't be nice at the expense of being real. Be real and be nice. If you're not nice you will push others away. If you're not real, you are pushing yourself away.

Don't be afraid to take your partner's hand during sex and place it wherever you want it to go.

Who Initiates Sex?

It is ideal when sex is initiated by each partner an equivalent amount of time. If you always initiate it, you wonder if your partner really is interested. If you are always on the receiving end, you might feel pressured and guilty about having to say no.

When a couple's desire for sex is very mismatched and one is highly sexed and the other isn't, it can get confusing as to what constitutes "initiating" sex. A person with a high-sex drive will interpret sexual playfulness (maybe she flashes him or grabs his bottom) as a clear desire for having sex when maybe she's just being playful. On the other hand, if your libido is sluggish, you might pull away from even small shows of affection for fear it might lead to something more.

It's essential that couples check out each other's code. Someone who enjoys sensual teasing or playfulness doesn't always want it to lead to sex. Is a passionate kiss a come-on? Is groping of any kind always an indication that sex is a must? Without a clear understanding, it's easy to misinterpret and get frustrated.

It's helpful for the highly sexually charged partner to cut back on sexual affection and simply show warmth without it becoming genitally focused. The partner will feel more understood, accepted, and less pressured and will be more open to initiating sex.

The Least You Need to Know

- About one-third of satisfied couples still wish their sex life could be improved.

- Avoiding your sexual concerns usually makes the problems worse.

- Talking about your sexual needs is easier than you think and pays rich rewards.

- Men should occasionally try to have sex the way many women want it (more romantic, more drawn out, more emotional), and women should occasionally do it the way a many men want it (quicker, more genitally focused, less emotional).

- If your sex drive is higher than your partner's, show more tender nonsexual affection; if your sex drive is lower, don't withdraw from playful, sexual affection.

Chapter 19

Affection and Intimacy

In This Chapter

- ◆ The signs that affection is dangerously low in your life
- ◆ The things men and women can learn from one another about affection
- ◆ The three components of real affection
- ◆ The do's and don'ts of sexual affection

This chapter is not about sex at all and yet, indirectly, it's got a lot to do with sex. It's about affection and caring and how they affect overall intimacy. When you're talking about friendships—affection and caring can be an important part of the relationship. However, if you're in a romantic relationship, then affection and caring is the cornerstone of a profound sex life. You can have exciting sex with someone you don't care about, but you won't have one drop of warm affection. Without warm affection, sex might be fun and interesting but it won't even be close to profound.

Given the choice, women often prefer hugging and holding to having sex. Why? Most women know that they can have sex if they really want it. But they can't always receive genuine affection when they want it. Also, women can more readily feel very close and connected to a partner without it having to turn into something sexual. It's a gift, really, to be able to connect so well with others.

Are We Friends Yet?

Do you show physical affection to your friends? If you're a female, you absolutely do. If you're a male, it is probably more subdued. Affection for men is less about being physical with each other than about doing things together as buddies. Men often good naturedly tease one another as a way to express their friendship.

> **Just Ask!**
>
> I often enjoy the company of my girlfriends more than my boyfriend, even though I love him. And he seems to have fun with his buddies in ways he doesn't with me. Is this a problem?
>
> Not necessarily. It's hard for one person to provide everything you need. How do you act differently with your friends than your boyfriend? Can you be more that way when you're with him? If so, you might start enjoying his company even more than you already do.

If a level of "affectionate friendship" is below par in a relationship, you will notice several of the following signs:

- Crankiness and irritability
- More complaining
- Sadness or boredom
- Disinterest in things that used to be enjoyable, including sex
- Frequent sighing
- More emotional distance
- Clinginess or neediness
- Over-involvement with work or childcare

These signs are also indications of clinical depression. This comes as no surprise because depression is often closely linked to the quality of one's relationships.

What Men Can Learn from Women

Each sex has a lot to learn about what the other feels comfortable with when it comes to showing affection. Guys, imagine the woman in your life is out with her girl-friends. She's having a wonderful time. What's she actually doing? Well, when she first meets up with her friends, they probably hug and kiss each other on the cheek. There is a lot of immediate conversation about how good everyone looks. In other words, women know how to give compliments and pay attention to details that matter to them. There is instantaneous smiling, chuckling, and maybe even laughter. If they go out for dinner or a drink the conversation is lively, entertaining, and very personal. They will talk about what's making them happy and what's making them feel insecure. Expressing their self-doubts is easy because it's met with understanding and support. There might be occasional touching of one another as the conversation gets animated. Physical contact is both instinctive and warm. When the evening is over, the women go home charged up, having had a great evening out.

But what do they come home to?

If there is a man waiting, he is likely to give her a quick kiss, if that. He might be busy with some project, or watching TV. If he took care of the kids for the evening, he might even be a bit disgruntled, depending on how the evening went. Even if he shows warmth and tenderness, there is likely to be a great disparity between what the woman received when she was out with her friends compared to what she's receiving from her man.

I'm not saying that men need to be more like women when it comes to attentiveness and affection. But men can learn a lot about what enlivens a woman's heart by paying attention to how she interacts with her female friends. Sprinkling a little of that same kind of attention on her now and then can go a long way toward achieving greater intimacy.

What Women Can Learn from Men

Ladies, imagine the man in your life is out having a great time with his buddies. What's he actually doing? Unless he's out for a quick beer after work, he's probably participating in some athletic event, watching a game on TV, or even helping a friend with some repairs. Whatever his interests are—even if they are

Intimacy Boosters

A word to the wise: Most men enjoy the company of their male friends because they don't feel judged even when they disagree. Men tend to be far more accepting of one another.

more solitary such as songwriting or gardening—he's likely to engage in them with friends from time to time.

Conversations among male friends aren't likely to get too personal. If they do, men aren't likely to discuss their flaws or insecurities. Men are more likely to talk about the "facts" of their lives and to tone down any references to how they feel about those facts. If a man does discuss a personal problem or asks for advice, the conversation is not likely to go on for long before the subject gets changed. But rather than feeling dismissed or uncared about, a man is likely to come away feeling better. Why? Because his friends, either directly or indirectly, give him the message: "You'll get through it. You'll figure things out." Male friends tend to give one another votes of confidence without getting too caught up in each other's problems.

Close Calls

Ladies, beware! Although male friends often display deep affection for one another by poking fun at one another—don't you do it. Good natured insults and verbal jabs that come from a woman to a man are not likely to be well received. He might chuckle along with you, but inside he won't like it.

Physical affection? A handshake and pats on the back tend to be the extent of any physical contact. A man might "feel" a lot of affection for another male friend, but he's not likely to display it physically.

What can women learn from this? Realize that when a man downplays his physical affection for you, it doesn't necessarily mean he doesn't care. He's just operating from his default drive and isn't mindful of what your needs are at that moment. You can ask for more attention and affection, and men are well advised to do more of it, but don't make him "wrong" for not showing enough affection.

How to ACT with Affection

First of all, affection involves a physical component. Perhaps that goes without saying but some people will claim that they feel affection for someone but rarely show it physically. Fondness is not affection. You can be fond of someone and hardly touch them. But if you feel affection, it must be shown by touch.

How much touch? There is no hard-and-fast rule. However, if for the most part your experience of affection is limited to sexual touch only, that's a very limited display of affection. Also if all you get is a perfunctory kiss or squeeze at the beginning and end of the day, there is no affection to speak of in your relationship. As a rule of thumb, the absolute minimum amount of affection in your relationship should be about eight times a day, with each of you initiating affection four times. That doesn't count sexual affection or lovemaking.

But genuine, intimacy-building affection goes beyond physical touch. It's really an attitude—a mind set. It involves three major components that form the mnemonic ACT:

♦ Attentiveness

♦ Caring

♦ Tenderness

By demonstrating these three qualities while adding physical touch, the quality of affection in your life will be strong. Let's look at each of these qualities more closely.

Intimacy Boosters

At least a few times a day, you and your partner should show physical affection that lasts 2 to 3 minutes or more. Cuddle on the sofa, give a foot or back rub, hold hands, or play footsy. The idea is not to limit affection to quick pecks on the cheek or lips. Take your time.

Attentiveness

This is an easy one to miss because most people think they do pay attention to the people in their lives, certainly the people they love. But if your eyes are glued to the TV for a half-hour television program, you've probably paid more attention to the TV show that day than you did to your partner. Waiting for your mate to pass the ketchup is not attentiveness. Neither is carrying on a conversation while doing some other activity at the same time.

When people feel that their partners are really paying attention to them, this is what they experience:

♦ Being valued for their opinion

♦ Being asked, sincerely, how they are doing

♦ Having them notice subtle emotions and moods and inquiring about them

♦ Being appreciated for the small sacrifices they make as well as the large ones

Exercise!

Take an hour or two and act as if your partner is a celebrity who you are totally enthralled with. Pretend that you are his or her personal assistant. Give your partner complete attention. What small things can you do that will make his or her day go easier? What can you anticipate your partner wanting or needing? The purpose of this exercise is to highlight just how inattentive you actually are, so you can work on being more attentive.

- Being listened to without criticism or judgment
- Having them aware of the small things they might want or need (such as a refill of coffee, a new jacket, help with some chore, and so on).

When you improve attentiveness, you are making the other person the centerpiece of your life. That person becomes number one.

Caring

Caring goes one step beyond attentiveness and involves actually doing something for the other person—going out of your way for that person. Attentiveness is recognition of some need while caring is tending to that need with a wish to be helpful or to demonstrate consideration.

If you are in a new relationship, being attentive and caring comes naturally. But if your relationship has settled into a rhythm, you might show less caring because you believe that your partner already knows you care. It can be eye opening to ask one another to make a list of at least 10 things that could be done that would demonstrate caring. Your list should contain the following:

- Things that would make your day go easier ("Please watch the kids while I take a long bath") or make you feel more special ("Write me a love note").
- The list should be very specific and easy to understand. Don't list things that are vague such as "Show me respect."

Exchange lists and try to do at least one thing from your partner's list every day, in addition to the usual ways you show caring. Be sure to modify your list regularly.

When you show caring toward someone by doing something thoughtful, you can actually feel more affection for that person. Fondness and affection doesn't just make you want to do caring things; doing caring things improves fondness and affection.

Tenderness

Tenderness involves warmth. It's a softening of the hard edges. A peck on the lips might be nice but not necessarily tender. A tender gesture has an added kindness to it, an extra spice of gentleness.

Someone who shows some form of physical affection but quickly follows it up with a harsh tone of voice or insensitive remark is not demonstrating tenderness. Tenderness reveals an underlying attitude that one's partner is precious and cherished. People who by nature tend to be abrupt, dismissive, or gruff in their tones don't make their dates or mates feel cherished. They might mean well, but might be unaware of how their tone is a turn-off. They need to make a very conscious effort to change their approach; otherwise there will be far less warmth in their life.

Sexual Affection: Do's and Don'ts

Sexual affection can be enjoyable and playful, a sign of real connectedness. But it's too often the primary way for some people, men especially, to show affection. When non-sexual affection is infrequent, sexual affection loses its power to connect a couple. The woman, typically, begins to feel more beleaguered than beloved, more a piece of meat than a mate. What she wants is tender, frequent, nonsexual affection to reassure her that her man truly loves her and is devoted to her.

A common, troublesome dynamic occurs when women, who are shown very little affection (unless it's of a sexual nature), start to feel unappreciated and used. They back away from not only affection but from sex. The man, feeling somewhat rejected, pushes for more sex with what he'd call sexual affection and what she would call "pawing" her. She resents it and backs away. Over time, he is less likely to show sincere, nonsexual affection and needs to have sex to feel reassured that she cares for him. It becomes a Catch-22 where neither party wins.

A good rule of thumb is that couples should show two to three times more nonsexual affection than sexual. Nonsexual affection is a sure-fire way to let your partner know that your depth of feelings go beyond obtaining sexual relief only.

Close Calls

People who have had several relationship failures are more likely to engage prematurely in sex or sexual affection (heavy petting) as a way to invite closeness and prevent another relationship failure. It can be a fatal mistake and one that leads to more rejection. Sexual affection should not come too soon in a new relationship.

Intimacy Boosters

Guys—are you not getting enough sex? For one month, dramatically increase the amount of *nonsexual* affection you provide (a hug or two here and there won't do) and decrease the amount of sexual affection. Then see what happens. She needs to know you care more about her than about sex.

Sexual Affection While Dating

After the sex in a relationship starts, it's hard to shut it down, unless the relationship itself ends. When a new relationship quickly develops into showing sexual affection and having sex, there is an increased chance it won't last.

Develop emotional intimacy first. Get to know one another's dreams, passions, and interests. Be friends. It's essential that there be physical affection as your relationship develops. After sexual intimacy begins, don't tolerate a reduction in nonsexual affection. Whatever you tolerate now will be so ingrained months or years from now that it will be harder to change. Research shows that when women put up with things that they didn't care for early on in a relationship, they were less happy later on than those that didn't put up with things.

Sexual Affection Within an Established Relationship

Sexual affection is a must. It makes you feel young no matter how old you are and it conveys the message "I think you're HOT!" Everyone needs to know they are attractive to their mates.

Sexual affection must be balanced with a great deal of nonsexual affection and other ways to show caring. It is not a good idea for a woman to withhold sex as a way to teach their mates to show more affection or caring. If a man is rejected sexually, he will doubt that he is loved and will pursue more sex to reassure himself that things aren't that bad. But a man needs to understand that if a woman doesn't feel cherished, she will naturally be less interested in having sex.

The Least You Need to Know

- Diminished affection can lead to depression.

- Fully feeling another's affection for you requires that they touch you.

- Double or triple the amount of nonsexual affection you show your partner.

- Sexual affection is a must in any quality relationship, but you must balance it with frequent shows of tender, nonsexual affection.

20

Leftovers at the Sex and Intimacy Buffet

In This Chapter

- ◆ How to identify the seven myths about sex and sexuality
- ◆ How to discuss your sexual history
- ◆ How to lovingly turn down sex
- ◆ How to deal when you dislike aspects of your partner's appearance

There is no such thing as sexual intimacy if you lack emotional intimacy with your partner. Sex, just for sex, with someone you have no real feelings for is hardly intimate. Anyone can go through the motions. That's why a sexual connection very early in a relationship can actually inhibit future romance and caring. Emotional intimacy is what makes sexual intimacy intimate. Emotional intimacy is the foundation of genuine sexual intimacy. The reverse isn't always true. When sexual intimacy comes first, emotional intimacy might never happen.

But after sexual intimacy begins, a whole new world of adventure opens up. And it's not just sexual adventure but emotional adventure, too. After sexual and emotional intimacy combine, your relationship is set on fire. You develop more specific wants, needs, and expectations of your partner. You're no longer casual friends. You're no longer just close friends. You're also lovers.

This chapter deals with a number of thorny issues and concerns that can crop up after sex becomes intimate sex. The goal is to help you sort through the issues so intimacy will be deeper and more profound in the relationships that really matter.

Seven Sexual Myths

Sexual intimacy that is cruising along can go into a skid when one or both partners believe certain things about sexuality that simply aren't true. Misinformation is a common cause of sexual problems. Here are some of the most common myths:

Myth: Frequent sexual fantasies are a form of unfaithfulness. *In fact, 95 percent of the adult population have daily sexual fantasies. People with the healthiest and most satisfying sex lives also fantasize the most. Still, about a third of people feel guilty about their sexual fantasies.*

Myth: Sex must always be great. *Fatigue, stress, and health problems interfere with sexual performance from time to time. Sex isn't always eye popping, particularly with an established partner. But it can be warm, intimate, and generally satisfying.*

Myth: It's a problem if a man loses his erection during sexual play. *Losing an erection, or partially losing it, isn't necessarily a sign of any problem. It can be a sign of relaxed comfort. If the sexual activity goes on a long time, a man might lose some of his erection, especially if some of the pleasures are not genitally focused. Women can lose their arousal, too. It simply is far less obvious.*

Myth: You shouldn't go along with sex halfheartedly. *You shouldn't be pressured into having sex. But if you're only somewhat in the mood, you might find that a little halfhearted sex is still good. Couples in established relationships often go along with sex when they don't feel like it, mostly to please their partner.*

Myth: Never be selfish when having sex. *Actually, to fully appreciate some of your sexual sensations, you must concentrate only on yourself once in a while. That's not self-ishness, that's necessity. Now and then, let your partner completely take over while you luxuriate in sexual ecstasy. Let your partner know what you want.*

Myth: Disinterest in sex is abnormal. *Chronic disinterest is abnormal. Occasional disinterest is common. Fatigue and stress play a big role, as does feeling disconnected from one's partner.*

Myth: Sexual experimentation is deviant. *Actually, at least half of all couples experiment with some new or different approach once in awhile. They are also more satisfied sexually than couples who don't experiment. However, one should never pressure a partner into doing something that he or she finds immoral or distasteful.*

It's difficult to be intimate when you're anxious or preoccupied. Intimacy involves openness and vulnerability, both of which are closed to some extent when you believe the wrong things about sex and sexuality.

The Book of Revelation: Discussing Your Sexual History

Jayne and Eric had been dating for two months. Jayne knew that the relationship was very close to becoming sexual. She had once been treated for a sexually transmitted disease and was horrified at the thought of mentioning it. But she did want to know if Eric had been treated, as well. She couldn't imagine how to start that conversation. Hardly the stuff of romance.

Guidelines to follow when you want to talk about sexual history:

1. Don't wait until you are in the midst of a passionate encounter before you bring up the topic. Your hormones will probably overrule your head.

2. Try to discuss the topic when your relationship is getting close to becoming sexual.

3. Don't bring up sexual histories within the first few dates. That's too presumptive.

4. Ask "What's the most number of people you've had sex with in any given year?" The higher the number, the greater the risk. A man with two to four lifetime partners has about a 3 percent chance of contracting an STD while a woman has a 5 percent chance. (Women are at higher risk because it is easier to be infected by a man than by a woman.) Someone with 20 or more lifetime partners has about a 30 percent chance of contracting an STD.

 Close Calls

Don't kid yourself. One in six Americans have had an STD at some point in their lives. STDs can happen to anyone. Raising the topic is no guarantee you'll be told the truth, but it's not as risky as not discussing it at all.

5. Be direct, be kind, be clear, be assertive. "I'm concerned about the risk of disease. Would you be willing to have a blood test? … I think it's important that we discuss our sexual histories before our relationship goes any further, do you agree?"

6. Use condoms until you know for sure.

> **" "   Just Ask!** _____
>
> *I'm being treated for genital herpes. When should I tell my girlfriend about it?*
>
> You have no obligation to say anything in the earliest part of your relationship when you are still getting to know one another and the chance of breaking up is still high. However, you do have an obligation if the relationship becomes sexual. Otherwise, wait until you've been dating exclusively (but before you become sexual).

Although you might be embarrassed by aspects of your sexual history, it's very likely that your partner has a similar history or has friends with a similar history. Honesty is important. Infecting a partner who had no idea there was a risk is an injustice and can kill your relationship.

How to Turn Down Sex Without Turning Off Your Mate

Millie was lying in bed, unmoving, eyes closed, showing disinterest in sex while at the same time trying not to hurt Shawn's feelings. He was caressing her in a way that clearly indicated he was interested in making love. "Should I just tell him no?" she thought to herself. After a few more minutes of uncertainty, Shawn finally rolled over and went to sleep. Now Millie felt guilty. Did she handle it the right way?

It isn't always a sure thing that your partner will accurately read your nonverbal message when you're not interested in sex. For one thing, people usually agree to having sex by using nonverbal communication. So the nonverbal message "Not now" might not be obvious. Also, if you're trying to be kind and not hurt feelings, your message might be ambiguous at best. Furthermore, there are many times a disinterested partner becomes interested with coaxing. Your partner might hear your nonverbal "Not now" but continues to push anyway because he hopes you'll change your mind.

> **CAUTION   Close Calls** _____
>
> Fatigue is the number one reason for turning down sex. Don't automatically take it personally if your partner isn't in the mood.

Ultimately, it's helpful to be able to speak your mind when you don't want sex. It can save a lot of aggravation. If your partner is generally thoughtful and kind, he or she will understand when you don't feel like making love.

How Best to Say It

If all is well in your relationship, you can probably get by with being physically non-responsive when you don't want sex and your mate will get the message without taking it personally. However, if the two of you have been disconnected lately or are overworked or overtired, a nonverbal message might be misinterpreted as being harsher than you intend. Open and direct is best. Ways to get your point across lovingly include the following:

- ◆ "I love you so much but I'm just not in the mood right now. I promise I'll make it up to you!"

- ◆ "Would you mind if we just cuddled this time?"

- ◆ "I know it has been awhile since we made love but now isn't the best time for me. Can we set a date?"

- ◆ "I fantasize a lot about us making love. But right now I have too much on my mind. Please understand."

The idea is to say something kind or perhaps offer an alternative. A kiss and a hug can make for a gentler turndown.

How Best to Not Say It

Anything harsh or unkind is a no-no. Remember, a partner wanting sex probably wants an emotional connection, too. Find a way to connect emotionally even if you won't connect sexually. The following statements should be tossed out of your repertoire:

- ◆ "Is sex all you ever think about?" (If you've said no to sex a lot lately, then sex probably is on your partner's mind. No need to be harsh.)

- ◆ "Can't you see I'm exhausted?" (Maybe not. Besides, you've probably had sex before when you were exhausted.)

- ◆ "Alright, alright, but let's make it quick."

- ◆ You say nothing but flinch roughly when you are touched.

Sexual intimacy is usually the kind of intimacy not shared with anyone else but your partner. Harsh turndowns can ruin that special connection.

What to Do When You Dislike Your Partner's Appearance

Physical intimacy can get derailed if something about your partner's appearance turns you off. Talking about it is very tricky. But saying nothing can make the problem worse if your opinion remains the same and you simply pull away from your partner more.

There are two things to consider when this issue arises. First, is your overall relationship quality high? Would you consider yourselves very happy together? If so, the two of you can probably withstand hearing unflattering comments. Second, is the physical feature you don't like something that is easily changed? Hair color, small weight loss, added muscle tone, eyeglasses, and clothing style can be changed quite easily. A large weight loss can be difficult to achieve. Wrinkles, sagging skin, or some skin conditions might only be fixable at great expense, if at all.

Chances are your partner wants to continue to look attractive for you and would be willing to make some modifications. It is unkind and unfair, however, to criticize something that cannot be changed.

The older you get, the more likely you will have to accept the physical changes that you and your partner experience. That's part of coming to terms with the aging process. (The alternative is to die young!)

If you are fairly young and you're dating someone who has a lot to say about your physical appearance, think twice about staying in the relationship. Ask your closest friends if the person you're dating is making a lot of sense or if he or she is just being fanatical, superficial, or controlling. There's a lot to be said for being liked for the way you already are.

Intimacy Boosters

If your partner is trying hard to change his or her appearance for your sake, quadruple the amount of physical affection you show.

Intimacy Boosters

Instead of emphasizing what you don't like (a certain hair color or clothing style, for instance), mention how sexy and attractive you think your partner would be if he or she tried something new. ("I think you'd look so incredibly sexy if you colored your hair darker!")

Sometimes learning to accept your partner's appearance might be harder than you think. If that's true for you, consider the following questions:

❑ Are you unhappy overall in your relationship? If so, you might be finding fault with a number of things you might otherwise overlook if you were happy.

❑ Are you a bit of a fanatic about your own appearance? If so, you might have very high standards that will be hard for anyone to meet.

❑ Are you unhappy with aspects of your appearance such as your weight, wrinkles, or saggy skin? If so, you might notice them more in your partner, too.

❑ Are you middle-aged or older? You might be experiencing a mild adjustment problem. Focusing on physical appearances is a sign you haven't accepted your age yet.

> **Just Ask!**
>
> *My boyfriend says I'm too fat. I'm five foot three and weigh 110 pounds. When we have dinner, he makes fun of me if I have anything other than a small portion of food on my plate. Any thoughts?*
>
> Yes, end the relationship. Your boyfriend sounds very controlling.

You do have an obligation to your partner to try, within reason, to look your best and stay healthy. People who let themselves go and show little care for their appearance and overall physical health are doing themselves and their partners a disservice.

The Least You Need to Know

◆ So much of what you think is a sexual problem, is probably something that is normal and common.

◆ It's important to discuss sexual histories before a relationship turns passionate.

◆ Fatigue is the number one reason for disinterest in sex, so don't take it personally.

◆ Learn to accept the physical qualities of yourself and your partner that really can't be changed.

Part 5

Intimacy Through Togetherness

It's hard to be fully intimate with someone unless you have the opportunity to do things together. Whether it's work or play, you have to spend time with people you want to get closer to, otherwise your connection level will be limited.

Intimacy through togetherness is a foundation of friendship. Meaningful conversation might also be a basis for friendship but many people, especially men, are more comfortable doing an activity with a friend rather than just talking.

The next few chapters will help you improve intimacy in your life through togetherness. This is especially important for people with hectic schedules who have precious little time to spend with loved ones or to nurture new (or old) relationships.

Chapter 21

The Power of Togetherness

In This Chapter

- ◆ Learning the two best ways to meet new people
- ◆ Determining your "Togetherness Quotient"
- ◆ Learning the tips to carve out more time together
- ◆ Knowing what to do when togetherness feels forced

You have to spend enjoyable time together with people you care about if you want to increase intimacy. And it's not enough simply to "be" together. It's important to actually do something fun or meaningful together that isn't only talking and isn't just sex.

If you are in a longstanding, comfortable relationship, you might not do as much together as you once did. And I bet your relationship has suffered because of it. Comfortable is fine, but if you're not careful it will turn into complacency (which is another word for boredom!).

If you aren't in a special relationship now or are just beginning one, the importance of spending time with the people you like and doing things you enjoy cannot be overstated. Certain activities, especially very fun ones or ones that get your adrenaline pumping, act as a bonding agent. They make you feel closer to whomever you are with.

Having friends is essential to your happiness and self-esteem. Friends need to talk and sometimes just hang out with one another even if there is little to do. But friends also need to get up and involve themselves in an activity once in a while.

All Alone and Looking?

Need a new friend? Looking for someone to date? Having a hard time meeting people? There are many lonely hearts in the world, but it isn't as easy as you might think to meet people you'll like and have something in common with.

Just Ask!

I have a great relationship with someone I've only met online. We feel very close to one another. Is it accurate to describe our relationship as intimate?

A soup and salad is one kind of a meal. A seven-course dinner is another. Your relationship is intimate up to a point. But other aspects of intimacy, including spending time together and sexual intimacy are not part of your relationship. If all you want is a friendship, talking is important but so is spending time together.

There are two things you must try to do, however, if you are hoping to increase your circle of friends. First, join groups that are involved with hobbies or interests that you find fascinating. You don't have to be an expert, just pick something that you've always had some kind of interest in. By meeting people with similar interests you have an automatic connection. Second, consider doing some volunteer work for an organization or cause that you admire. You're likely to meet a class of people who are giving, compassionate, dedicated, and who possess similar interests as yours.

Just Ask!

Any other ideas on how to meet people? I'm tired of bars, online services, and local dances.

Have an interest in the arts? Many communities have an arts council that needs members. Or join a community theater group. Even if you have stage fright you can help out behind the scenes with props, painting the sets, concessions, or publicity. It's a brief commitment that only lasts for as long as the current show. And people of all ages participate in theater.

Most community colleges offer semester-long and even one-day courses in a whole variety of areas. If you always wanted to take a writing course or learn how to do certain crafts, such courses are offered everywhere. Many of the national hardware store chains also offer mini-trainings in certain home repairs such as putting up wallpaper or tile. Larger communities have many events happening every weekend. Check the local papers and make a point of attending one or two new and interesting events every month. If you do things that you know you'll enjoy then you can't lose, even if you don't happen to make a new friend or two right away.

These same ideas can also be put to use if you are in a relationship. As a couple, no matter how old you are or how long you've been together, it's important to try new things or go to new places now and then. When a relationship has gone stale it's usually because the couple no longer has fun together and the usual humdrum activities take up all their time.

> **⚠ CAUTION**
>
> **Close Calls**
>
> Unsure if you and your partner have enough enjoyable time together? Answer this: When was the last time the two of you laughed hysterically together? If you can't remember, you are in dire need of some fun together-time.

Togetherness Is Not a Fast Food Drive-Through Activity

Imagine having an intimate conversation where you really open up and talk about what matters most. The other person is listening intently to all you have to say and for the first time in a long time you actually feel heard. Sounds nice, huh? Now imagine that same scene is about to start again. This time, however, you have 10 minutes and you'd better make it snappy because the listener has other things to get to.

Would the second situation really feel intimate? Of course not. But that's what it's like for many people these days when it comes to spending quality time together. They have precious little time to spare so togetherness is squeezed into small spaces.

Couples in established relationships fare the worst. Because they see one another regularly

> **⚠ CAUTION**
>
> **Close Calls**
>
> It isn't the presence of conflict that predicts a failed relationship or friendship. It is the absence of positive emotions. People who spend very little meaningful time with friends or lovers miss out on opportunities for positive emotion, and may lose the relationship in the process.

and perhaps live together, they take one another for granted. They assume that because they breathe the same air and likely sleep together, that there "Togetherness Quotient" is just fine. But it probably isn't. Take the following quiz to see what your "TQ" is.

1. We have regular date nights.

   Mostly True_____ Occasionally True_____ Mostly False_____

2. We spend a lot of our free time doing things separately.

   Mostly True_____ Occasionally True_____ Mostly False_____

3. We have about 20 minutes of "quality couple time" almost every day.

   Mostly True_____ Occasionally True_____ Mostly False_____

4. We don't usually spend much time with one another's friends.

   Mostly True_____ Occasionally True_____ Mostly False_____

5. We're good at coming up with creative things to do or going to interesting places.

   Mostly True_____ Occasionally True_____ Mostly False_____

6. Much of the time I like to do my thing, and my partner does his/her thing.

   Mostly True_____ Occasionally True_____ Mostly False_____

7. We really enjoy each other's company.

   Mostly True_____ Occasionally True_____ Mostly False_____

8. I wouldn't mind vacationing without my partner.

   Mostly True_____ Occasionally True_____ Mostly False_____

9. I miss my partner when I'm having a good time and he/she isn't there.

   Mostly True_____ Occasionally True_____ Mostly False_____

10. If we had a lot of unexpected free time to spend together, we wouldn't know what to do.

    Mostly True_____ Occasionally True_____ Mostly False_____

Scoring: For all the odd-numbered statements, score five points for Mostly True, three points for Occasionally True, and one point for Mostly False.

For all the even-numbered statements, score one point for Mostly True, three points for Occasionally True, and five points for Mostly False.

Scores can range from 10 to 50.

10–20: Very low togetherness. A great deal of change is needed to improve intimacy in this area.

21–30: Togetherness time needs improving. Intimacy is less than what it should be.

31–40: Good. You spend your time together fairly well. Some areas might need a little work.

41–50: Excellent. You are likely very good friends and intimacy is strong.

If your TQ is between 10 and 30, you need to have much stronger levels of intimacy in the other three areas (thought, talk, and touch) otherwise your relationship will probably be less than satisfying. The problem is that all four areas of intimacy interact to some extent. If you have low quality time together, for example, you probably don't communicate as well, either. Conversely, if your TQ is between 31 and 50, you can afford to have some occasional lapses in intimacy in the other areas without it adversely affecting your overall level of intimacy.

Role Overload

The biggest reason for inadequate amount of time together is role overload—your responsibilities as lover, parent, adult-child to aging parents, worker, financier, and friend simply take up too much of your energy and time. People are simply too busy and their personal relationships, not their jobs, suffer the fallout. More than 60 percent of young mothers are also employed. Most women do more of the house chores and childcare than do men, even if the women work full time outside of the home. The average woman today is busier by about 12 hours a week than the average woman was in the 1980s. All that time comes at the expense of the couple's relationship.

After role overload takes hold, a predictable pattern emerges:

♦ If people are too busy, romance and time together gets put aside …

> **Intimacy Boosters**
>
> If a young couple with kids has little time together, the partner who does the least amount of housework or childcare needs to increase his or her share. That frees the other partner up to have some R&R and allows the couple to have more free time together, too.

- This creates more emotional distance ...

- This creates irritability and a sense of being neglected or unappreciated ...

- This makes time together even less gratifying ...

- This leads to spending more energy on career or children or hobbies because the relationship is less fulfilling

This vicious cycle takes hold until the couple realizes they must spend more time together on a regular, daily basis, making sure that some of that time is very enjoyable.

Role Confusion

Men and women have yet to completely shed their gender-role stereotypes, but they are trying. Most men born before 1980 had fathers who, for the most part, adopted a more traditional role as breadwinner rather than as caretaker. These young men are now trying to become more involved in childrearing than their fathers were, but with not a great amount of support from employers.

And many women are very clear that they want to have their careers as well as family. However, research shows that these women are very hard on themselves when it comes to grading their role as parents. They feel guilty for not doing enough for their kids even though they are probably doing more than their male counterparts. If a young mom must miss a child's ballgame because of work, she feels terribly guilty. If a young dad must miss a game, he feels some regret but is able to convince himself that by earning a living he is caring for his family.

Tips for Finding More Time

When you're too busy, something has to give. If it's the relationship, you'll be sorry. Here are some tips for finding more time to spend with one another:

- Say no to low-priority tasks. Some things really can wait.

- Ask friends or family for more assistance on home projects or babysitting.

- Make ordinary, mundane activities more special. Instead of dinner together, make it a picnic. Pay bills while having a cup of tea together. Listen to fun music together while doing chores.

◆ If you haven't the time to do something enjoyable together, do it part way and finish it later. Watch half a movie today, the other half some other night. Go out for coffee or ice cream if you have no time for a nice dinner out.

◆ Turn off the TV and the computer. It eats up a huge part of time that could be used for other more important things.

Basically, when it comes to scheduling time, your relationships need to come first. Otherwise you're likely to have no time left over at the end of the day for the most important person in your life.

Forcing Togetherness: Shouldn't It Feel Natural?

Every couple and every pair of friends eventually develops a rhythm to their relationship. The relationship "flows" in fairly predictable directions. This is terrific when it comes to feeling at ease with one another but this rhythm can create staleness in the relationship, too. When the rhythm is set, you know what to expect. You know what your partner is likely to be doing when you get home from work. You know what kind of sex moves he or she will make. You know if you're likely to be going out on a Friday night or staying home. You know what he or she will say "yes" or "no" to.

The rhythm in your relationship promotes stability. But what if you want to bring about change? Anytime you want to change something that has a longstanding history to it, you will be up against a counter-force that tries to maintain stability and prevent change. Chronic dieters know this story all too well. Weight loss is met by metabolic resistance, creating a plateau or even weight gain. The same is true in relationships.

Let's say you want to change the rules about who does what housework and how often. Good luck. In a week or so things will be back to normal. Let's say you and your partner want to have quality together time every day. Well, why haven't you up until now? You haven't because you both fell into a pattern of relating that didn't allow for that time. Perhaps time after work is spent watching TV or doing chores or looking after the kids. And when that's finished, it's time for bed. To carve out quality time together, you have to alter your schedule in a way that feels unnatural. You miss your time in front of the TV or you feel guilty spending a little less time with the children.

The effort to make a change for the better almost always puts you out of your comfort zone. Ever convince yourself you'll wake up an hour earlier each day to exercise?

How many times has that failed? Stepping out of your comfort zone isn't easy, even when you know that the changes you need to make are important and beneficial.

If you and your partner (or good friend) realize that you need to spend more quality time together, don't expect it to be a smooth transition no matter how good your intentions. The force that resists change and maintains stability is similar to the force of gravity. It is powerful. People mistakenly assume that changes should be easy and comfortable. If they aren't, they worry that something must be wrong. "Maybe he doesn't really want to be with me" is a common reaction. Although that's possible, it's much more likely that spending more time together has disrupted your comfort zone. You have to hang in there and keep making the desired changes until the new ways feel comfortable. Eventually, you can stabilize at that new level.

> **⚠ CAUTION**
>
> ### Close Calls
>
> The happiest couples find time for togetherness regardless of their hectic lives. If you're having a hard time making time for your partner, it might be because your overall level of satisfaction is a bit low. Togetherness is even more important then.

Here are some things to keep in mind as you reorganize your relationship to create more togetherness:

- Expect setbacks. But remember, you can't have a setback unless you've first made progress.

- Anticipate what might predictably happen that would derail your efforts and come up with a backup plan.

- Expect the reorganization of time together to feel a bit awkward and unnatural at first.

- Be willing to give up something to make more quality time. If you just "squeeze each other in" to a busy schedule it won't work long term.

- If you want more date nights with each other, take turns being in charge of planning. That way it won't always fall in one person's lap to do the grunt work.

Intimacy can prosper if you make time together that is meaningful, occasionally fun, and at times exhilarating.

The Least You Need to Know

♦ Togetherness doesn't automatically create intimacy; there must be a rush of emotions to really connect you to someone else.

♦ Role overload (too much to do) is the biggest obstacle to intimacy.

♦ Togetherness combined with hysterical laughter makes for a great bonding experience.

♦ If you've been disconnected and attempt to make more quality time with your partner, don't simply squeeze that person into your hectic schedule. Give something else up.

♦ Don't be surprised if making more time for your partner feels a little strained at first; it can take a period of adjustment.

Chapter 22

Friendship and Togetherness

In This Chapter

- ◆ Discovering what friendship and togetherness means to men and women
- ◆ Being a couple and best friends
- ◆ Learning the secret ingredient to making the most of togetherness
- ◆ Feeling together when you must be apart
- ◆ Overcoming the excuses for not finding time together

Intimacy, in its fullest, includes togetherness. When a romantic relationship or a friendship must be maintained long-distance, it's being kept alive by the memories of past togetherness and the promise of future togetherness. Phone calls and e-mails are wonderful and do help keep the connection going, but intimacy has a greater chance of being deeper when you are physically together.

Sharing your life with someone on a regular basis, whether it is a friendship or something more, is a vital part of healthy intimacy. There is no question you can feel a deep love for someone whom you rarely see when you are separated by a physical distance. But it is hard. And intimacy and love do not always co-exist. When they do, when you experience profound love and complete intimacy, you have found heaven. But more commonly we have intimacies with people we care about but do not necessarily love, and we love people whom we do not share the kinds of intimacies we should.

The power of togetherness in shaping intimacy cannot be overstated. People often take togetherness for granted. They assume that because they are in the physical presence of someone for so many hours a week that they have plenty of opportunities to express caring and love and to make moments together more intimate. But the majority of people fall short in this area.

This chapter helps you sort out what being friends and lovers is all about. Should romantic couples also be best friends? The answer may surprise you. This chapter also reveals a powerful but often hidden force in relationships that can make or break "intimacy through togetherness." People who are unaware of this force can slowly destroy their relationships without ever knowing exactly how or why. People who become aware of this force can dramatically improve the quality of their togetherness without having to expend much effort.

What Does It Mean to Be a Friend?

Most people know friendship when they feel it. It is a feeling of liking someone a lot and wanting to spend time with that person. As friendships deepen there is a sacrificial devotion, a willingness to go the extra mile for one another; to be there when it counts. Friends also think about each other. They wonder how the other is doing. They worry when they know their friend is going through a rough time. They offer practical help when they can as well as emotional support.

Just Ask! _____

My partner and I don't get out much anymore. We're usually too tired by the end of the week. Any suggestions?

Forget spontaneity. Make plans. Purchase a gift certificate to a movie theater or several local restaurants. Because it's already paid for, you'll have more reason to go. If there is another couple you enjoy going out with, make plans weeks or months in advance with them.

Friends enjoy being in one another's presence. Time together is usually pleasant, sometimes joyful, sometimes painful, but always meaningful. Friends can argue and disagree and maybe even hurt one another. True friends make up rather quickly.

When you are with a friend you rest easily. Even somewhat boring small talk has a feeling of contentment to it. When friends must move away from one another there is a genuine sadness and grief. But there is a deep sense of wishing one another well; of wanting the friend to be happy in life even if you cannot be together as you had been.

Close friends who are not lovers share three and a half of the four pathways to intimacy. They share intimacy through thought—they think about each other in positive ways and look forward to their next time together. They share intimacy through talk—they inquire how the other is doing and really care about the answer. They share intimacy through togetherness—they do things together, things that are often fun or helpful to one another. Lastly, they share an intimacy through touch. But friends who are not lovers do not have a sexual relationship. They will show affection, however, even if it's just an occasional pat on the back or hearty handshake. Sometimes the affection is very physical and loving.

When friends become lovers they think that all they need to add is sexual intimacy and Voilà!—they have a perfect relationship. But it doesn't always work out that way. When friends become lovers the qualities that made them friends can diminish somewhat over time if they're not careful. They might take one another for granted. One way is in the quality of their togetherness. For many men, the sexual aspect of the relationship tends to supercede other intimate aspects. Men would rather have sex than have a heart-to-heart talk, for example. The trick is to maintain a healthy friendship when friends become lovers if the relationship is to be a long and happy one.

A Woman's Idea of Friendship

If a woman's best girlfriend is going through a difficult time, the woman would want to hear all about it. And not just once or twice or now and then. It would be a regular topic of conversation. She might offer advice, but advice-giving would always take second place to simply giving emotional support. Women friends are not just comfortable and at ease with one another. They truly enjoy one another's company. If they do something together, the something that they do is secondary to the fact that they are together.

Female friends are not shy about showing physical affection. It comes easily and naturally without any forethought. In fact, if physical affection is restrained and formal it's unlikely that the women would consider their friendship as deep or meaningful.

Being understood is probably at the root to a feeling of friendship for women. Women want to be known and they want to know their friends. It's hard to imagine a woman having a deep friendship where there is not some form of self-disclosure. (That's where male-female relationships often suffer. Men are less adept at self-disclosing.)

> **Intimacy Boosters**
>
> Togetherness only adds to intimacy when what you're doing together either reveals or reaffirms (in a positive way) who you are.

When it comes to male-female romantic relationships, a woman's sexual intimacy is based on her felt sense of being understood and cherished. In other words, her sense of friendship with her mate is the basis for the degree of sexual intimacy they share. The degree to which she feels cherished is in part due to the quality of the "togetherness" with her mate.

A Man's Idea of Friendship

If a man's best male friend is going through a hard time he would likely talk about it with his friend but not necessarily very deeply. If he sensed uneasiness in the air he'd likely keep his words brief, supportive, and optimistic. The conversation might possibly go deeper but it wouldn't automatically be that way. Physical affection, if it happened at all, would likely be a pat on the back or a hand on the shoulder.

To the friend going through the hard time, such a style of interaction would be welcome and not viewed as lacking. If a man's closest male friend shows a kind of subdued support for him, he knows it is another way of being told "I have faith that you'll get through this." It is recognition of one's strength. Furthermore, some men are very much aware of how hard it can be for their friends to be emotionally in touch, so they view any effort by their buddies to be supportive as positive and meaningful however shallow it might appear to others. "Jim never says much," a man might say of his best buddy. "But I know he cares."

> **CAUTION Close Calls**
>
> If you anticipate having some time off together, even if it's just a day or weekend, make sure you plan in advance how you'll spend that time. Otherwise, you each might have different expectations when the time arrives.

Togetherness is a big part of friendships to a man. Watching a ballgame on TV together can be a form of intimacy even though there is not a lot of interaction. That's why a man who watches *Star Trek* reruns with his romantic partner might feel a strong sense of togetherness with her whereas she may feel only a weak sense.

Men are more tolerant of other men's ways. Their friends can be loud, obnoxious, rude, or self-centered and the guys still might get a kick out being in each other's company. That sense of lightness, of not needing or expecting a great deal from a friendship, can carry over to a romantic relationship. The average guy, to his mind anyway, overlooks a lot of annoying things about his partner. "My needs are simple," a man might say. So when his partner has higher expectations of him, he can get resentful. "I'm so accepting of her, why can't she be more accepting of me?" he wonders. Women want more depth to their relationships whenever possible. Men get comfortable with the status quo.

Can a Couple Really Be Best Friends?

The stereotypes of what friendship means to men and women don't apply to everyone. But if they do in your case, you might find it a struggle to be best friends with your current or future partner. Rather than emphasize where your mate is letting you down in the friendship department, concentrate instead on being "good" friends.

A good friend will still go out of his or her way for the other but expectations are a bit lower overall. What this means specifically is that men need to reach out more to the women in their lives with conversation and affection (not just sexual affection) and women need to accept that a man who isn't listening to her every word might still love her deeply.

Just Ask!

Sometimes I'd rather not have my girlfriend accompany me when I'm with my friends. Is something wrong with that?

Not necessarily. It's normal and appropriate to have some alone time with your friends, apart from your girlfriend. But dig a little deeper. Do your friends like her? Do you have fun with her when she tags along? If so, you have nothing to worry about. If not, think about what changes might be needed.

It's also very important for the couple to do things together on a somewhat regular basis. Togetherness is like a spoon that stirs the rest of your intimacy needs. The right kind of togetherness (having fun, showing interest in one another, accomplishing something as a team) adds to your sense of connection and affection. It also gives you something to talk about (or something to do while you talk about other things).

Some people have no friends nearby that they consider to be dear or close. They have a host of acquaintances and are friendly with many others but lack a real, close, solid friendship. When that happens, they might consider their spouse or lover to be their best friend. However, that doesn't mean it is a high-quality friendship. I've listened to many husbands, for example, describe their wives as their best friend but yet they spend little quality time together and there is very little emotional intimacy. If you want to be better friends with the person you sleep with, you have to treat that person the way you would treat a close friend. You have to do things together, self-disclose, go out of your way for one another, and laugh and have fun. What's missing in your friendship?

The Secret Ingredient to Making the Most of Togetherness

It was so subtle that Frank missed it completely. Angela had come up to him, rubbed his back affectionately, and mentioned that dinner was almost ready. Frank was thumbing through an owner's manual and mumbled a response. He didn't look at Angela. She walked away.

Angela wasn't mad at Frank and Frank wasn't mad at Angela. There was no hostility in that brief interaction. But it was one of many similar interactions the couple shared. What was wrong with it? Angela had made a small attempt to connect and was ignored. She didn't take it as a harsh rejection. But neither did she try it again later. In fact, she felt less connected to him the rest of the night but didn't realize why. That was a missed opportunity for connection. When it happens too often in a relationship, the couple loses their desire to connect in small ways and then in bigger ways.

Such a failed attempt at connecting can happen in a variety of circumstances. Maybe you start to ask a question and you get hushed because your mate is in the middle of something. But then he or she never asks what it was about later. Or one of you starts to tell a funny story and it looks like the other really isn't listening so you stop. One of you kisses the other with passion but gets a weak kiss in return. You inquire about the weather and get a grunt for a response. These things happen in all relationships. But when they happen too often, the friendship aspect of the relationship starts to corrode.

Why do such things happen in the first place? One of you wants a connection at the same time the other wants some personal space. That's not unusual. But if a couple only connected at times when both were in the mood to connect, the relationship would be weaker than it should. It's important to connect, even in small ways, when one or both of you isn't in the mood or is preoccupied. Regular small gestures of affection, attentive listening, and thoughtful responses work to build a sense of closeness with the one you want to be intimate with.

Completing the Circuit

Your relationship is like an electrical circuit. When one of you makes a small bid for attention and the other one is receptive, it's like completing the electrical circuit. It adds light, power, and energy to the relationship. "Completing the circuit" isn't hard. The person wanting some space often overlooks the fact that he or she could still respond positively to the other's overture with very little investment of time and energy. When Angela rubbed Frank's back all he needed to do was to rub her hand or say "Thank you" or give her a kiss. It would have added to their sense of togetherness. Instead he ignored her and she had no intention of doing that again for him, at least not that day.

Intimacy Boosters

When you and your partner are spending time together and trying to build intimacy, pay attention to those small bids for attention or affection. They are like dollar bills in a jar that add up significantly over time.

Many Ways to Ignore Your Lover

Take several days and pay close attention to the number of times your partner makes a small attempt to connect with you. Notice how you respond. You may be surprised at just how often you come across as disinterested or downright rejecting. Because many couples have precious little quality time together, ignoring those few small bids for attention can seriously weaken the relationship over the course of months and years.

Do you or your mate feel lonely at all these days? If so, you can probably bet that you've missed many opportunities for brief, positive connections.

As an exercise, do your best to notice and respond favorably to every attempt your partner makes to connect to you. If you really are busy and unable to make the most of the interaction, you can still be positive and warm. Also, look for gaps in your time together where you can make a connection, however brief. Try this for two weeks and see how this affects your overall attitude toward your partner.

Long Distance Togetherness

If long distance is keeping you apart from the one you love, it's important to add to the sense of togetherness even when you can't be together. Of course, connecting via phone calls, e-mails, and instant messaging help. But *what* you talk about when you connect can add to an even greater sense of togetherness.

For example, if your partner has access to a computer, take some digital photos and send them via e-mail. Take photos of your children's report cards, drawings, and so on. When you discuss how your day went, be more detailed and specific than you might otherwise be. For example, if you went out to a restaurant, be descriptive of what it looked like and what you ate. Men especially may be less inclined to offer such details, but it really helps add to a sense of togetherness. It only adds a few minutes more to the conversation but it's well worth it. If you are a man listening to all these details, be patient. See it as a form of intimacy, because that's what it is.

> **Intimacy Boosters**
>
> If one of you has been away for several weeks or more, expect a readjustment period upon reuniting. When you are accustomed to being apart, it can take a day or two to get used to being back together.

The more you know what your partner's forthcoming day will be like, the more you can think about it during your day and ask about it later on. If your partner has a meeting, for example, try to think about that right when the meeting is happening. If you're on the phone with one another at night, check to see if you can each look up at the moon. Or synchronize your watches and say something such as, "Tomorrow between two and two-fifteen I'll be thinking only of you." That way you can enjoy a kind of spiritual connection.

Poor Excuses for Not Having Time Together

How much time together do you need to increase overall intimacy? That's not possible to say. Good friends can get together once in a while and perhaps chat via email or telephone periodically and maintain their relationship. However, if you're one half of a couple, you need a minimum of about 20 minutes a day of quality "connecting time" plus periodic outings where you can enjoy one another's company. And that's the bare minimum. Couples that are busy raising kids can sometimes feel like a team ("Here, you give him a bath while I read her a bedtime story …") and that sense of teamwork can add to a sense of closeness. But couples need alone time together, too.

There are dozens of excuses people give for not making time together. But there are four principal excuses:

- It costs too much.

- But what about the kids?

- I'm too busy.

- I'm too tired.

The validity of these excuses is not in question. Probably all these excuses are true, much of the time anyway. But if they occur too regularly, you have lost sense of your priorities. Furthermore, you might have it backward: these four reasons don't get in the way of your togetherness; your lack of sufficient togetherness creates the conditions for these four reasons to exist. If you don't spend time together, you will focus on work, chores, or the kids too much. And if you are too tired, it might be because you suffer from a mild depression, which can easily be the result of too little intimacy in your life.

The truth is that successful couples seem to find the time to be together despite crazy schedules and the demands of home life and career. You must choose to make time for one another. Period.

The Least You Need to Know

- Spending meaningful, regular time together is essential for a high level of intimacy.

- The more you fit the stereotype of male or female, the more difficult it will be for you and your partner to be best friends.

- Be receptive to the small bids for attention your partner or friend makes.

- Take the time to find creative ways to connect when you must be physically apart for any great length of time.

- If you don't have sufficient time to be with your partner, you are making excuses.

Chapter 23

Intimacy, Togetherness, and Family Politics

In This Chapter

- ◆ Learning what to do when your family disapproves of your partner
- ◆ Assessing if you're at risk for having divided loyalties: a quiz
- ◆ Determining if you are the family scapegoat
- ◆ Coping with uncomfortable family gatherings

It seems that all it should take is some warmth, a felt sense of "chemistry," some love, perhaps a dollop of sex appeal, and then add the final ingredient—togetherness—and you have the makings of a wonderful friendship or romantic relationship. But it's not always that simple. Sometimes "politics" get in the way. By that I mean the tensions that build when various people you care about (your family and best friends) don't always agree with your choice of whom to be intimate with.

When that happens, you feel the strain of having divided loyalties. Should you listen to your best friend when she tells you that the guy you're interested in is a loser? If you parents or siblings have their doubts about your judgment, should you heed their advice?

This chapter tries to guide you through the political minefields that can appear when all you want is to build a close relationship with someone special. I will reveal hidden traps you definitely want to avoid and suggest ways to minimize the damage that can happen when well-intended loved ones try to put a wedge between you and your newfound intimate friend.

Divided Loyalties

Brett and David are a gay couple. Both of their families accept their lifestyle and have made efforts to make both men feel at home when they visit. But there is a problem. Brett's family thinks David is too self-centered and that he has a mean streak. Brett has mentioned to his family how on several occasions David said some cutting remark that seemed totally out of line. David always apologized later, but Brett often felt hurt and attacked. His family didn't like it. They believed that Brett, who is very friendly, outgoing, and compassionate, doesn't deserve to be with someone like David.

Brett always countered by pointing out David's good traits. Yes, David was rough around the edges but there was a kinder side as well. When Brett needed a new transmission for his car, David had no problem helping to pay the bill. When Brett was tossing around the idea of switching careers, David was all for it, even if it meant that Brett would have to return to school and perhaps get a lower-paying job in the interim. Couldn't his family appreciate that about David?

Brett and David aren't the only ones who have a public relations problem with their relationship. Family politics is a strain for many people trying to build or maintain a relationship with someone the family hasn't completely welcomed with open arms. If the pressure is too great it can cause a rift between the couple or a rift between the couple and the family, or both.

> **CAUTION**
>
> **Close Calls** _____
>
> Think twice about making critical comments about your friends or romantic partners in front of family members. It can poison their views, at least somewhat, and create conflicts where none is necessary.

But situations that result in divided family loyalties don't just happen. They are typically an outgrowth of earlier, unresolved issues and family dynamics that are being perpetuated now under a different context. Let's put it another way. Imagine that your family life growing up was about as good as it gets. You now have a close relationship to your parents and siblings. Now imagine that one of your siblings is involved in a relationship with someone you dislike. Would you go to war over it?

Probably not. You might speak to your sibling about your feelings or you might not. But you would probably honor your sibling's choice and do your best to be respectful whenever possible. You wouldn't go out of your way to be rejecting or attacking. Instead you'd be polite and gracious whenever you saw them together and you would hope for the best. But if there were any old, unsettled family issues, all bets would be off. Anything could happen to upset the family apple cart.

Are You at Risk? Take the Quiz

Some people have a greater chance of choosing a partner where friends or family might seriously disapprove. Respond to the following statements to see if you are at risk for being torn between two loyalties.

1. I have often been the family scapegoat.

   Mostly True_____ Mostly False_____

2. My relationship with my parents and siblings has always been pretty strong.

   Mostly True_____ Mostly False_____

3. At least one of my parents has had an addiction or been emotionally difficult to live with.

   Mostly True_____ Mostly False_____

4. Members of my family know when to step back and mind their own business.

   Mostly True_____ Mostly False_____

5. I usually do whatever I can to keep the peace.

   Mostly True_____ Mostly False_____

6. My family is willing to offer advice but then allow me to make my own decisions.

   Mostly True_____ Mostly False_____

7. There has been power struggles in my family.

   Mostly True_____ Mostly False_____

8. I am rarely tense or ill at ease when with my family.

   Mostly True_____ Mostly False_____

9. Members of my family can be very judgmental and have a strong need to be right.

   Mostly True_____ Mostly False_____

10. My partner enjoys the company of my family.

    Mostly True_____ Mostly False_____

The more you answered "Mostly True" to the odd-numbered statements and "Mostly False" to the even-numbered statements, the greater the odds you and your partner will be embroiled in some divisive family issue. The more you answered in the reverse, the probability is high that even if your family has misgivings about your choice of partner everyone will show goodwill and civility.

Intimacy Boosters _____

The better you get along with your partner's family, the greater the closeness between you and your partner. Try to establish a personal, one-to-one relationship with as many members of the family as you can. Spend some time alone with them even if only for a brief bit of time. Send thank you notes and cards when appropriate.

Are You a Scapegoat?

Remember Cinderella? She was looked down upon and never could do anything right in the minds of her stepmother and stepsisters. Yet it was always clear to those who heard the story that Cinderella was the healthy member of the family. Scapegoats are members of the family who are easy to focus on as a source of family strain or unhappiness. Sometimes the scapegoat actually does act out in an unhealthy manner and sometimes the scapegoat is someone who always does their best and is helpful to others but somehow is ridiculed and unappreciated.

The issue is not whether the scapegoat actually is a troublemaker. The issue is why. Often, when the family structure is dysfunctional, such as when one parent is an alcoholic or abusive, someone in the family will call attention to the dysfunction by acting out or by developing symptoms such as depression, anxiety, or a variety of physical ailments. However, that person will be labeled as the troublemaker or "sick child" when in actuality he or she is the sacrificial lamb.

When a scapegoated child grows up and has an intimate relationship, family members might have a hard time viewing that person as capable and responsible. They are likely to find fault with the scapegoat's choices in life (career, love interest, financial investments). But by focusing on the scapegoat, family members avoid looking at the more fundamental reasons for their unhappiness or frustration in life. They avoid looking at themselves and their own role in the perpetuation of family misery.

If you have a history of being scapegoated by your family, that doesn't mean you are simply being misunderstood and victimized. Often, because of a lingering depression or low esteem, people who've been scapegoated will not make the best choices when it comes to relationships. If this describes you, you have a dual burden: you must try to enhance your self esteem and look at the ways you are creating problems in your life; while at the same time you must be prepared to not get the full support from your family.

Steps to take if you have a history of being scapegoated:

◆ Set up boundaries with those who often find fault with you. Refuse to talk about issues that only result in your being criticized.

◆ Remain connected to your family but only to a degree that you feel most comfortable. Don't give in to pressure to conform to their views if you don't already agree with them.

◆ Consider some brief psychotherapy to help you through the maze of conflicting feelings and outside pressures.

◆ Don't make any complaints about your partner, however small, to those people who disagree with your choice in partners.

◆ Don't add to your partner's sense of unease by speaking ill of your family at times when there is no need to do so.

◆ Accept the fact that members of your family may never fully understand or appreciate you.

◆ Never act out of spite.

Keep in mind that when there is a fundamental, unresolved problem within a family such as alcoholism or marital unhappiness, there is an increased risk for some members to become scapegoated. Sometimes the scapegoat role changes hands and the black sheep of the family becomes more acceptable while another member assumes the role of the black sheep. This doesn't mean that the former scapegoat is now free. It just means that the fundamental problems in the family have not been resolved.

Fun at Family Gatherings (When You'd Rather Not Be There)

Let's pretend that you and your partner are about to spend an afternoon with family members and that family politics will add to the stress and strain of the gathering. Let's also assume that someone in your family doesn't have as positive feelings toward your partner as you would like. Now what?

 Just Ask!

My parents insulted my husband and now he refuses to ever see them again. He gets mad when I take the kids to visit them. What should I do?

Are your parents willing to apologize? Is your husband willing to look at the larger picture? It's unreasonable for you and your children to stop seeing your parents. He needs to understand that and he needs to understand that not seeing his in-laws doesn't solve anything; it just perpetuates ill-will. The sooner one side can break the ice the better.

Your goal in these gatherings is not to convert anyone to your beliefs. It is to find a way to get along and make the most you can out of the gathering. After all, there will likely be plenty more gatherings in the future. Here are a number of guidelines to follow.

- Stick together most of the time. Don't leave your partner at the hands of those who might find a way to be critical or dismissive.

- Make a point of saying something publicly that is positive about your partner.

- If possible, repeat something positive that your partner said to you in private about a family member.

- If your partner is publicly criticized, don't be neutral. Be willing to leave if you must.

- Be polite. Say something positive and kind to others when appropriate.

Acceptance is a fundamental attitude. If your family is not accepting of you and your partner, you are not likely to make any headway if you return the favor by failing to accept your family for who they are. Acceptance doesn't mean you like what is happening. It means that you will not emotionally oppose a situation that is unlikely to change. When you accept your family even though they are making life difficult for you, all it means is that you will cease trying to convert them to your point of view. It doesn't mean that you must put up with their constant criticism. You can leave the situation and, if need be, limit how often you see your family.

When Family Pressure Gets Intense

Remember Brett and David, the gay couple who was feeling some pressure from Brett's family? They didn't like David's personality and wished Brett and David were not together. When such pressures get too intense, a rift can develop between partners. Someone might make an ultimatum: "It's your family or me." David didn't go quite that far, but after a while he told Brett he'd no longer accompany him to family gatherings. That put pressure on Brett. If he went to visit his family, he'd hear "Where's David?" and try to come up with excuses for David's absence. He was afraid that if he told his family the truth then matters would only get worse. Eventually Brett applied pressure on David to come with him to visit his family. He argued that visits were not that frequent, they wouldn't stay long, and it might ease the tensions. But David disagreed. He felt like Brett's family was against him and he hated the idea of trying to pretend that all was well. What's the best way to handle the situation?

For such matters, it takes a great deal of maturity on everyone's part. Mostly, it requires everyone being willing to find some merit in everyone else's attitudes. For example, can David understand that Brett's family might object to someone making harsh criticism of Brett, as David has done? Can the family understand Brett's position that David has redeeming qualities?

Close Calls

If you're dating someone who easily finds fault with your family and urges you to pull away from them, end that relationship.

In their case, this is what happened. Brett explained to his family that David felt uncomfortable in their presence because of their stated dissatisfaction with their relationship. He also explained that although he would visit them and maintain his relationship with them, he'd also be visiting them a little less often because he has an

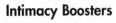

Intimacy Boosters

If you really cannot stand your partner's family despite efforts by your partner to get you to think otherwise, try to go along to as many family visits as you can. Kindness and consideration toward your partner is essential for intimacy to blossom. He or she should show kindness to you by understanding when you choose not to attend a family gathering.

obligation to David, too. This led Brett's parents to call David on the phone. They explained that they were willing to honor Brett's choice in who to be with and asked him to please start visiting them again. David agreed. David also told Brett that he would try to work on reducing his mean streak.

In the worst cases, one side completely cuts themselves off from the other. Sometimes this separation is necessary, especially if certain family members are so toxic that any kind of contact results in misery. However, emotional cut-offs can be avoided if each side is willing to put aside "being right" for the sake of getting along.

The Least You Need to Know

♦ You don't have to really like your partner's family in order to just get along.

♦ Try to accept your family and your partner's family for who they are, even if they annoy you.

♦ Don't poison your partner's mind against your family and then expect him or her to be happy and at ease in their presence.

♦ Always speak positively about your partner to members of your family.

Chapter **24**

Dynamic Togetherness

In This Chapter

♦ Learning the three factors for dynamic togetherness

♦ Separating is essential for quality togetherness

♦ Balancing separateness and togetherness: a quiz

♦ Letting your weaknesses draw the two of you together

Like so many situations in life, togetherness is all about attitude. How you think about togetherness dictates what you'll do about togetherness. Although it's true that some people prefer to be left alone, the vast majority of people need to experience intimacy with others to have a satisfying life. And that intimacy must involve togetherness.

But how much togetherness is optimal? And what about the quality of the togetherness? When friends and couples disagree about the terms of togetherness, they get cranky with one another. In fact, if any romantic couple seems to be irritated with each other for no obvious reason, the underlying reason is probably that they haven't had enough time together.

The key problem with togetherness is that there also must be time to be separate. Too much togetherness is like too much perfume or cologne. It can make you gag. Too little togetherness can be even worse. But it's a sure bet that every group of friends or every romantic couple has a different view on how often to be together. For couples especially, there is a constant push and pull where one person wants more time together and the other wants a little less. Couples who are experts at achieving satisfying intimacy don't get into tugs of war over this issue. They know how to work as a team to meet each others' needs without getting into a battle for supremacy.

This chapter reveals the key factors that create not just ordinary togetherness but dynamic togetherness. And it gives away a secret that will help all couples and friends improve the quality of their togetherness.

What Is Dynamic Togetherness?

Dynamic togetherness isn't about pizzazz. Moments together that are filled with heart-pumping excitement and magic are wonderful to experience now and then. But real-life togetherness doesn't work that way day to day. Dynamic togetherness is often about feeling "at home" with whoever you're with. Dynamic togetherness is powerful but in a subtle way. It's like a large, quiet engine that does its job beautifully without calling attention to itself.

Dynamic togetherness has three ingredients:

Intimacy Boosters

Couples who attend religious services or pray together regularly, stay together more than other couples.

◆ Acceptance of the idea that each person's needs for separateness and togetherness must be fairly addressed.

◆ A willingness to ask oneself, "What's it like for my partner (friend) to have me around at this moment?"

◆ A willingness to tolerate a little selfishness once in a while.

Intimacy will be blunted when even one of these conditions is absent. But achieving a state of dynamic togetherness isn't that difficult.

Balance the Need for Togetherness and Separateness

People who are unsuccessful in relationships often slip up in this area. They either push for togetherness to such an extreme that they push the other person away, or they withdraw from togetherness and try to carve out as much separateness as possible. In either case, the underlying issue is the same: the person wants to preserve a sense of self. For the former, their sense of self is wrapped up in their connection to others. In other words, they feel selfless unless they are in a close relationship. For the latter, getting too close to someone means they risk losing their sense of self. So they pull away, wanting to be in a relationship but only a little bit.

Going to either extreme is a mistake. But finding a comfortable middle ground is very difficult for many people in a relationship. Much of the time, people in a relationship get into tugs of war over where to draw the line between connection and disconnection. If the wars get intense, it usually results in some form of name-calling. "You're too needy," is the claim of the person wanting more space. "You're too cold and aloof," is the claim of the person yearning for more togetherness. Who's right? No one. Turning it into a right versus wrong debate will not resolve the issue. It will only inflame it.

This issue will never get solved entirely. At best it will only be managed. It's like a trick knee that you must be mindful of because it acts up every so often. When the two of you are in sync with how much togetherness you want, it's only a matter of time (hours or days, typically) before you are out of sync. You manage this issue by calling on your goodwill toward one another and on your willingness to give at least as much as you get.

A common mistake you might make when trying to be accommodate your partner's need for more closeness or more distance is to be accommodating only after it's requested. Sometimes it's a good idea to give your partner what he or she wants without having to ask. So if you tend to be the one who likes to carve out space for yourself, make a point of initiating some togetherness time so your partner isn't always the one to do it. The more you give your partner what he or she wants in this area, the less it will have to be taken.

Read the following checklist and see how many statements apply to you. The more you can check off, the more likely you will not have a problem balancing togetherness and separateness with your partner.

❑ I do not usually feel threatened or annoyed by my partner's individual pursuits.

❑ When my partner wants more time for us together, I see that as important.

> **CAUTION**
>
> **Close Calls** _____
>
> Do you give more than you get in your relationship? That's okay to a point. If your share of the giving is more than 60 percent and your share of the getting is under 40 percent, resentments will build.

❏ I am not more emotionally dependent on my partner than he or she is on me.

❏ I don't have to struggle to get my needs for togetherness or separateness met.

❏ I would not describe my partner as possessive or jealous.

❏ I wouldn't mind if my partner had interests and hobbies that were different from mine.

❏ We don't usually battle over who's going to get their way.

A common paradox is that many people with a strong need for closeness and togetherness find themselves attracted to people who are more aloof—and vice versa. What's really going on is that each person is disavowing either a need for togetherness or a need for separateness and is attracted to a person who displays that need. It's a way of getting what deep down you know you need—more togetherness or more separateness—without having to take ownership of that need. That sets the stage for bickering and disappointment. It's so much simpler if you can simply recognize that togetherness and separateness are both necessary for a healthy, intimate relationship.

Intimacy Boosters

If your best friend or partner wants to try a hobby that you don't find interesting, be encouraging anyway. It will add to overall goodwill.

"What's It Like for My Partner Right Now?"

Dynamic togetherness must include some form of empathy. Togetherness doesn't mean much if all you're interested in is what *you* are getting out of the deal. Specifically, it's important to understand the impact you're having on your partner. What's it like for him or her to have you around right now? Are you a joy to be with or are you a pain in the neck? To succeed at this you must put aside your wants and needs for the moment.

Intimacy Boosters

If ever you're in doubt as to the impact you're having on your partner, give him or her a hug and a kiss or say something sweet or romantic. If it's received well, you know you're having a positive impact. If it's not received well, you know it's time to ask, "What's the matter?"

Right now is your partner: Happy? Sad? Bored? Content? Tired? Lonely? Aggravated? Excited? Wishing for some togetherness? Wishing for some time alone?

If you're not sure of the answer, you need to find out. If you are sure and the answer is in the negative category, what are you willing to do? You're not responsible for making your partner feel better, but you do need to examine what impact you're having and make some changes if necessary.

Tolerating Some Selfishness

Selfishness happens. Your partner cannot be expected to always make sacrifices for your sake. Once in a while you or your partner will miss the boat when it comes to being thoughtful or generous. But having a tolerant partner does not give you license to be selfish. The rule "Do unto others as you would have them do unto you" is the best rule to follow when it comes to intimacy and togetherness.

Togetherness After an Argument

Melanie put it this way: "After an argument Bill and I just don't connect. We go off to our separate corners and wait for the other to make the first move. But even then, after one of us has broken the ice, it still takes us awhile to enjoy being together."

Mending fences with proper words certainly helps. But it's vital to regenerate that "togetherness feeling" that you once had. Often people just wait for the good feelings to reappear, but that can sometimes take longer than is healthy. The other problem with waiting is that the lack of togetherness can cause yet another argument. Furthermore, when you're off by yourself reviewing how right you are and how wrong your partner is, you're filling your head with negative ideas about your partner.

Just Ask!

After an argument, I'm always the one to break the ice. My husband never does. It isn't fair. Any suggestions?

He probably feels he was the more-injured party. You probably disagree but that is likely how he feels. He might have a build-up of resentments, too. So even though your last argument might not have been major, it probably stirred up some old issues for him and now he's being stubborn. Ask him what the underlying issues are. (Hint: He probably feels disrespected and/or underappreciated.)

If you cultivate the attitude of dynamic togetherness, you won't allow disagreements to interfere with intimacy. To improve a sense of togetherness after an argument, you mustn't let too much time pass before you make some kind of overture. An apology, a warm kiss or show of affection, or some thoughtful gesture are common ways of extending an olive branch.

After the ice has been broken and it seems like the two of you are on your way to feeling more connected, do something enjoyable together. It doesn't matter what it is. Go to a movie or go out for a bite to eat. Take a walk. Just do something that you might do if you were already feeling very connected. Humor also helps, but not everyone can pull that off. If nothing else, try to smile more. It can help shape the tone of your togetherness.

What Brings You Together: A Magical Idea

When you're in a special relationship, what is it that unites you? You might say it is your love or devotion. You might say it is having common goals. Probably everybody would answer that question by pointing to their strengths.

But people who end up happy and peaceful in their friendships or romantic relationships allow something else to unite them: their weaknesses. It is a unique concept. Letting your weaknesses bring you together is more than simply tolerating one another's faults. It is finding a value in those faults. It is telling yourself that *because of* those faults (not just *in spite of* them) you wish to get closer to your partner.

Chances are your partner's faults turn you off in some way. That's normal and not necessarily a bad thing. But if you want to improve the quality of your togetherness, it helps to actually find a way to accept and perhaps *love* those faults. I'm not suggesting that you love such things as alcoholism or abuse. I'm talking about the more routine behaviors that we find annoying and that detract from time together with those we love.

Exercise!
Think of someone (not your partner) who is a close, dear friend or someone you very much admire even from afar. Now think of some of the annoying traits and weaknesses your partner has. Finally, imagine that the friend or person you admire possesses some of those qualities. Would it turn you off? Or would you find a way to see those qualities as somehow more acceptable? If you find them acceptable, how did you do that? How did your thinking change? Can you give your partner the same kind of consideration?

The key to allowing weaknesses to bring the two of you closer together is to realize that your partner's faults probably shed light on your own faults. That can happen in two ways. First, it might very well be that what you dislike about your partner are qualities that you possess but cannot see. We are often blind to some of our more hidden weaknesses. However, others see them plainly. After you identify your partner's faults such as "He's too selfish … She's too needy … He's too irresponsible …

She's too rigid … He's too controlling …" and so on, switch pronouns. Could you say the same of yourself? If you don't think so, ask a few trusted friends and see what they say. You might be surprised to learn that they think you need some improvement in the same areas you think your partner needs improvement.

A second way that your partner's weaknesses can shed light on your weaknesses is to ask yourself what virtues you need to improve to be more tolerant of your partner. Maybe you need to improve your levels of patience, forgiveness, charity, or humility. By focusing on *your* areas of weakness, you can draw your partner closer to you and practice strengthening those qualities in yourself.

Dynamic Togetherness: Making the Most of Small Things

Many couples complain about having very little quality time together. They mention how they are too busy taking care of the home or the kids. But those busy moments, with a little creativity added, can have a powerful effect on togetherness.

Commonly, such things as housework, yard work, and childrearing have a neutral or slightly negative impact on a couple's quality of togetherness. Sometimes the negative impact results from resentment that one partner isn't doing his or her fair share of the workload. Such resentment usually results in poorer-quality togetherness later on when the couple has a chance to be alone.

Maggie's husband John rarely helped with housework. Granted, he worked about 60 hours a week, but Maggie still wished he'd help out more. He'd often ask her to watch a movie with him, and she'd decline because she knew that after the movie she'd have to finish the housework while he got ready for bed. She chose to get the housework done at an earlier hour and miss her time with him. A simple solution would be for John to assist her with the housework so she'd have time to enjoy the movie with him. That's an example of dynamic togetherness in action.

Some couples can make housework drudgery a forum for a pleasant time together. They put on an enjoyable CD for background music or they take time out for a nice lunch. In other words,

> **Exercise!**
>
> Next time you and your mate are driving together, discuss ways to make ordinary chores or mundane time together turn into something more fun. Get creative. Come up with three different ways to make gardening or housekeeping a more pleasant time for the two of you.

they try to find ways to feel like a couple when they are involved in activities that could easily be boring or stressful.

Very often, a nicely worded compliment while a partner is in the middle of some aggravating chore can make the difference between simply occupying the same room and having real "togetherness."

The Least You Need to Know

◆ True togetherness is about feeling at home with the person you're with.

◆ Dynamic togetherness includes awareness of the moment-to-moment impact you're having on your partner.

◆ Don't allow too much time to pass after an argument before you mend fences.

◆ What you dislike about your partner is sometimes a trait that you possess but don't see.

Part 6

Intimacy During Trying Times

When intimacy stays alive and strong during difficult times, the difficulties seem easier to bear. But for many people, stress creates problems in intimacy which only adds to the overall strain. Intimacy requires connection, sharing, and caring. But under severe pressure, many people withdraw into themselves and have a difficult time expressing themselves or extending any kind of caring.

The next few chapters discuss some of the more common stresses people experience that can have a negative impact on intimacy. You'll learn what you can do to improve closeness during trying times.

Chapter 25

Stress and Intimacy

In This Chapter

- ◆ Understanding your problems on two levels
- ◆ Noticing when your anxieties interfere with intimacy
- ◆ Using intimacy to soothe anxious feelings
- ◆ Coping with emotions and how they affect intimacy

Most of the time stress has a negative impact on the intimacy in your life. Stress makes you worried, depressed, or irritable, and takes a toll on your sex life, too. Did you know that the part of your nervous system that is in charge of sexual arousal shuts down whenever you feel stressed? (If it didn't, our species would have died off eons ago because cave dwellers would have continued having sex when danger approached.)

The irony is that intimacy is often a stress reducer. If you can find a way to make a close connection with someone you care about when you are contending with life's hardships, you can actually reduce your overall levels of stress. (Stress is not a negative event; it is your response to that event. The more effectively you respond, no matter what the event, the less stress you will experience.) The problem is that many people instinctively act in ways that oppose intimacy when they are stressed. They get irritable, they withdraw, they complain, they worry, and they have a harder time feeling empathy for others because they are so wrapped up in their own concerns.

This chapter helps you understand the specific ways that stress affects intimacy and how you can maintain intimacy even when your world turns upside down.

Two Levels to All Your Problems

A Level I problem is whatever has "gone wrong." Maybe you have a financial or health crisis, for example, or perhaps something broke and needs repairing. At Level I, you do your best to solve your problems and often come up with commonsense ideas to achieve that goal.

Level II problems include anxiety, depression, and a "bad attitude" that occur from having a Level I problem.

> **Intimacy Boosters**
>
> Whatever major stresses you might be facing, let your partner know that you have faith the problems will be overcome. Say "I trust in us to eventually do the right thing." Optimism is important for bringing you closer during difficult times.

A Level II problem happens when your emotions over a Level I problem interfere with your functioning and makes your problems worse. When a Level I problem is chronic, such as a debilitating illness or long-term unemployment, Level II needs the most attention. Typically we think that if our original problems were to simply vanish, our Level II problems would vanish, too. But if problems are longstanding, the reverse is usually true: until we better manage our emotions, we might never be able to solve the problems that led to those emotions.

Kyle and Kate lived together for a year when Kyle was laid off from his job. Weeks of unemployment turned into months. Kyle became more depressed and the couple argued more often. Kyle's depression became so bad that he didn't have the energy to keep applying for positions. Therefore his unemployment dragged on and he became even more depressed. In this case, Kyle's Level II problem (his depression over being unemployed) interfered with his ability to find a new job. It was only when he sought treatment for his depression that he was able to begin his job search with more enthusiasm.

A Level I intimacy problem might be that you and your partner are too busy and have too little time together. Or perhaps your communication skills need improving. Or maybe you've gotten into a rut and your sex life has become routine and uninspired.

If you remain at Level I, you and your partner might be able to put your heads together and devise a plan to correct your intimacy problems.

But intimacy problems at Level I often create bigger intimacy problems that lead to Level II problems. If you feel hurt or rejected, you might be less cooperative when trying to solve a Level I intimacy problem. You might become demanding or start blaming your partner for everything that isn't right. You might have doubts about your compatibility and hesitate when you should be plowing ahead with ways to improve your problems.

Overcoming Level II Problems

If you can reduce your intense emotional reactions, your problems might seem much more manageable. Your goal is to always keep intimacy in mind. You can use intimacy as a way to reduce your troublesome emotions. Or you can find other ways to reduce those emotions so that you can relax and become more intimate. Either way, when intimacy is strengthened, stress always diminishes.

If your Level I problem is not about intimacy (maybe it's a financial or health problem) you can use intimacy to reduce your overall stress, which will also help you deal with the problem more effectively. Here is a partial list of ways to allow intimacy to reduce your tension levels.

> **Close Calls**
>
> If you withdraw from your partner during trying times, you will have two problems: the original problem and the emotional distance you have created. Stay connected when times are rough.

- ◆ Go out with friends. Talk about your worries for a limited amount of time then sit back and enjoy the company.

- ◆ Find something to do with someone you love that will make you laugh hysterically.

- ◆ Cuddle on the couch for at least 20 minutes.

- ◆ Put aside your worries for the moment and really listen to someone else talk about their life and concerns. Don't interrupt with comments about your plight. Just be there for the other person.

- ◆ Give and receive a lot of extra affection.

- Exercise with someone. Go out for a long walk.

- Call some old friends you haven't spoken to in a long time.

- Leave notes for the one you love that reveal why that person matters to you.

If you need some time for yourself to cope with whatever is troubling you, by all means take that time. But don't do so in a way that feels rejecting to others. Ask them to understand that you need time alone and show them appreciation. Regardless of how much time you think you need for yourself, you still need to take others into consideration. Make sure you spend time with those you love even if you're feeling distracted and preoccupied.

When Level II emotions get the better of you, you need to take extra steps to calm down.

Reframe Your Problems

The most common (and counterproductive) view people take when they're going through hard times is to see themselves as victims. If intimacy issues are the problem, it is rare that only one person is responsible for the state of the relationship. You're better off looking inward and examining the ways you contributed to the current situation. Try to view your problems as challenges rather than as threats. See yourself as a survivor, not as a helpless victim.

The most important way to reframe your problems is to realize that all problems are temporary. Even if you suffered a permanent disability, the real problem is not your disability but your overall attitude. When you learn to adjust to your situation and find ways to appreciate what you still have, you will discover that your stress will have automatically lessened.

End the Downward Emotional Spiral

If your negative emotions are intensifying, you can bet that you are engaging in catastrophic thinking: assuming the worst. This leaves you no choice but to feel overwhelmed and agitated. Most of the time our catastrophic thoughts are much exaggerated. By assuming the worst we are really preparing ourselves in advance for all possibilities. But because most of the assumptions are too extreme and unlikely to happen, we end up feeling stressed for no valid reason.

Catastrophic beliefs typically start with the words "What if ...?" You might worry "What if she leaves me? ... What if he cheats? ... What if it doesn't work out? ... What if we can't pay our bills? ..." and so on. These questions become obsessions that can never be answered with certainty but only with trust and faith. And the more worried you are, the less you want to rely on trust and the more you want hard answers that are impossible to know for sure.

Just Ask! _____

My husband worries about everything. When I tell him he's not thinking rationally he just gets mad. Help!

Thank him for trying to be protective. Tell him it must not be easy being so anxious all the time. Then tell him that you simply choose not to anticipate problems that usually never arise anyway and that you are happier for it.

Catastrophic beliefs usually include an unstated negative belief about yourself (or others) such as "I won't be able to handle it ... I'll never be happy again ... I'm a loser ... No one will want me ..." and so on. These views must be challenged. Are they really true? Is it true that you will never be able to handle it even a little bit? Has anyone else gone through what you fear might happen? Have they coped? Is it absolutely, positively true that no one will ever want you again? Can you know that for sure? By challenging the negative statements you begin to take the air out of those inflated negative beliefs and start to think more realistically. This will lower your stress.

The Five Ways You Cope

Think of a time from your childhood when you were very worried or frightened. Maybe one of your parents had a serious health problem. Maybe you had to move to a new school and make new friends. Perhaps you suffered some kind of abuse. Did your parents get a divorce? Now try to remember what you did to cope with that situation. Did you withdraw? Cry? Adjust easily? Call attention to yourself by acting out? Try to please everybody and not make waves? Fight with others? Chances are that your approach to coping with your childhood problems is similar to what you do now under high stress. When our problems are especially difficult to deal with, many of us regress and rely on older and often less mature coping patterns.

Sheila's mother was an alcoholic and Sheila was the eldest of four kids. As a child she assumed the responsibility of caring for her younger siblings. Now an adult, Sheila still puts aside her wants and needs for the sake of others. This has caused problems with intimacy because she tends to over-function and be too giving in her relationships while asking for little in return. She ends up feeling used, unappreciated, and always stressed. She feels hurt easily, even by her girlfriends, because she is always by their side when they need emotional support but they are too busy when she could use some TLC.

Rick has a different coping style. His parents were good providers but emotionally distant and Rick grew up fending for himself emotionally. If he had a problem at school or with friends or if he felt insecure and unsure of himself, he never asked for support or advice. As an adult Rick is very self-sufficient. But intimacy is a problem because he rarely talks with his wife about what is on his mind. If he is upset about something he just "handles it" in his own way without involving anyone else. Although he is a good provider, like his parents, he has also become emotionally distant.

When problems arise or your life is in some kind of emotional turmoil, you will cope in one (or more) of five ways. I call these the "Five Fs."

- **Fight.** You deal aggressively with your problems. You also have a tendency to blame or criticize others or use force to get your way.

- **Flee.** You withdraw, run away from the issues, avoid talking, or deny that certain problems exist.

- **Freeze.** You procrastinate on deciding what to do. You might be unable to think straight or you are indecisive.

- **Fold.** You surrender, give in, or submit to the will of others.

- **Face your fears.** You tackle the problems squarely without making yourself or others feel miserable in the process.

Each of these coping styles has an impact on intimacy.

Fighting

A fighting resolve isn't a bad thing. But many people overuse this approach and become harsh and difficult to live with as they are trying to cope with life's difficulties. "Fighters" tend to be blamers. They often feel that life is very unfair to them so they feel entitled to be angry. They like to control situations and other people. They believe they know what is best so they tend to overlook other people's ideas on what to do.

Someone with a fighting coping style pushes others away when they don't always mean to. Others feel disrespected. Warmth is not always part of the relationship. Fighters don't trust easily. For intimacy to blossom, fighters must be willing to examine the negative impact they are having on others. They simply come on too strong and can be selfish under stress. A good exercise for fighters during trying times is to take time during each day and focus only on meeting the needs of others in the family in a loving, generous, and joyful way.

Fleeing

People who flee when faced with conflict or major stress try to avoid the issues. They might tune out their partners during conversations. They might drink to excess or get occupied with busy work that distracts them from their problems. They might develop physical complaints or "suffer in silence." Basically they try to shut down their awareness of problems.

People who flee from conflicts can enjoy personal relationships but intimacy will suffer. You can't get close to someone when you must avoid certain topics. If you withdraw from conflict, underlying issues might not get resolved and resentments can build.

To improve intimacy, people who flee from conflict need to be willing to tolerate emotional discomfort for the purpose of gaining closeness.

Intimacy Boosters

If you don't feel comfortable talking about areas of conflict in your relationship, write requests on a slip of paper and place them in a jar. After a week (or whatever time you choose) draw out the slips and have a brief discussion that focuses on steps you can take to mend the situation.

Freezing

People who freeze up during adversity can't think straight and are usually afraid of making the wrong decision. They procrastinate until they have no choice but to take action. If your partner uses this coping style you might feel you are living with a child, at times. When times are tough, you might have to make all the decisions and not rely on your partner for help.

Intimacy requires emotional risk-taking and vulnerability. People who freeze up during hard times dislike taking risks. They might hesitate to make emotional commitments because they need to be absolutely sure they're choosing the right person.

Exercise!

Afraid to take emotional risks? This exercise is safe but helpful. Lie down on your back. Have your partner kneel behind you and place his or her hands under your neck. Next your partner should lift your head and massage your neck with his or her fingers. However, you are to completely relax and allow your head to be lifted without any assistance from you. It should feel like dead weight in your partner's hands. The more your neck tenses up as you try to lift your head and assist your partner, the more you need practice letting go and trusting others.

Folding

Folding is helpless surrender. It is giving up. People who easily cave in to pressure tend to get depressed easily because they don't see themselves as having any influence over the important events in their life. "Folders" might try to cope but will give up quickly if their efforts don't bring immediate results.

Folders are pessimistic. They take things very personally and see negative events as having a lasting impact. In contrast, they view positive events as temporary.

Intimacy is stifled when you have a folding coping style. Intimacy requires connection. It is hard to really connect with someone who is depressed and pessimistic. Often, partners of people who are depressed have to take on extra burdens.

Folders must learn that outcomes are often a result of process. Persistence usually pays off. Giving up always results in not getting what you want.

Facing Fears

Nobody's perfect. You might face fears head on and still do some degree of fighting, fleeing, freezing, or folding. But facing fears is the only legitimate and healthy way to deal with them. Someone who faces fears has the best chance for achieving a high level of intimacy in his or her personal life. Intimacy itself can be somewhat frightening and often a risk. You risk being rejected or ridiculed by revealing more of who you are to someone. But failing to take that risk keeps you from experiencing a profound level of closeness.

When Facing Fears Works Against Intimacy

Some people face fears all the time, but intimacy is not their strong suit. They are risk-takers by nature. They love the thrill of danger. They might engage in dangerous sports activities, always pushing the envelope and risking injury. They take situations right to the edge and see how much they can get away with. These people might lead very exciting lives and are highly adventurous by nature. But they are too busy for intimacy. In some ways, exciting adventures replace intimate relationships. Such people may have close friends and be very passionate, but it can be difficult to keep up with them. Personal relationships might be very intense but might also lack depth or commitment. After these people have achieved something, they need to move on to something greater.

You might say that these people are fearless except when it comes to deep intimacy—then they have to pull back. On the surface their relationships might appear very intimate and very intense, but they are very self-focused people. They need a great deal of stimulation, and settling down with one full-time partner isn't easy for them.

If you are in a romantic relationship with someone like this, be prepared to take second place to high adventure activities. If you think you can persuade your partner to make you number one, you'll become very frustrated. If you need a lot of personal space in your relationships and you also enjoy excitement and adventure, this relationship might work for you.

The Least You Need to Know

- You cannot effectively manage chronic problems unless you have a handle on your emotions.

- Improving intimacy will lower your overall stress.

- View difficult times as challenges, not as threats.

- However you coped as a child during very anxious or troubling times will likely be how you cope now when times get tough.

Chapter 26

Intimacy and Chronic Illness

In This Chapter

- ◆ Four ways to improve intimacy when there is a chronic illness
- ◆ Intimacy and cancer
- ◆ Intimacy when couples have a chronically ill child
- ◆ Intimacy and depression
- ◆ Intimacy and anxiety disorders

A chronic illness is often defined as one that lasts longer than six months. The more years you live, the likelihood is close to 100 percent that you or someone you live with will suffer a chronic illness or injury. (Contrary to common sense, the majority of people with a chronic illness are under 65 years of age.) About one-third of Americans report some form of chronic pain. You probably know someone close to you who has suffered from heart disease or cancer. About one in nine Americans currently has a serious anxiety disorder or clinical depression.

Chronic illness affects your lifestyle, your self-esteem, and your relationships. Intimacy often diminishes when chronic illnesses arise, but it shouldn't have to be that way. In fact, maintaining intimacy can help you cope with illnesses that otherwise can wear you down.

This chapter provides general guidelines on how to maintain or restore intimacy when chronic illness takes hold.

Intimacy Expectations When Illness Strikes

Tom suffered back pain after a car accident. It was not a major injury but his discomfort was intense at times and interfered with his enjoyment of everyday activities. As months rolled by, Tom complained more and more. Discussions with his wife Jill often centered around how he was feeling. They did fewer things together because he didn't want to aggravate his condition. Their sex life diminished somewhat, too. All in all, intimacy through talking, touching, and togetherness was adversely affected. The couple didn't even realize it until months later when it became obvious that they were crankier with each other and just not getting along.

Fortunately for Tom, his condition slowly improved. But there were two aspects of his situation that are common in terms of intimacy. First, Jill didn't always know whether to be supportive or to keep quiet and not mention his injury. She wanted him to know she cared but she didn't want his injury to be the centerpiece of their lives. For his part, Tom gave mixed signals. On some days he wanted more help and understanding from Jill. On other days he wanted to do more for himself. Because his condition fluctuated day to day, it wasn't easy for Jill to know what he needed.

A second effect was that as Tom slowly improved, Jill became more negative. You'd think she'd have been thrilled that he was getting better. She was happy, but months of frustration and worry had taken their toll. Now that he was on the mend, she felt freer to express feelings that she suppressed before.

In general, all four areas of intimacy must be examined when someone has a chronic illness. Chances are at least two, if not all four areas, are far below optimal levels. Here's why, and what you can do about it:

CAUTION

Close Calls

If your partner has chronic pain, it is wise to be kind but not overly helpful. Allow your mate to do as much as possible for him or herself. Nonverbal pain signals (grimacing, sighing, and so on) are best ignored unless they are out of the ordinary. Being over solicitous will cause you to burn out and might keep your partner from being as independent as possible.

CAUTION

Close Calls

Never complain that your partner's illness or physical pain is "all in your head." It will only make him or her feel resentful and misunderstood.

❏ Intimacy through thought. If you have a chronic illness you might fill your head with worry and preoccupations with the effects of the illness. It's essential to make sure that time is spent thinking in positive ways about your situation and your relationship. If your partner is the one with the illness, think about the qualities of your partner that make him or her special. Give the benefit of the doubt when he or she is in a bad mood. Illness can take a toll on one's general disposition. If you are the one who has an illness, think about the needs of your partner and ways that you can meet some of those needs despite how you feel.

❏ Intimacy through talk. Let your partner know on a daily basis how you are feeling (keep it brief and to the point) and what you might like or need. If you need help, ask for it. If you want to do more for yourself, say so. Don't expect your mate to read your mind. Make sure you have pleasant chats about topics unrelated to things you worry about. Make sure you mention how physically attracted you are to your partner, especially if physical activity is limited in some way.

❏ Intimacy through touch. If physical pain interferes with affection and sex, find ways to include some kind of physical connection in your relationship. Use your imagination and don't always wait until you feel better to be sexual or affectionate. Body massages, back rubs, or showering together can replace some sexual activity if need be.

❏ Intimacy through togetherness. You can still do things as a couple even if you are more limited than you once were. Make a point to go out together as often as you can, even for small amounts of time. Find interesting things to do together at home.

If intimacy in one area is harder to achieve, try to bolster intimacy in another area. Never allow a chronic illness to thwart devotion.

Intimacy Boosters

When chronic illness has become a burden, concentrate on doing something for your partner with as great a sense of love and devotion as possible. Act as if this is the last act you will ever perform. It will lighten your heart and add to a deeper sense of warmth in the relationship.

Intimacy and Cancer

The statistics are heartening: the five-year survival rate for prostate and breast cancers is about 80 percent. Still, almost half of all breast cancer survivors and 70 percent of prostate cancer survivors experience a reduction in sexual desire or functioning. For example, radiation can kill cells in the vaginal wall, which results in diminished lubrication. This can make intercourse uncomfortable. But it is important to try to maintain as much of a sex life as you can. Many couples avoid physical closeness altogether when sexual desire is reduced. This is a mistake. Even if your physical relationship must be limited for the time being, physical closeness of any kind can be rewarding. Lying together naked in bed and simply holding one another can be a very loving experience.

When the diagnosis of cancer is made, couples and friends are understandably worried and frightened. But studies reveal that a week after the diagnosis about half of all couples have yet to discuss their emotional reactions with one another. They fear making one another upset and they sometimes don't know the best thing to say.

By far the best way to talk about the situation is to admit the feelings that are most obvious. Denying that you are scared or worried is not believable. One of you might always try to be the optimist and insist that all will work out. Although optimism is healthy, your partner knows that you are also concerned. If you insist that all will turn out fine, you might inadvertently make it hard for your more-worried partner to express fears to you. He or she might instead worry in silence.

Just Ask!

I'm engaged to be married and my fiancée has breast cancer. What's the best way to be encouraging?

Before you offer optimistic forecasts, show that you can listen well. If she talks about her fears, tell her "It's normal to feel afraid" and don't try to talk her out of her feelings. If she knows that she can talk to you and be heard, not challenged, she will feel very loved and supported.

There are two types of assistance someone with cancer requires. The first is practical. They need help getting to and from appointments, they often need help changing their dressings, and they might need help with routine daily activities. But they also need emotional assistance. They need to know they can talk about their concerns if need be. And they need to offer *you* emotional assistance, too. They know that you are worried and they might want to hear about your apprehensions. Don't try to hide your concerns in the name of being helpful.

Many men tend to help out with practical matters as a way to offer assistance but they underestimate the value of offering emotional support. Try to offer a balance of emotional and practical support. If you can't, see if others (friends and relatives) can pick up the slack.

CAUTION **Close Calls**

If your partner has cancer and asks how you are coping, don't reflexively say "Don't worry about me, I'm fine." It's okay to mention that you have worries and fears. You will not sound discouraging. Your partner knows you are having a stressful time of it and wants to be helpful to you. Being open about some of your concerns allows him or her to do just that.

Caring for a Chronically Ill Child

About 15 percent of all children have some kind of medical illness or disability that is chronic. These can range from mild allergies to severe deformities. The more severe the condition, the more taxing it can be for the parents. Ironically, the divorce rate for parents of children with special needs is lower than the national average. This might be because divorce is not very practical in such cases even if the marriage is unsatisfying. But it can also be that these parents find a way to show devotion to one another as they both share a difficult circumstance.

Statistically, when a child has a chronic disability or other special needs the men cope better when they have an adequate amount of attention from their wives. The women, on the other hand, often wish that the men took a greater role in the ongoing medical care of the child. These women feel overburdened by doctor's appointments and other medically related activities. For such couples, if the men took a greater role in the day-to-day care of the child, the women would have more free time to devote to the men.

Raising children is a demanding job. But when a child has special needs the parents often have less time for one another and are more fatigued. Fatigue is the number one reason for an unsatisfying sexual relationship.

The more intimate a couple can be, the more energy they have to cope with routine family burdens. When a child has special needs, the parents must be especially capable communicators. Otherwise frustrations, misunderstandings, and resentments will fester and cause unnecessary complications. Such couples are advised to "touch base" regularly about matters that are constantly being updated. Working together as a team is important for the emotional welfare of everyone involved.

Depression and Intimacy

Depression can be treated with counseling and medications. Still, many people suffer for months on end before some relief is obtained. Depression definitely affects intimacy. For one thing, sex drives are usually reduced when one is depressed.

Depression can be triggered by a loss of status (such as a job loss) or a cutoff from a close relationship. A depressed person tends to show less affection and is less adept at listening. Both of these consequences reduce intimacy, which in turn can add to the depression.

Wanting a depressed partner to "snap out of it" is an understandable but naïve sentiment. Severe depression has a biochemical component and often requires medication to alleviate it. Criticizing a depressed partner will only make the situation worse. Depressed people tend to be highly self-critical as it is. Fault-finding will only add to their misery.

Exercise!
If you're depressed and your sex drive is low, aim to raise it just a notch or two. Rate your level of desire on a scale of zero to ten with zero meaning no desire at all. Then ask yourself what you would do differently if your desire was two points higher. Then try to act that way regardless of how you feel. You will discover that pushing yourself just a little doesn't take that much effort and the outcome will at least be some kind of sexual or affectionate encounter rather than none at all.

A depressed person needs gentle encouragement and understanding. Yes, they must try to push themselves, too. When they feel like staying in bed or doing very little activity, it helps if they force themselves to follow some kind of structure during the day. Even achieving one or two small tasks they might not otherwise accomplish is preferable to doing nothing.

The couple should examine all four areas of intimacy (intimacy through thought, talk, touch, and togetherness) and concentrate on adding something to each of these areas. Even a small but positive improvement can make a big difference.

Anxiety Disorders and Intimacy

Anxiety disorders are now more prevalent than depression. A common anxiety problem is called Panic Disorder. (Women are twice as likely to be diagnosed with this problem compared to men.) People suffering from this can feel surges of strong anxiety accompanied by such sensations as heart palpitations, sweating, jitteriness, or a fear that they might be dying.

When these attacks are frequent and severe, two of three people develop a condition known as agoraphobia. Agoraphobia is when a person starts limiting the places they will travel or go for fear of getting a panic attack while there. So a person suffering from agoraphobia might drive only short distances from their home or avoid checkout lines, movie theaters, or any place where a quick and easy exit is not possible. If left untreated, panic and agoraphobia can create serious limitations in a person's life, which then interferes with their relationships.

Couples where one person has a diagnosed anxiety disorder often experience greater discord than other couples. Often, the nonanxious partner grows weary of the limitations imposed by the anxiety on the relationship. Arguments are more frequent and each person feels misunderstood. Not only are conversations (and therefore intimacy via talking) compromised, but the couple cannot travel far together because of the agoraphobia. This leaves their sexual relationship as the main path to intimacy. However, that path is usually blocked because sexual desire is often diminished (especially for women) when a couple is not getting along.

Just Ask!

My wife gets panic attacks. Are there some key things I should say—and not say—when I'm with her and she gets these attacks?

Yes. Tell her that although she is very uncomfortable and panicked, what she is experiencing is an intense feeling, that's all. Remind her that it will take at least several minutes for the sensations to start to go away. Tell her to try to breathe normally, letting her abdomen fill with air as she inhales. If she doesn't want to go somewhere you had plans to go, encourage her to go part of the way. Complete escape or avoidance might reduce her anxiety now but it perpetuates the underlying disorder. Better that she tolerate some degree of discomfort while facing a fear than avoid the situation altogether. Never tell her that she is just seeking attention or that she is being irrational. Never force her to go somewhere when she is feeling overwhelmed. Never tell her that you are sick of her anxiety problems.

It's helpful for a couple to attend therapy sessions together so the nonanxious partner can learn the best way to encourage a fearful partner to overcome the anxiety. Usually, goals are set whereby the fearful person goes into places that create anxiety but does so taking small steps. For example, a person who fears waiting in check-out lines would choose a line at a time of day when the store is not busy. As her confidence increases, she can then choose lines that take longer and longer to get through. It helps a great deal to have a partner who is cooperative and supportive; otherwise the process can become too burdensome.

Even small gains in overcoming anxiety can be a cause for some celebration, especially when the couple worked together to make progress.

The Least You Need to Know

- Most chronic illnesses occur in people under age 65 and can have a detrimental effect on intimacy.

- If intimacy is adversely affected in one area, it's important to bolster intimacy in other areas.

- Don't try to instinctively cheer a partner up with optimistic forecasts without first listening to what his or her concerns are.

- People with a chronic illness need practical support as well as emotional support.

- People with chronic illnesses need to do as much as they can for themselves. Don't be too solicitous with your partner.

27

Intimacy During Difficult Life Transitions

In This Chapter

- ◆ Sustaining intimacy after the baby arrives
- ◆ Surprising findings about intimacy at midlife
- ◆ Continuing intimacy after the loss of a parent
- ◆ Rebuilding intimacy after the death of a child

Just when you think you've settled into some sort of intimacy rhythm, something happens in your life to disrupt things. Transitions in life (such as becoming a parent, finding or losing a job, or the death of a loved one) almost always affect intimacy. But whether intimacy is affected positively or negatively depends on many factors.

A key factor is your own personality. When you are sad or worried, do you instinctively want to draw closer to others or withdraw? It's not uncommon for one person in a relationship to want to increase intimacy and connect more during stressful times and the other to want to find some solitary time. Mutual understanding and the finding of common ground is essential in these cases.

This chapter discusses some of the most common life transitions that people face and how to make sure that intimacy remains as strong as possible during these times.

Intimacy and Parenthood

Parenthood is a bit of a paradox. Studies show that becoming a parent adds depth and purpose to people's lives. If you want a meaningful life, say the researchers, becoming a parent is one way to have it. But if you want a life that is *happy*, well, parenthood might not be your first choice. Day-to-day measures of happiness fall after the birth of the first child. Some studies show that the rate of happiness stays lower until after the last child leaves home. Being a parent doesn't mean that you will always feel unhappy. But you will feel more stressed and stress can deplete you of some of the joy that otherwise might be part of your life.

Intimacy levels between parents don't necessarily plummet after their baby is born, but intimacy is experienced very differently. Fatigue puts a major dent in their sex life. And as a couple you are more likely to reduce your socializing and going out together. But togetherness will increase in other ways as you each care for the baby and try to "be a family." In some ways, intimacy isn't so much lost as it is rearranged.

> **CAUTION**
>
> **Close Calls** _____
>
> Intimacy suffers if you try to get as much work done as possible in the home and office and still refuse to put some chores lower down on your priority list.

Studies show that couples drift somewhat to more traditional roles after a baby arrives. This means that men view themselves as the provider, even if the woman has a fine career. And women with careers feel very pressured to be the best mothers they can be while working hard at their jobs—a challenge that is unrelenting. Maternal guilt often leads to moms devoting as much time as possible to their kids, often at the expense of the couple's relationship.

There is another paradox. The men who complain the most about lack of intimacy after a baby arrives are not the most intimate to begin with. In contrast, men who cultivated intimacy in all four areas (thinking, talking, touching, and togetherness) before there was a baby seem the most capable of getting along with less intimacy after the baby's birth. The reason for the paradox is simple when you look a little closer. Men who complain most about a drop-off in intimacy after the birth of a baby are mostly upset over a decline in sex. They were less likely to experience intimacy through talking and togetherness to begin with so they did not notice a change in those areas after the baby arrived. Men who can tolerate less of a sex life (mostly for reasons of fatigue) when there is an infant find other avenues of intimacy. Those other avenues might not always be as appealing as sex but they have a positive impact nonetheless.

If you want to keep intimacy at its optimal level when you are also contending with the wonders of parenthood, the following four "B-A-B-Y" steps will help.

◆ "B": Build new and creative ways to be intimate.

◆ "A": Appreciate one another.

◆ "B": Believe in your future together.

◆ "Y": Yield to one another's requests whenever possible.

These four steps are examined more closely.

"B": Build New and Creative Ways to Be Intimate

Doing things together as a family is very important for bonding. It's also a way to view each other not only as partners but as parents. Seeing each other in action trying to be a mommy or daddy can draw you closer if you let it. Yes, you will have to get used to a little less sex. Reread Chapter 17, "Hot Intimacy" and you will learn many fast and easy "recipes" for wonderful, sexy, and romantic encounters that take very little time.

If you are weak in one of the four areas of intimacy (thinking, talking, touching, and togetherness), now is the time to build up the weak spots. Spend 10 or 15 minutes a day in conversation that you wouldn't otherwise have. Don't have the time? It doesn't have to be a special moment with just the two of you. Chat while one of you is feeding or bathing the baby. Talk while fixing dinner. Take a few extra minutes before you fall asleep. Improving intimacy any way you can will help make up for the loss of intimacy in other areas.

CAUTION

Close Calls

Working couples who adopt a "masculine" philosophy of not expressing feelings, showing less affection, and concentrating on career advancement, are more dissatisfied in life.

Intimacy Boosters

Guys, want a night out with your mate after the baby has arrived? You should plan it all. Find a babysitter, pick a place to go, pick a day and time. Overlooking these details or assuming the other person will take care of them often results in disappointment.

"A": Appreciate One Another

Now is the perfect time to increase the number of compliments you give. Women especially might be feeling less attractive after giving birth and need to hear that they are beautiful and physically desirable. Even if they respond by putting themselves down ("I'm not beautiful, I'm fat!") they still need to hear the compliments.

Compliment each other on how well you are doing as new parents. It's normal to feel unsure of yourself as a rookie parent. Praise can be a confidence builder.

Show appreciation by biting your tongue when you might want to complain. Expect the house to be more cluttered and dinners to be hurried. Expect to arrive later at certain functions. Expect to have less money to spend on frivolous things. Complaining about such things won't help because they will occur anyway. If it's really important on occasion to have a spotless home or to arrive on time for something, be willing to make the sacrifices necessary to bring it about, even if you have to make most of the effort. That's just how it is when you have an infant on the scene.

"B": Believe in Your Future Together

It's easy to feel worried and disheartened when stress is continuous and your romantic life has taken a hit. Instead of imagining the worst-case scenario—the two of you drifting apart with no time for one another—envision the two of you happy and committed. Focus on the things you can now look forward to as a family. Talk about your future and your dreams. Make plans, even if they seem fanciful. Find something to look forward to whether it's something special to do the next day, a vacation next year, or a bigger house in five years.

"Y": Yield to One Another's Requests

Okay, this step is aimed mostly at men. I'm not saying that women shouldn't yield to requests. In fact, women tend to yield a great deal, which is why they don't need this advice.

Men are more likely to be uncooperative and disagreeable when it comes to managing a household after a baby arrives. Even if the man and woman both work, women tend to assume more of the childcare and housework responsibilities and are overburdened and exhausted as a result.

If a woman asks for help with something or makes a suggestion on how to make life easier or simpler, the man is probably better off yielding to her wishes. Nobody should be a doormat. But a cooperative effort is essential if intimacy is to thrive after a baby is born. An overworked and underappreciated mom will definitely have little interest in sex and affection or togetherness, and the man will soon feel shut out. When a man does his share of the housework and childcare, a woman sees that as caring about *her*.

Yielding doesn't mean completely giving in. It means a willingness to see some merit in what the other wants and finding creative ways to meet those needs. The goal is to find a way to cooperate, perhaps through compromise, but not to stubbornly refuse to yield.

Intimacy and Midlife

Midlife crises are overstated. Sure, you might find a 50-year-old guy wanting to buy a red Corvette and date young women but these cases happen less often than commonly thought. The transition to midlife can be an exciting time for many people. One reason is that they have the ability to make more choices. People in the 40 to 60 age range are less concerned about climbing the corporate ladder and earning money for a down payment on a home. If they are stressed and very busy it's often because they have purposely chosen to make their life that way, and they don't regard it as stressful so much as challenging.

Just Ask!

My husband wants to change careers. I worry it will add more stress and lower our income at least temporarily. Does changing a career help or hinder one's marriage?

There are too many factors to consider. If you can't pay your bills, your stress levels will increase. But if your husband is unhappy at his current job, his misery can affect you, too. Research shows that men who change careers are actually happier than men who remained in the same occupation for 20 years. Men who switch careers have a greater sense of control over their lives and feel more productive in the work they do.

Intimacy changes during midlife. One common finding is that middle-aged men, less worried about providing for a young family, become more nurturing. Family time becomes more important than work time. This is an age where many men think about retirement. In contrast, middle-aged women tend to be more assertive. A woman who held back her career for family is now free to explore new ground and often wants to do just that. Ironically, at a time where many men look forward to coming home at night to a quieter house and having time together with their partners, the women are busy pursuing outside interests.

This change in attitude is called "gender expansion" by researchers, where men allow more feminine qualities to be expressed and women show a more masculine side. This tends not to be a problem for the majority of couples. However, it is a problem for a certain group of men. Men who always perceived their fathers to be weak and ineffectual and their mothers as domineering and aggressive seemed to suffer more when their wives became more assertive. Psychologically, these men unconsciously worry that they will turn out just like their fathers and that their wives will become like their mothers.

To not feel threatened by "gender expansion," couples must view these changes in a positive light. Any expansion of capabilities is usually a good thing. Women might naturally view men being more supportive as a favorable change, whereas men might have to work harder to see assertiveness in the women as more positive.

The sex life of middle-aged couples can be very rewarding. Although any sense of novelty might have worn off, many couples report that their sex life possesses a depth and warmth that was not always present in younger days. As a couple gets older and their physical appearances change, it's nice to still feel attractive to one's partner despite extra pounds and wrinkles.

Intimacy After a Loved One Dies

Death of a loved one causes us to grieve. There is no common pattern to grief, and it is a mistake to assume that one should grieve in a particular manner for a certain length of time. Sexual intimacy during grief is usually replaced by other forms of intimacy. When grief is intense, one's sexual appetite as well as one's appetite for food can vanish.

How someone's death affects the intimacy of a couple depends on two factors: the current level of satisfaction within the couple's relationship, and the level of devastation of the loss. Broadly speaking, couples whose relationship was less than satisfying who are now grieving the loss of someone who was beloved (such as a parent or close friend) will experience much more strain.

The area of intimacy that probably needs the most attention during grief is intimacy through talk. Some people (men especially) may not wish to talk much and prefer to spend time alone or doing some form of physical activity. But his partner is likely grieving, too, and may want to talk. If this is the case, she might want to spend some time conversing with others for her sake so she is less reliant on her partner for conversation. However, some kind of periodic conversation between the man and the woman should be expected and is important.

The person less desiring to talk is probably afraid of losing control of his emotions. It's not a good idea for the woman in this case to say "It's okay to cry" when he is weeping. It will just draw attention to something he feels very uneasy about. (And if he is not upset about showing his emotions, no comment that it's okay to cry is necessary.) Giving him a tender hug is fine. Asking if there is something you can get for him is also nice, even if he declines the offer.

There are ways to talk about the deceased in a manner that doesn't lead to intense emotions. A passing comment such as "I wish dad was still with us" or "Aunt Marie would have loved this restaurant" is a way to bring up the person's memory and perhaps have a brief conversation.

> **Exercise!**
>
> If discussing your grief is too uncomfortable and you fear losing emotional control, write out your feelings several days in a row for about 20 minutes each time. You can do this when you are alone. After the fourth day you might discover that you feel a bit lighter and that talking about how you feel, even a little bit, is easier.

If partners have opposite ways of dealing with grief, it isn't a good idea for either one to try to force the other to do something they don't want to do. A talker shouldn't insist that a nontalker express feelings. But a nontalker shouldn't expect a talker to remain silent. Ideally the couple will find some common ground.

As a rule of thumb, it is a mistake to think that talking about a deceased loved one will only make people upset. Even if a person cries at the memory, such expressions of feeling are usually helpful and healing. You can take your cue from others as to whether the conversation should continue or be brief.

Loss of a Parent

A parent's death can bring about many mixed emotions. How well a person copes with the death of a parent depends on the quality of their relationship, the timing and manner of death (a tragic, sudden death is usually harder to deal with than a death that is expected from normal causes), and the quality of emotional support available to those grieving. A partner who is insensitive during this time makes a mark on the relationship that might never wear away with time. You only have one opportunity to be lovingly supportive when a partner's parent dies.

You should probably show more physical (nonsexual) affection toward a grieving partner in the weeks following the death of a parent. Pressure for a sexual connection should be absent. Take your cue from your partner on when sexual intimacies are desirable and appropriate.

Intimacy Boosters

If your partner's parent died, you might find some suitable pictures and have them framed for your mate. Gestures that show caring and sensitivity will be warmly received.

If a marriage or relationship has been less than satisfying, a parent's death is often a springboard for taking a sober look at one's own life and the value of making the most of your years on Earth. There is a slight increase in the divorce rate following the death of a parent. Many people decide that being happy in life by having the best partner is more important than struggling with a relationship that isn't working well.

Loss of a Child

When a child dies, no matter what the age, parents suffer the most extreme grief anyone can suffer. Unlike the death of a parent, where at least one of the partners is perhaps somewhat less grieved, both parents are devastated by the death of a child and often have a hard time being supportive for one another because they are each so lost in their own unbearable sadness. The death of a child is a life-transforming event. No couple is ever the same. The question is whether their devotion to one another will eventually be deeper and more profound or whether they will slowly disconnect from each other.

In the weeks following the death of a child, many couples experience the following within their relationship:

♦ A dramatic reduction in communication. *Talking about the child is too painful and ordinary topics seem too unimportant. Brief, supportive, and loving comments such as "I love you … You were such a wonderful mother … Let me make you some tea …" are essential.*

♦ Absence of all sexual interest. *Holding one another and brief shows of tender affection are important. Find time every day to hold one another, even if just for a minute or so.*

◆ A tendency to go off by oneself and think. *Time together feels joyless because of the loss, and people often want to be alone. Take time to do some things together whether it is going for a walk or even going to the supermarket. Don't expect to feel any joy or contentment. Do it as a sign of your devotion.*

◆ A loss of joy in things that once gave pleasure. *It's still important to do some things that might be a little pleasurable. Plan your vacation, visit with close friends, and try to follow some routine.*

◆ An increase in feelings of guilt or blaming others. *Never blame your partner for anything he or she did when the child was alive. Never criticize the person's parenting role. Realize that disciplining children or telling them "No" is a normal and responsible part of parenting. Regretting certain actions is commonplace but a distortion. It's best to recall the good times and the love that was present.*

Over time, conversations might resume as "normal" living takes hold. It's not unusual for one parent to want to talk about the child and various memories more than the other does. Do your best to try to meet one another's needs, realizing that grief affects different people in different ways.

Just Ask!

My stepson died recently and my husband feels uncomfortable visiting the grave. I go to the grave myself and wish he would come with me. What should I do?

Perhaps your husband would be more comfortable planting a tree or small garden in his son's memory. The two of you could stroll to that tree as a way of showing remembrance. Or you could make a charity contribution once a year in his son's name. These are two ways that the two of you can do something together.

Resuming a sexual relationship can be awkward. Couples may feel guilty allowing themselves to have sensual pleasure after a child has died. Some might lose their sex drive altogether. If sex becomes an issue, it's best to start slowly. Begin with a lot of physical holding that includes some sexual touching but doesn't necessarily lead to orgasm. Body massages allow for some sexual arousal without leading to intercourse. Over time, intercourse may seem like a normal next step. Abandoning all sexual intimacy is a mistake. But it can take time to resume lovemaking.

The Least You Need to Know

◆ The more intimate you are before the birth of your first child, the easier it is to cope with fatigue and some loss of togetherness after the baby's birth.

◆ Men who do their fair share of childcare and housework after a baby is born have a more satisfying sex life.

◆ Men tend to become more nurturing in middle age and women tend to become more assertive.

◆ Giving more physical (nonsexual) affection when your partner is grieving the death of a loved one is helpful.

◆ Don't be afraid to bring up the memory of a deceased loved one for fear it will make people upset.

Chapter 28

Intimacy After the Affair

In This Chapter

- Learning the three key reasons people cheat
- Implementing the phases of recovery after an affair
- Controlling intense arguments and mood swings
- Asking yourself three questions after being betrayed
- Holding on to issues a year after the affair ended
- Rebuilding love and devotion

The statistics vary but are not encouraging. One-quarter to one-half of all married men will eventually cheat on their wives. Slightly fewer women will cheat on their husbands. These numbers are misleading to some extent because a significant portion of infidelity occurs when the marriage is nearing an end anyway. But a huge number of couples face the crisis of infidelity every year, and many wish to repair their broken relationship.

Rates of infidelity are higher for nonmarried couples. Although it might seem less of a betrayal when people aren't married, cheating can still have a devastating impact on a dating or live-in couple.

This chapter specifically focuses on how a couple torn apart by infidelity but who wish to keep their relationship alive can rebuild trust and intimacy. It reveals common pitfalls these couples face and what can be done to improve the chances that love and devotion will be resurrected.

Why Do People Cheat?

Perhaps dozens of reasons exist for why people cheat. But they boil down to three:

- **Weaknesses in character.** Some people have a history of cheating and have a roving eye. Other people tend to be self-centered and don't feel a lot of empathy for others. They have an easier time cheating because they don't consider the affect it will have on their partners. Some people give in to impulses and have a difficult time delaying gratification.

- **Problems in the primary relationship.** The more dissatisfied you are with your partner, the greater the odds you will develop a relationship elsewhere. Although infidelity is a poor choice for coping with an unhappy relationship, many who choose this path believe they have already tried other ways to make their relationship work.

- **Opportunity.** Sixty years ago most women did not work outside the home and families owned only one car. Now the majority of women with young children are employed and people travel many miles to work. An increasing number of affairs happen between co-workers. It's common for people who would never have imagined themselves betraying a partner to discover they have developed strong feelings for people they see everyday. All it takes is one weak moment.

> **Close Calls**
>
> After the two of you decide to work it out, never throw up your hands and say "It's over!" when you hit a rough patch. Such a sentiment may be understandable, but it is also highly destructive. If commitment is weak, choose a timeframe for which you'd be willing to work on the relationship without giving up no matter what.

The Phases of Recovery

There are three main phases you go through when trying to recover from the effects of infidelity. These phases tend to overlap but most of the time you will be devoting your energy to the specific phase you are in.

- Phase One: The Rollercoaster Ride

- Phase Two: Sluggish Co-Existence

- Phase Three: A Rebirth of Love and Devotion

Your intimacy experiences will vary within each phase. Most people experience all three phases, and many get stuck in phase one or two and find it hard to advance.

Phase One: The Rollercoaster Ride

This phase can last for months. It is marked by intense swings in mood and attitude, mostly by the betrayed party. One minute there can be intense loathing and contempt, followed by pangs of fear that the relationship might not survive. Feelings of bitterness toward the unfaithful partner can be followed by intense feelings of love and passion. It isn't unusual for couples to report having the most passionate and unrestrained sex ever on one day and yet spend the next day barely communicating.

At this phase nothing the unfaithful partner says can be believed. The betrayed partner is constantly preoccupied with worry and fear that the two lovers might find a way to reconnect. At this phase the betrayed partner might give in to endless searches for evidence that the affair isn't over. Cell phone bills are checked as well as computer entries (chat rooms) and e-mails. Odometer readings are secretly compared before and after the unfaithful partner drives somewhere, just to double-check that the mileage is appropriate for the intended destination. Hunting for evidence sometimes becomes an obsession that the person can't stop even though they might want to.

This phase is also famous for interrogations where the unfaithful partner is asked repeated questions as to what actually happened, when, where, and why. The betrayed partner actually tries to keep such thoughts to herself when possible, but the dam eventually bursts and there is an outpouring of anguish in the form of questions. These interrogations can happen anywhere and at anytime—usually when it is least convenient—such as late at night or right before leaving for work. If the unfaithful partner balks at having yet another

Close Calls

If you must search for evidence of guilt, do it sparingly. Because you can never prove innocence (only that no data to support guilt was uncovered), this approach can become addictive. It's best to do infrequent, random checks and then stop all checking within a month or two.

Close Calls

If your partner had an affair and you want to repair the relationship, be careful who you talk to for support. Telling your family or parents, for example, might help you cope with stress now but might turn your parents against your partner for years to come. Talk to a therapist or a few trusted friends, if need be, but be discreet.

conversation, it is seen as more evidence that he or she is trying to hide something or is at least highly insensitive to the partner's pain.

Exercise!

If interrogations must happen repeatedly, it is wise to schedule them for specific days at specific hours. The interrogation should not last more than one hour at a time. The frequency can vary. At first, the betrayed partner might want these conversations to occur daily or every other day. Eventually they can occur once a week, once a month, and then not at all. For this to be effective, the betrayed partner must promise not to make interrogating comments at any other time. If new questions or evidence surfaces that is important to discuss, it should be written down and discussed at the agreed upon time. The unfaithful partner must agree to be receptive to the question and honest in all answers. This means no sarcasm, no eye-rolling, no sighing, no refusing to answer on the grounds that you answered the same question before, and so on. Cooperation is key. Done properly, these scheduled discussions allow the betrayed partner the opportunity needed to vent and ask questions. But it also allows the unfaithful partner room to breathe because such discussions won't happen spontaneously at inopportune moments.

Because this phase is intense and can last for months, the unfaithful partner often grows weary and starts to resist being cooperative, sensitive, and understanding. He often says something such as, "I know I did a terrible thing but I can't go on like this!" Such a comment usually makes the betrayed partner feel uncared about and righteously indignant. It leads to more conflict. The unfaithful partner is better off saying "It's understandable that you are still very hurt and angry and very emotional. I'll be glad when we can get past this part because all I want is for us to feel better about our relationship."

Phase Two: Sluggish Co-Existence

As the rollercoaster phase starts to diminish, the couple is left exhausted and unsure if the relationship is worth it. Each side has now suffered a great deal both from the affair and the emotional aftermath. The betrayed partner may still not have all the answers but has reached a point of resignation and grim acceptance. The unfaithful partner is disheartened and wonders if he or she can ever be truly happy again.

As this phase begins, time together is not so much open conflict as it is quiet, uncomfortable co-existence. The unfaithful partner tries to be thoughtful and caring. His actions are sometimes appreciated but sometimes ignored. Still, occasionally the couple has a very nice day together. They smile and laugh or have a surprisingly pleasant time. Lovemaking might have resumed or it might still be on hold. If it occurs each partner is very self-conscious and preoccupied. "Is he thinking about ... *her?*"

If there are children in the household, they offer the couple many opportunities to perform routine family tasks and give the appearance of normalcy. Kids are a great distraction.

The turning point at this phase happens when each partner realizes that they simply are not as happy as they should be and that it is time to begin letting go of what happened and working at rebuilding love and joy.

Phase Three: A Rebirth of Love and Devotion

Aspects of this phase usually begin in the earlier phases but with not as much gusto and determination. Here the affair has been put in some kind of perspective that makes it tolerable. It might be viewed as an aberration, a weakness of character, or as a consequence of not having made their relationship as strong as it should have been. Regardless, there is a renewed promise of fidelity and a commitment to address relationship issues early—before they become too big.

Trust is on the rise in this phase. The injured party learns that trust must, by definition, involve a leap of faith. One might have reason to mistrust but is willing to act trusting. The injured party regains trust by thinking "If I felt more trusting, how would I act today?" and then starts acting that way. The betrayed partner realizes that the *feeling* of mistrust might come back now and then but it need not be acted upon.

The unfaithful partner continues in this phase what was started in phase two. He examines what it was he liked about being in the affair and finds a way to bring those qualities to this relationship. What did he do differently during the affair that was positive for a relationship? Can he do that now in this relationship?

The Affair One Year Later

After the couple is back on track they might still encounter reminders of the tough time they once had. For example, they might hear about someone they know getting a divorce over an affair. Or they might watch a movie where a character has an affair. Celebrities often make news by their indiscretions and that can be a painful reminder to some couples.

After Helen's affair, Jim had to drive by a motel on his way to work that Helen used with her lover. Eventually he took a different route to work but still the couple would drive by it occasionally on their way somewhere and it always made them uneasy.

Certain "anniversaries" are often remembered. "It was a year ago today I found out about the affair," a partner might say. Or, "Remember how lousy last Christmas was? I'm glad this one is better."

> **Intimacy Boosters**
>
> If you made it through the recovery phases, make a renewed commitment to each other. Renew your wedding vows or have some kind of ritual that is meaningful to each of you. It's a way of drawing a line between the past and the future.

If the "other woman" or the "other man" lives in the vicinity or still works with your partner, painful reminders can be more frequent. Eventually you run into the other person in the mall or gas station and it can be an uncomfortable moment for all.

The best way to handle such situations is to say something kind or make a tender gesture of affection, especially to the betrayed partner. Saying "Get over it!" or "It's no big deal!" at such times won't win you any brownie points and might put you in the doghouse for a day or two.

Rebuilding Intimacy Through Thought

If you are the betrayed partner you must find ways to think more positively and hopefully about the scarred relationship. This means recalling how you fell in love and contemplating the qualities of your partner that you know are good and worthwhile. This task is hard, especially at phase one. But in phase two, when much of your anger is spent and you have made a decision to make the relationship work, this task gets easier. It means seeing your partner as human; as capable of being hurtful and making poor judgments.

This is not the time to think pie-in-the-sky thoughts and pretend all will work out fine and that your partner is a wonderful human being. Honesty is essential. But honesty demands that you emphasize the good as well as the not so good points about your partner.

Questions you need to think about:

- ◆ "In my heart, despite my hurt and pain, do I want to remain committed to this person who betrayed me?" (Yes or no.)

◆ "In my heart, despite my hurt and pain, am I willing to act trusting toward this person?" (Yes or no.)

◆ "In my heart, despite my hurt and pain, do I honestly know that I would never have betrayed him (or her) as I have been betrayed?" (Yes or no.)

◆ "In my heart, despite my hurt and pain, am I willing to offer forgiveness even though I may never forget?" (Yes or no.)

If you listen to your heart you will come up with a yes or no answer. All the gray areas in between won't matter.

If you are the unfaithful partner, you also must improve intimacy through thought. It begins by shutting down opportunities to see or talk with the lover so you can begin reorienting yourself toward your partner. You need to think about why your affair was wrong, not why it was justified. Especially at night as you fall asleep, veer away from thinking about your lover and try to replace those thoughts with images of your partner. See him or her in the best possible light.

Intimacy Boosters

Forgiveness is a decision, not a feeling. It begins with a willingness to wish well for the person who hurt you or to wish that the person finds peace or gains a better understanding of the human condition. It continues as a choice to act with a forgiving attitude even though anger may exist for some time.

Just Ask!

I know my partner still thinks fondly of the woman he had an affair with. He misses her, too. How should I react?

It's very common for someone to truly miss the person they had an affair with. Unless the affair was purely for sex, the average person will develop strong feelings of caring or love. Your best bet is to simply accept that and not try to argue about it. Your partner might want to speak with a therapist so he can better cope with his feelings.

Rebuilding Intimacy Through Talk

If you are the betrayed partner, you eventually must realize that no answer to "Why?" will ever be good enough. In fact, you might never feel you've gotten to the bottom of why the affair happened and what it all entailed. Asking such questions is typical in the first phase of recovery but it eventually becomes a wasteful, tiresome endeavor. Your goal is to shift conversations so that you focus on what is working and what is improving, not what went wrong. You also need to set aside hours or days when you simply won't talk about the affair at all. This helps you build up strength to cope with it.

If you are the unfaithful partner, it can be kind and helpful to initiate discussions about the affair even though you'd rather put the whole thing behind you. Your partner needs to talk about it once in a while, and he or she hates having to be the one to initiate those talks.

Rebuilding Intimacy Through Touch

This can be a difficult process. If you are the betrayed partner you will often have very intense mixed feelings about being touched or receiving any form of sex or affection. The angrier you are about the affair the more you will reject any affectionate advances by your partner. However, if the affair left you feeling afraid of losing your partner, you might initiate many physical encounters and actually crave them.

A typical scenario is for the unfaithful partner to lie in bed and put his arms around his mate, hoping to show affection or perhaps to make love. The betrayed partner flinches or pulls away. She doesn't want to be touched. Yet at the same time she wants to be touched. One woman put it this way to her husband: "Just because I pull away from you 12 times in a row doesn't mean I don't want you to try a thirteenth time."

If you are the unfaithful partner, this scene of being rejected can be frustrating and disheartening. If your advance is rejected, say that you understand but ask if you can show affection anyway. If the answer is still no, say that you will ask again later because you want to be able to have some kind of physical contact. Persistence, if done with sensitivity and understanding, will probably pay off.

Rebuilding Intimacy Through Togetherness

This might be easier than the other three pathways to intimacy. Even if you're not getting along well and the hurt of betrayal is still strong, you still have to be in the same room with each other now and then. In fact, if your partner was the one who was betrayed he or she might want you around as often as possible because of a lack of trust.

Getting away together to some romantic hideaway is usually not a good idea in the beginning phase of rebuilding the relationship. It will only bring up vivid images to the betrayed partner of romantic encounters the two lovers had. However, a getaway can still be good idea if you lower expectations. Don't expect to have a wonderful time. Don't expect the betrayed partner to be enthusiastic and happy. But time alone in a different environment might help clear your heads and allow for some degree of pleasant companionship that might otherwise be lacking.

The Power of Emotional Acceptance

Ultimately the affair must be accepted. This doesn't mean it is approved of. To accept it is to stop being emotionally opposed to the reality of it. When you keep asking, "Why did you do it? How could you have done such a thing?" your questions reveal that you have yet to emotionally accept reality. Initially such questions need to be asked. Eventually there must be some resignation as to what happened and a willingness to stop asking why.

Acceptance is actually a way of letting go. When you refuse to accept something that has happened, you are still holding on to it. People in shock after a tragedy will say "I can't get it through my head that it happened." That's a normal response to trauma but it also keeps the memory alive as the person tries repeatedly to integrate what happened into his view of the world. After it has been accepted the process of letting go has begun.

As an exercise, make a list of the main aspects of the affair that you can. List what happened and when. Next, list your emotional reactions to those events. Then list the good and bad qualities of your partner. Finally, list your hopes and fears for the future. Now go back to each item and read it. Then say to yourself, "I accept it." Accept each aspect of what happened. Accept each emotion you feel. If you don't like accepting any of it, say "I accept that I don't like accepting it." If you need to, go back and re-do this exercise every day. You should notice a reduction in your overall stress. You should notice that you breathe easier at the end of the exercise, too.

The Least You Need to Know

◆ Affairs don't have to end a relationship.

◆ The emotional rollercoaster ride after the affair has been exposed can last months.

- Answers to "Why?" may never seem good enough.
- You must act trusting before you can start to feel trusting.
- Forgiveness is a decision, not a feeling.
- Ultimately, an affair must be emotionally accepted.

Answers to the "What Sexual Intimacy Means" Quizzes in Chapter 16

Quiz Number One: For Women Only

1. Men usually want to have sex just to "get their rocks off."

   False. This is a close call but the correct answer is False. Sure, if you just started dating a guy and he wants to have sex, it isn't because he loves and adores you. However, if you are in a loving, established relationship his motives for sex go much deeper than having an orgasm.

   As you know, a man can get sexually aroused very quickly, more quickly than a woman. Getting some kind of relief is definitely part of a man's conscious thinking after he's up and at 'em. However, he really wants to feel closer to the woman, and having sex is the easiest way for him to experience that closeness at a more profound level. One way to tell if his motivation for having sex is more than just physical release is to pay attention to how he treats you later. Often, in the hours after making love (or the next morning), a man will show more tenderness and affection. He will be "softer" and happier. These are clear indications that he felt a strong connection that went beyond sex.

2. When a man shows sexual affection, he is really after one thing.

   False. On occasion he is definitely hoping that sexual affection will lead to some kind of bump and grind. But more often than not he is being playful. It's his way of saying he is attracted to you. The belief that he is only after one thing stems from a dynamic often found in relationships: when sex hasn't happened for a while, a man might show sexual affection as a nonverbal way of saying "Now? Later? Soon? Please???" At these moments, sex is his number one priority. Generally speaking, when the frequency of sex is at tolerable limits, sexual affection by a man should best be interpreted as playfulness.

3. "Quickies" for a man are almost always about sexual release only.

   False. By now you know why. Men love the spontaneity of quickies. They are aware that a quickie might not have as much zing for a woman if she needs more time to get aroused. But he loves that she would do that for him anyway. To a man, a quickie is playful and just plain fun. Watch how he treats you afterward. Chances are he'll be more attentive, thoughtful, and loving. (If not, he needs to read this book.)

4. Most men would have sex with any number of women if they knew they could get away with it.

   False. Trick question. Some men might give in to this, especially if there is a great deal of "fraternity boys" peer pressure. But this question taps into the sentiment that men are mostly animalistic Neanderthals. The correct answer is False. The average guy shows a lot of restraint, and if he is in a committed relationship he isn't willing to risk losing that relationship for some kind of immature ego boost.

5. If a man feels "owed" when his woman hasn't had sex with him in a while, it shows that he is immature.

   False. Most of the time it shows that he is feeling rejected. What might come across as his sense of entitlement is really a sense of hurt (he'd never use that word but it fits). In his mind, wrong as he might be, he looks at all he does for the woman he loves and feels that she should therefore want to have sex with him. When this issue arises repeatedly, the underlying problem is that he is focusing on sexual intimacy as the main pathway to closeness while the woman is focusing on the other pathways. If he would spend more effort building up intimacy through talk and togetherness and showing more nonsexual affection, the tides would turn in his favor.

6. A man who keeps pushing for sex, despite hints by his partner that she's not interested, is being selfish.

   False. Most of the time he's worried. He needs reassurance that he is loved and desirable, so with every sexual turn-down his fears increase and he becomes more impatient and demanding for sex. It isn't the best way to handle his emotions but it's often all he thinks of doing. He'd be better off asking "What's wrong?" and listening with an open mind. For that matter, the woman is advised not to simply say no to sex when she is really displeased with some other aspect of the relationship. She's better off saying, "I want to make love but I can't when I'm feeling upset about …"

Quiz Number Two: For Men Only

1. When a woman fondles her man sexually, gets him aroused, and then leaves him high and dry, she is being an insensitive tease.

   False. Guys, look at it this way. Practically every time she touches you down there you're going to get aroused. If she had to have sex with you every time you got erect, well, you'd be having sex a lot more than really works for her. Her alternative (not fun) is to never touch you there unless she wants sex. What would you rather have? No touch at all unless sex follows? Or she touches you more often even though it might not always result in a romp in the hay?

   Most of the time when she leaves you high and dry she's not being a tease. She's really saying that she wants to give you some pleasure but she's not in the mood for sex. That's not so bad, is it? If you get mad and call her a tease she won't touch you there at all unless she wants to have sex. You don't want that, do you?

2. If a man wakes up aroused and rolls over to press against his woman, she should (much of the time, anyway) follow his lead and want to have sex.

   False. Guys get aroused fairly easily. Erections upon awakening are common. But arousal for women takes more time. For her to follow your lead is sometimes asking a lot, especially if she's tired and not physically able to get aroused as quickly. Cut her some slack. Cuddle up close if you want and enjoy the sensation but don't expect that she should get excited, too.

3. Foreplay typically means caressing the woman's breasts and genitals and kissing her until she seems ready for intercourse.

    False. Foreplay is all about attitude, not just sensual stimulation. If you have sex on a Friday night, foreplay probably started (in the woman's mind) on Friday morning at the earliest and might have even begun days before. To a woman, foreplay is about thoughtfulness and attentiveness as much as it's about sexual arousal. The kinder and more thoughtful you are during nonsexual moments, the more ready she will be for you when it's time for sex.

4. Helping the woman out with daily chores and responsibilities and freeing her up so she has time for herself should have little to do with her level of sexual desire and passion.

    False. Guys, you probably know the reason why by now. Helping her out so she has more time for herself and you is a wonderful gift that will make her more hot for you. Yes, once in a while for both men and women sex is just for the sake of sex. But on average, a woman's overall connection to her man is what drives her sexual desire. For a man it tends to be the opposite: his sexual desire uncovers his deeper need to connect to his woman.

5. There's no need to flirt with a woman you already have a steady relationship with.

    False. Flirting is a neat way of saying "I think you're sexy and beautiful and hot." Flirting with her from across a crowded room is a tantalizing way to make a connection even if you're both preoccupied talking to other people. Flirting made dating fun, so have fun with your partner now, too, and flirt some more.

6. A man is ready to make love when he has a full erection; a woman is ready to make love when she is lubricated.

    False. It's also a bit of a trick question. A woman is ready for intercourse when she is lubricated. But her readiness for "making love" depends on other, non-sexual factors. Making love is a more profound experience and requires a deeper connection than the connection required for simply having sex. So, if you want to make love to your woman, you have to "think outside of the box." You have to treat her with loving kindness and make her feel cherished. Yes, every couple will get into a rut sooner or later and take one another for granted. But for love-making to be the most profound, you have to step out of that rut and show her you cherish her.

Great Resources and Books

In this appendix, I list some of my favorite books on relationships plus two organizations that supply great material on issues related to intimacy. Any of these references would be a superb addition to your library.

The Sex Starved Marriage by Michele Weiner Davis

This is an easy-to-read book that's filled with useful information about low sexual desire. Reading it will take the stigma out of having low desire while offering pages of solutions to get those engines purring. It offers medical and psychological reasons why sexual desire might be low. It's easy to flip through if you're interested in certain topics only, and it's very guy friendly.

What Women Want Men to Know by Barbara De Angelis

Men would enjoy this book as well as women. It's very easy to read, and there are lots of lists and easy-to-find tips. Men would enjoy this book because they can open to any page and probably learn something they can apply immediately to their relationship. Women will like it because it validates what they really think and want men to understand.

How Can I Get Through to You by Terrence Real

This book—one of my personal favorites—is a highly readable guide on communication. It provides many real-life examples and is written at times like a novel. It discusses what the author calls the five relationship skills needed to improve communication and shows how men and women don't always speak the same language. It's not a book for the casual reader. It should be read cover to cover to fully appreciate it.

How to Say It for Couples by Dr. Paul Coleman

Okay, I wrote this book, but I believe it to be one of the most useful books you'll find on communication. It is written to provide tips you can use immediately. There is no fluff. The first part of the book describes the five most essential keys to effective communication. The remainder of the book reveals 100 different stressful scenarios the average couple faces and gives explicit advice on what to say and how to say it (as well as advice on what not to say). It's a book that's meant to be read and re-read as you move through various life transitions.

The Lost Art of Listening by Michael Nichols

The author has some amazing ideas on how to be a better listener. His writing style is very friendly, down to earth, and wise. Reading this book is like listening to a good friend. It's also a great book for simply browsing through because no matter what page you land on you will read something that captures your imagination and makes you think. If you think you are a good listener, read this book and you'll become a much better listener.

Relationship Rescue by Phillip C. McGraw, Ph.D.

Okay, Dr. Phil doesn't need any more publicity, but this book deserves to be read. His shoot-from-the-mouth style is evident in his tone but that helps you take what he is saying seriously. He pulls no punches. You will undoubtedly come away with several new ideas to apply to your relationships.

The 30 Secrets of Happily Married Couples by Dr. Paul Coleman

Oops, that's me again. The original version and the updated version (coming in 2006) get to the heart of the matter very quickly and provide solid tips and exercises that will put your relationship on the road to better happiness. The premise is simple: What do happy couples do that other couples don't? After you realize that happy couples do things a little differently than the average couple—and I provide you with exercises to help you bring those qualities into your relationship—happiness can be a big part of your marriage, too.

The Relationship Cure: A Five Step Guide to Strengthening Your Marriage, Family, and Friendships by John Gottman

Dr. Gottman is a highly acclaimed researcher and has done more to advance our understanding of how relationships work than any other researcher in the past 20 years. It's well worth reading anything he has to say.

The Verbally Abusive Relationship by Patricia Evans

Not a pleasant topic, but an important one. You cannot experience genuine intimacy in an abusive relationship. Still, so many people remain in these relationships in part because they don't recognize the signs. This book is an eye opener and an essential guide for anyone who might think they are in an abusive relationship.

How One of You Can Bring the Two of You Together by Susan Page

This is a useful book packed with ideas on how to jumpstart (all by yourself) a relationship that has lost its energy. It forces you to think about ways you might unwittingly be creating distance in your relationship and how to change directions.

The Complete Idiot's Guide to a Healthy Relationship by Dr. Judy Kuriansky

You can't go wrong reading this book. Dr. Kuriansky, a best-selling author and popular radio talk show host with years of experience, offers advice on a broad base of issues faced by people wanting to have the healthiest relationship they can. Browse through the catalog of other *Complete Idiot's Guide* books for similar topics of interest.

Sacred Marriage by Gary Thomas

This book has a definite spiritual focus. It is well written, highly informative, and not at all preachy. The author's insights into his personal life as well as his understanding of marriage and intimacy make this a book worth owning and reading more than once. If you want to add a spiritual depth to your relationships, this book will open your eyes.

House of Affection by Wendy Wood Kwitny

An outstanding book of prose and poetry that will capture your heart. It is a true-to-life love story. The author's husband was an award-winning journalist who died of cancer. Wendy Wood Kwitny writes with such grace and power that it's hard to put this book down. It is a memoir of their final months together and a beautiful tribute to her husband and the love they shared with each other and their two boys. It is inspiring and reveals what love is all about. Reading it will open your soul. Magnificent.

Marriage

This bimonthly magazine is published by International Marriage Encounter for all couples, married or not. It contains no advertising and is published by a not-for-profit organization. The editor, Krysta Kavenaugh, is dynamite. Every issue is packed with advice and articles and reprints from top-selling books and is focused on a theme such as romance, communication, finding time together, and so on. The magazine is flashy, colorful, and easy to read. It also occasionally touches on spiritual themes without being preachy. I keep copies in my waiting room and have to keep replacing them because my clients take them. You can contact the magazine at 1-800-MARRIAGE or visit them at www.marriagemagazine.org. You'll be glad you did. A great gift idea, too.

The Centering Corporation

This is another not-for-profit organization that carries hundreds of publications related to issues of grief and loss of any kind. I include it here because so many people struggle with intimacy when they or someone they love experience a loss. It is a family run organization, and they are all genuinely nice people. Call them at 402-553-1200 (Omaha, Nebraska) for a catalog. There is something for everybody.

Index